THE GREAT STATE OF
TEXAS
ALMANAC
2 0 0 6

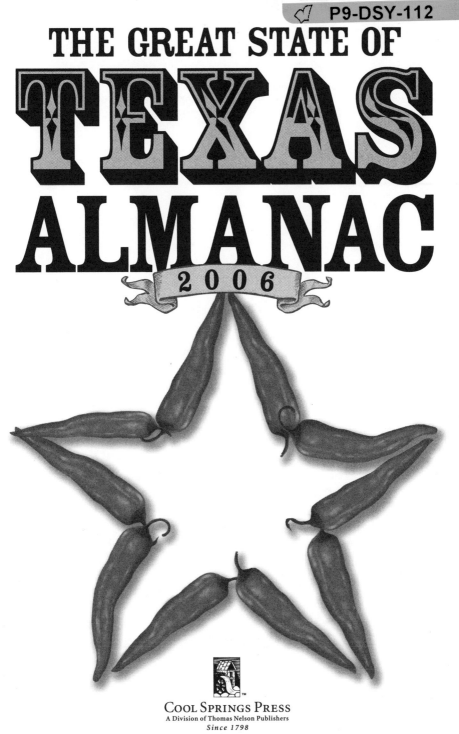

COOL SPRINGS PRESS
A Division of Thomas Nelson Publishers
Since 1798
Nashville, Tennessee

Published by Cool Springs Press, a Division of Thomas Nelson Inc., P. O. Box 141000, Nashville, Tennessee, 37214.

First printing 2005
Printed in the United States of America
10 9 8 7 6 5 4 3 2 1

Managing Editor: Carol Pierce Olson, Waynick Books
Cover & Interior Designer: Dennis G. Deaton
Garden Content Illustrators: Dennis G. Deaton; Bill Kersey, Kersey Graphics
Contributing Writers: James A. Crutchfield, Carol Pierce Olson, Roger S. Waynick

Cool Springs Press books may be purchased in bulk for educational, business, fundraising, or sales promotional use. For information, please email **SpecialMarkets@ThomasNelson.com**.

Visit the Cool Springs Press website at **www.coolspringspress.net**

ACKNOWLEDGEMENTS

The Editors of *The Great State of Texas Almanac 2006* would like to acknowledge the work of all those who contributed to this project. Specifically, we would like to thank Dennis Deaton for his great design and fabulous artwork. Thanks to Jim Crutchfield for his great writing and insight into Texas history. A huge thank you to Carol Olson for her project management and her dedication to assembling the many pieces of the puzzle and her positive attitude. And finally, we would like to thank Billie Brownell and the staff at Cool Springs Press for their assistance in getting this almanac to press.

DEDICATION

This new almanac is dedicated the people who live in the Great State of Texas, whether they truly live there or only live there in spirit.

TABLE OF CONTENTS

WELCOME

The book you are holding was created to celebrate the lifestyle and culture that has made Texas unique. From the early days when Texas was a wild wilderness to today, Texas has always had a spirit that others have wanted to emulate or be a part of. Even though many other areas have tried, there is not another Texas...and that is the way Texans want it!

We have tried our best to provide you with short articles and stories that represent many aspects of life in Texas. You will find a bunch of stories celebrating the rich history of the state throughout the book, but there is not a chapter dedicated exclusively to history. We intended to have a history chapter, but we quickly realized that whether we were writing a business article or one on high school sports, history was intertwined throughout them. And that says a lot about Texas... history is something to be proud of, not something to run from!

There is humor throughout the book that we hope you like as well. A great sense of humor is common in Texas whether you live in the dry Panhandle or along the humid Gulf Coast. Much of what we included may require a discerning Texas eye to understand, so we would suggest you not give this book as a gift to your cousins in New York. They just will not get it!

Finally, we want to tell you that a new edition of this book will published in the fall of each year. We look forward to unearthing more interesting and humorous facts and information about the Great State of Texas. We invite you to join us.

The Legend of Brushy Bill Roberts

Most everyone knows the story of Billy the Kid, right?

Well, maybe not, if some Texas history aficionados have their way. The traditional story is that Billy met his Maker on July 14, 1881, at Pete Maxwell's ranch near Fort Sumner, New Mexico. Sheriff Pat Garrett was the shooter and the lawman testified that the Kid was buried nearby. End of story for nearly seventy years.

In the late 1940s, in the small town of Hico, Texas, a private investigator by the name of William Morrison chanced upon Brushy Bill Roberts, an old-timer who reluctantly admitted that he was, in fact, Billy the Kid. Desiring no publicity, the elderly man had kept his story secret for years, but when seriously questioned, he told the following tale.

He was born in New York City, as was the Kid. His real name was William Henry Roberts, and he had migrated to Texas as a youngster to be with his father who had ended up in Hico following the War Between the States. The old man readily recalled all of the well-known facts of Billy's tumultuous life, and according to one researcher, Judge Bob Hefner, "95 percent of Brushy Bill's story" was corroborated.

Brushy Bill claimed that Pat Garrett had actually shot another man that night at Fort Sumner and pronounced the corpse to be Billy the Kid so that he could collect reward money. According to Bill, he was tired of being a fugitive from justice, so he simply rode away from the incident and left the world believing that he had been killed. The old man never lived to see the furor that his bizarre claim would cause in the historical community. He died in Hico in 1950, just short of his 91st birthday.

You can examine the evidence for yourself and make your own determination whether Billy the Kid and Brushy Bill Roberts were the same man. At the Billy the Kid Museum, located on Hico's Main Street, you will find all sorts of exhibits and reading material about the historical mystery. For more information, call 254-796-4244.

HOW DID DAVY DIE?

John Wayne was the perfect Davy Crockett. With his coon skin cap flying in the wind and his musket raised high above his head, Crockett/Wayne was the ultimate American hero. Wayne's influence on America and the West has been preserved forever through his films, but, even though there has been no debate as to the valor that Crockett showed at the Alamo, there has been a great deal of controversy over exactly how David Crockett and some of the other defenders of the Alamo really died. The traditional version of the events that occurred during the wee hours of the morning of March 6, 1836, describes the great bravery of the Americans during the last hours in the doomed mission and repeats the story of how every one of them fought bravely to their last breath. This is what most of us learned in our school books, and it is the vision of the epic drama that most Texans support.

An account of Davy Crockett's last days, although probably embellished by the patriotic writer, was published the year after the events at the Alamo and told of Crockett running about the mission grounds "encouraging the men to do their duty." He also led a sortie from the fort where he and his party were attacked by six Mexicans. The book reports that he shot one of the foes with his rifle, two others with his pistols, and severely wounded a fourth with his sword. Days later, as the final Mexican assault upon the Alamo commenced, Crockett and the others "all fought like bloodhounds and Col. Crockett's body was found in an angle of two buildings with his dagger in his hand, and around him were lying seventeen dead Mexicans, eleven of whom had come by their deaths by his dagger, and the others by his rifle and four pistols, which laid beside him."

That is the John Wayne story, but in 1975, the translation of the diary of a Mexican army officer who accompanied Santa Anna at the Alamo was published in the United States. Written just six months after the mission's fall by José Enrique de la Peña, the journal caused a furor among historians, many of whom claimed it to be forgery. De la Peña's account paints a much different view of the fate of many Americans, including Crockett, during the final minutes of the Mexican slaughter at the mission.

According to the journal, an "unpleasant episode" occurred "after the end of the skirmish," which many of Santa Anna's men considered to be nothing short of murder. The episode affected the soldiers strongly and "contributed greatly to the coolness" among Mexican army troops when their commander congratulated them on their victory.

"Some seven men had survived the general carnage," wrote de la Peña, and had been placed under the protection of a high-ranking Mexican officer. "Among them was one of great stature, well proportioned, with regular features, in whose face there was the imprint of adversity, but in whom one also noticed a degree of resignation and nobility that did him honor," wrote the diarist. He continued that the individual was "David Crockett, well known in North America for his unusual adventures."

De la Peña then explained that despite the protection order that had been extended to Crockett and his companions, Santa Anna, "with a gesture of indignation... ordered his execution." Several of Santa Anna's staff officers were horrified and refused to obey their general's edict, but others "in order to flatter their commander, and with swords in hand, fell upon these unfortunate, defenseless men just as a tiger leaps upon his prey." According to the diary, even though Crockett and the others were ruthlessly tortured before they were killed, they "died without complaining and without humiliating themselves before their torturers."

Regardless of how Crockett and the others died—whether their deaths occurred

The Bastrop family was important in Texas history. Three Bastrop men signed the Texas Declaration of Independence, eleven died at the battle of the Alamo and sixty or so lost their lives at San Jacinto.

in the fury of hand-to-hand combat or they were murdered as prisoners of war—the fact remains that they went down in a blaze of valor seldom encountered in the annals of military history. They are true heroes of Texas! ★

REMEMBER GOLIAD!

In an event which has sometimes been overshadowed in the history books by the earlier defeat at the Alamo, some 300 to 350 Texans were executed by the Mexican army at Goliad on March 27, 1836. The Texans, under the command of James W. Fannin, Jr., were caught while retreating to Victoria on March 19, forcing their surrender to General José Urrea. Contrary to Urrea's orders, General Santa Anna ordered that all of the captured prisoners be put to death. The cold-blooded murders of Fannin and his men added fuel to the flames in the minds of the revenge-crazed Texans, who satisfied their blood lust the following month when Sam Houston defeated Santa Anna at San Jacinto.

A Bevy of

TEXAS GUNSLINGERS

During the years following the War Between the States,
Texas was filled with drifters, ex-soldiers, lawmen, and outlaws.
Here are a few of the more famous gunslingers—
both good and bad—who called the Lone Star State home
at one time or another.

Clay Allison

Clay Allison was born in Wayne County, Tennessee, in 1841 and when the War Between the States began, he joined General Nathan Bedford Forrest's cavalry, sometimes serving as a scout. Captured at the Battle of Shiloh, he soon escaped and eventually gravitated to Texas, where he was briefly employed by Charles Goodnight as a cowboy. He spent considerable time in northern New Mexico and southern Colorado, had several serious scrapes with the law while there, and purportedly killed several men throughout the region. In 1880, he returned to Texas, where he established a ranch in Wheeler County in the Panhandle. Following his life of violence, he died in July, 1887, near the town of Pecos, when he fell from a freight wagon and fractured his skull. Allison's brother, John, also crossed paths with the law, but he was not as well known.

Sam Bass

Outlaw Sam Bass was truly a legend in his own time. Born in Indiana in 1851, he moved to Texas in 1870 and worked for a few years as a cowboy and assistant to Denton County Sheriff William F. Egan. The young man soon fell in with a bad crowd, however, took up a gun, and began robbing stagecoaches. His success led to an even more profitable career as a train robber and, during a fifty-day period in 1878, he and his gang held up four trains within twenty miles of Dallas. The law caught up with Bass in July 1878 at the small town of Round Rock in Williamson County. As the result of a botched bank robbery in which one of his own men had betrayed him, Bass was severely wounded in the back and kidney. He died on July 21, his twenty-seventh birthday. Bass is buried in a small cemetery in Round Rock.

"Long-Haired Jim" Courtright

Born in Sangamon County, Illinois, in 1845, Timothy Isaiah ("Long-Haired Jim") Courtright served in the Union Army during the War Between the States and later migrated to Texas where he scouted for the army. He was elected city marshal of Fort Worth in 1876 and was one of the local officials who pursued Sam Bass and his outlaw band in Denton County two years later. After living a while in New Mexico where he served as a mine guard, he returned to Fort Worth. It was there, in February 1887 that he got into a fracas with Luke Short when Short protested Courtright's demands for protection money from his partners at the White Elephant Saloon. Courtright drew his pistol, but the weapon became entangled in Short's watch chain, at which time Short methodically discharged several shots into his adversary, killing him instantly.

John Wesley Hardin

The son of a preacher and named after the famous Methodist churchman, Hardin was born in Fannin County, Texas, in 1853. He killed his first man when he was only fifteen years old and, over the next three years, he murdered thirteen more. During the next few years, his path crossed and crisscrossed Texas, until in 1874, he passed through Brown County, killing

Clyde Barrow
AND
Bonnie Parker
(Bonnie and Clyde)

The woes of the Great Depression brought out the bad sides of many Americans. Among them were the notorious Texans known as Bonnie and Clyde. Clyde Barrow was born in 1909 in Teleco, Texas, one of eight children born to poor dirt farmers. He dropped out of grammar school and pursued a life of petty crime until 1930, when Bonnie Parker entered his life. Bonnie, born in 1910, came from a laboring family, but was a smart student in school. Nevertheless, soon after she met Clyde, she helped him break out of jail, and the pair's criminal career was born. For the next four years, the lovers caused havoc in communities all over Texas and the Midwest, killing at least twelve people in the process. Famed Texas Ranger Frank Hamer finally caught up with the outlaws on May 23, 1934, near Plain Dealing, Louisiana, and the two were killed in a hail of gunfire.

Deputy Sheriff Charles Webb along the way. Texas Rangers finally caught up with him in 1877. He was tried the following year and sentenced to twenty-five years in prison. While in jail, Hardin attempted several unsuccessful breakouts, but in time moderated his habits, read extensively, and was eventually named superintendent of the prison Sunday school. Granted a full pardon in 1894, by the following year he had slipped back into his old ways and was killed in El Paso by another gunman, John Selman.

Jim Miller

For a devout Methodist churchman who didn't drink, smoke, or curse, Jim Miller lived a wild and woolly life. Born in Arkansas in 1861, he moved to Robertson County, Texas, as a small child where he lived with his grandparents. During various phases of his life he worked as a Texas Ranger, real estate agent, gambler, city marshal, and deputy sheriff, but along the way he murdered at least a dozen men, one of whom many authorities believe to have been Sheriff Pat Garrett, the killer of Billy the Kid. For most of these crimes, he escaped prosecution, but in February, 1909, the law caught up with him in Oklahoma when he was arrested for the murder of a well-known and respected citizen of Ada. After requesting that his diamond ring be returned to his wife in Fort Worth, Miller was hanged at 2 a.m. on April 19, 1909.

John Selman

John Selman was born in Madison County, Arkansas, in 1839 and, at an early age, moved with his family to Grayson County, Texas. When the War Between the States began, he joined the 22nd Texas Cavalry, but deserted less than a year and a half later. He was later elected a lieutenant in the Texas militia, but was subsequently tried on the desertion charge and fled. By 1870, he, along with his wife and son, had moved to New Mexico. Back in Texas within two years, he became involved in a vigilante movement and participated in several needless killings. In the meantime, he had turned to rustling cattle and other unlawful activity. His most notable claim to fame was his fatal shooting of outlaw John Wesley Hardin in El Paso in August 1895. Less than a year later, Selman himself was killed by Deputy U. S. Marshal George Scarborough.

Luke Short

Upon meeting Luke Short, one observed that he was indeed, short. Standing only five and a half feet tall and weighing 125 pounds, the diminutive gunfighter was born in Mississippi in 1854. Moving with his family to Texas when he was two, he became a cowboy as an adult. Contact with gamblers in the trailhead towns convinced the impressionable youngster that card playing was more profitable than driving cattle. Subsequently, Short worked in several of the West's more infamous saloons, including the Long Branch in Dodge City. He eventually moved to Fort Worth, where he bought into the White Elephant Saloon. There, in February 1887, while arguing over the "protection" money that "Long-Haired Jim" Courtright was trying to extort from the saloon's owners, Short shot and killed Courtright. Short died in 1893 of dropsy and is buried in Fort Worth's Oakwood Cemetery, just a few feet from the grave of Courtright.

The oldest original existing courthouse in Texas sits in the town of Comanche in Comanche County. The log structure, affectionately known as "Old Cora," was built in 1856.

The Largest Cities in TEXAS *by Population*

Population	Place Name	Population	Place Name	Population	Place Name
1,953,631	Houston	104,197	Wichita Falls	50,702	Flower Mound
1,188,580	Dallas	94,996	Midland	48,465	Edinburg
1,144,646	San Antonio	91,802	Richardson	47,152	Bedford
656,562	Austin	90,943	Odessa	46,660	Pharr
563,662	El Paso	88,439	San Angelo	46,005	Euless
534,694	Fort Worth	86,911	Killeen	45,444	League City
332,969	Arlington	83,650	Tyler	45,408	Mission
277,454	Corpus Christi	80,537	Denton	44,503	Rowlett
222,030	Plano	77,737	Lewisville	43,554	Allen
215,768	Garland	73,344	Longview	42,059	Grapevine
199,564	Lubbock	67,890	College Station	41,521	Texas City
191,615	Irving	66,430	Baytown	39,018	Haltom City
176,576	Laredo	65,660	Bryan	37,646	DeSoto
173,627	Amarillo	63,328	Sugarland	37,640	Pearland
141,674	Pasadena	61,136	Round Rock	36,811	Conroe
139,722	Brownsville	60,603	Victoria	36,494	New Braunfels
127,427	Grand Prairie	57,755	Port Arthur	36,385	Spring
124,523	Mesquite	57,564	Harlingen	36,273	Hurst
115,930	Abilene	57,247	Galveston	36,081	Duncanville
113,866	Beaumont	55,649	The Woodlands	35,958	Coppell
113,726	Waco	55,635	North Richland Hills	35,757	Atascocita
109,576	Carrollton	54,514	Temple	35,082	Sherman
106,414	McAllen	54,369	McKinney	35,078	Huntsville
		52,913	Missouri City		

10 *Things you will never hear a Texas woman say......*

1 My daddy spoils me too much.

2 Are these jeans too tight?

3 I really do not want to live in Highland Park.

4 Truthfully, I was not pretty enough to be a cheerleader.

5 I hate riding in pickup trucks.

6 I think my hair is just too big today.

7 Excuse me, where is the mall?

8 Tight t-shirts are tacky.

9 A man in Bermuda shorts makes me weak in the knees.

10 He is just too rich.

BILLY DIXON'S MILE-LONG SHT

I f Billy Dixon was proud of one thing in his life it was the fact that he was a respected buffalo hunter, or, more specifically, a hide hunter. Although he was only twenty-three years old, he had already won the admiration of hunters many years his senior. He was known all over Texas, Kansas, and the Indian Territory for his marksmanship and his ability to bring down staggering numbers of buffalo in the course of a single day.

On June 29, 1874, however, Dixon wasn't thinking about buffalo. Instead, the young hunter was concerned about his safety and that of his twenty-five or so companions. For the past three days, they had been holed up at a remote hunters' camp in the Panhandle called Adobe Walls, fighting off a brutal attack by Comanche, Kiowa, and Southern Cheyenne warriors under the leadership of Isa-tai and the notorious Quanah Parker. Three men had already succumbed in the fierce fighting which pitted the handful of hunters against nearly seven hundred Indians. The warriors had also shot and killed most of the hunters' horses and cattle and, had it not been for the thick walls of sod used in the construction of the camp's buildings, more casualties would likely have occurred.

For two days after the initial attack, the hunters' compound had been fairly quiet. One man had slipped away to Dodge City for help, while a burial detail interred the three dead men in a single grave. The hunters had also disposed of the rotting carcasses of the cattle and horses as best they could. The Indians, in the meantime, had completely surrounded Adobe Walls, showing themselves from time to time to remind the men inside that escape was impossible.

While several hunters surveyed the plain around camp, they noticed some warriors silhouetted against a slight rise in the prairie about a mile away. One of the observers was Dixon, who had lost his prized Sharps rifle several days earlier while crossing the flood-swollen Canadian River. Billy reached and picked up James Hanrahan's .50-caliber Sharps and fiddled for a moment with the rear sight. He aimed the rifle at a lone Indian perched upon his horse who was sharply outlined against the skyline. The big Sharps belched flames and smoke. Neither Dixon and his companions, nor the crowd of warriors could believe their eyes at what happened next.

"I took careful aim and pulled the trigger," Billy wrote later, and

"...we saw an Indian fall from his horse."

"we saw an Indian fall from his horse." The hunters then observed the spectacle as two Indians rescued the body of the fallen warrior and pulled it to safety. The remarkable shot was too much for the attackers and they soon left Adobe Walls to the hide men. Once they were out of sight, one curious onlooker paced off the distance of Billy's shot and found it to be 1,538 yards–nearly seven-eighths of a mile!

Out of the dramatic battle at Adobe Walls, the legend of Billy Dixon was born. Although he repeatedly acknowledged that he had been lucky, the young man's marksmanship became a favorite subject for storytellers forever after. Billy went on to become a distinguished scout for the 6th U. S. Cavalry under the command of Colonel, later General, Nelson Miles and was awarded the Congressional Medal of Honor for "skill, courage, and determined fortitude" displayed during another fight in September, 1874. Unfortunately, Dixon's prized medal was later rescinded when guidelines for the granting of the award were defined to cover members of the military only and not civilians.

Dixon later served as the first sheriff of Hutchinson County, but eventually moved to Oklahoma. In subsequent years, he returned to Texas where he died near the New Mexico border on March 9, 1913.

Texas Independence by the Numbers

On March 2, 1836, four days before the Mexican assault on the Alamo, fifty-nine men met in a small building in the infant town of Washington-on-the-Brazos to sign the **Texas Declaration of Independence**. In addition to the momentous occasion, Sam Houston, one of the session's organizers, had something else to celebrate: he turned forty-three years old on the same day. Most of the signers were Americans, but a few were foreign. Here is a list of the origins of the signers.

Place	Number of Signers
Tennessee	11
Virginia	11
North Carolina	9
Kentucky	6
Georgia	4
South Carolina	4
Pennsylvania	3
New York	2
Texas	2
Mississippi	1
Massachusetts	1
England	1
Scotland	1
Ireland	1
Canada	1
Mexico	1

➤ The Sharps Rifle ➤

Billy Dixon wasn't the only legend spawned on that fateful day in June 1874 at Adobe Walls. The reputation of the already popular Sharps rifle jumped a few notches as well. The Sharps had seen lots of action by both sides in the War Between the States, but its use during the 1870s and 1880s as the weapon of choice among hundreds of hide hunters scouring the Great Plains in search of the ever-dwindling bison herds insured its elevated position among firearms of the times. To the buffalo hunters, the rifle's beauty was its ability to fire a heavy bullet several hundred yards with complete accuracy.

PRESIDENTIAL ELECTION RESULTS

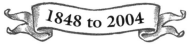
1848 to 2004

1848

Lewis Cass	(Democrat)	10,668	70.29%
Zachery Taylor *	(Whig)	4,509	29.71%
		15,177	

1852

Franklin Pierce*	(Democrat)	13,552	73.07%
Winfield Scott	(Whig)	4,995	26.93%
		18,547	

1856

James C. Buchanan *	(Democrat)	31,169	66.59%
Millard Fillmore	(Whig)	15,639	33.41%
		46,808	

1860

John C. Breckinridge	(Democrat)	47,548	75.49%
John Bell	(Constitutional Union)	15,438	24.51%
		62,986	

1864

U.S. elections were not held in Texas in 1864.

1868

There was no presidential voting in Texas in 1868 because the state had not been readmitted to the Union and was not officially part of the United States during Reconstruction.

1872

Horace Greeley	(Democrat)	66,546	57.07%
Ulysses S. Grant *	(Republican)	47,468	40.71%
		116,594	

1876

Samuel J. Tilden	(Democrat)	104,755	70.04%
Rutherford B. Hayes *	(Republican)	44,800	29.96%
		149,555	

1880

Winfield S. Hancock	(Democrat)	156,428	72.99%
James A. Garfield *	(Republican)	57,893	27.01%
		214,321	

1884

Grover Cleveland *	(Democrat)	225,309	69.26%
James G. Blaine	(Republican)	93,141	28.63%
		325,305	

1888

Grover Cleveland *	(Democrat)	234,883	65.70%
Benjamin Harrison	(Republican)	88,422	24.73%
		357,513	

1892

Grover Cleveland *	(Democrat)	239,148	56.65%
James B. Weaver	(Populist)	99,688	23.61%
Benjamin Harrison	(Republican)	81,144	19.22%
		422,155	

1896

William Jennings Bryan	(Democrat)	234,298	48.05%
William McKinley *	(Republican)	167,520	34.36%
		487,576	

1900

William Jennings Bryan	(Democrat)	267,432	63.12%
William McKinley *	(Republican)	130,651	30.83%
		423,716	

1904

Alton B. Parker	(Democrat)	199,799	71.06%
Theodore Roosevelt *	(Republican)	65,823	23.41%
		281,188	

1908

William Jennings Bryan	(Democrat)	224,110	73.39%
William Taft *	(Republican)	70,458	23.07%
		305,357	

1912

Woodrow Wilson *	(Democrat)	222,589	72.71%
Theodore Roosevelt	(Progressive)	28,853	9.43%
William H. Taft	(Republican)	26,755	8.74%
Eugene V. Debs	(Socialist)	25,743	8.41%
		306,120	

1916

Woodrow Wilson *	(Democrat)	286,514	76.92%
Charles E. Hughes	(Republican)	64,999	17.45%
Allen L. Benson	(Socialist)	18,969	5.09%
		372,467	

1920

James M. Cox	(Democrat)	288,767	59.34%
Warren G. Harding *	(Republican)	114,538	23.54%
James E. Ferguson	(American)	47,968	9.86%
		486,641	

1924

John W. Davis	(Democrat)	484,605	73.70%
Calvin Coolidge *	(Republican)	130,023	19.78%
Robert M. LaFollette	(Progressive)	42,881	6.52%
		657,509	

1928

Herbert C. Hoover *	(Republican)	367,036	51.77%
Alfred E. Smith	(Democrat)	341,032	48.10%
		708,999	

1932

Franklin D. Roosevelt *	(Democrat)	760,348	88.07%
Herbert C. Hoover	(Republican)	97,959	11.35%
		863,392	

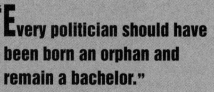

"**E**very politician should have been born an orphan and remain a bachelor."

Former First Lady, Lady Bird Johnson

1936

Franklin D. Roosevelt *	(Democrat)	734,485	87.08%
Alfred M. Landon	(Republican)	103,874	12.31%
		843,482	

1940

Franklin D. Roosevelt *	(Democrat)	840,151	80.69%
Wendell L. Wilkie	(Republican)	199,152	19.13%
		1,041,168	

1944

Franklin D. Roosevelt *	(Democrat)	821,605	71.42%
Thomas E. Dewey	(Republican)	191,425	16.64%
		1,150,331	

1948

Harry S. Truman *	(Democrat)	750,700	65.44%
Thomas E. Dewey	(Republican)	282,240	24.60%
J. Strom Thurman	(States' Rights)	106,909	9.32%
		1,147,245	

1952

Dwight D. Eisenhower *	(Republican)	1,102,878	53.13%
Adlai E. Stevenson	(Democrat)	969,228	46.69%
		2,075,946	

1956

Dwight D. Eisenhower *	(Republican)	1,080,619	55.27%
Adlai E. Stevenson	(Democrat)	859,958	43.98%
		1,955,168	

1980

Ronald Reagan *	(Republican)	2,510,705	55.28%
Jimmy Carter	(Democrat)	1,881,147	41.42%
John Anderson	(Independent)	111,613	2.46%
		4,541,637	

1984

Ronald Reagan *	(Republican)	3,433,428	63.61%
Walter Mondale	(Democrat)	1,949,276	36.11%
		5,397,571	

1988

George Bush *	(Republican)	3,036,829	55.95%
Michael S. Dukakis	(Democrat)	2,352,748	43.35%
		5,427,410	

1992

George Bush	(Republican)	2,496,071	40.56%
Bill Clinton *	(Democrat)	2,281,815	37.08%
Ross Perot	(Independent)	1,354,781	22.01%
		6,154,018	

1996

Bob Dole	(Republican)	2,736,167	48.76%
Bill Clinton *	(Democrat)	2,459,683	43.83%
Ross Perot	(Independent)	378,537	6.75%
		5,611,644	

2000

George W. Bush *	(Republican)	3,799,639	59.30%
Al Gore	(Democrat)	2,433,746	37.98%
Ralph Nader	(Green)	137,994	2.15%
		6,407,637	

2004

George W. Bush *	(Republican)	4,518,491	61.20%
John Kerry	(Democrat)	2,825,723	38.27%
		7,382,897	

* Denotes the national winner.

Texas Ethnicity (2000)

Ethnic Group	Number	Percent
Anglo	11,074,716	53.11%
Hispanic	6,669,666	31.99%
Black	2,421,653	11.61%
Other	685,785	3.29%

(2000 Statistical Abstract of the United States, Census Bureau)

Republic of Texas Elected Officials

Presidents	Vice Presidents
David G. Burnet	**Lorenzo de Zavala**
Mar. 16, 1836 - Oct. 22, 1836	Mar. 16, 1836 - Oct. 17, 1836
Sam Houston	**Mirabeau B. Lamar**
Oct. 22, 1836 - Dec. 10, 1838	Oct. 22, 1836 - Dec. 10, 1838
Mirabeau B. Lamar	**David G. Burnet**
Dec. 10, 1838 - Dec. 13, 1841	Dec. 10, 1838 - Dec. 13, 1841
Sam Houston	**Edward Burleson**
Dec. 13, 1841 - Dec. 9, 1844	Dec. 13, 1841 - Dec. 9, 1844
Anson Jones	**Kenneth Anderson**
Dec. 9, 1844 - Feb. 19, 1846	Dec. 9, 1844 - July 3, 1845

1960

John F. Kennedy *	(Democrat)	1,167,932	50.52%
Richard M. Nixon	(Republican)	1,121,699	48.52%
		2,311,670	

1964

Lyndon B. Johnson *	(Democrat)	1,663,185	63.32%
Barry Goldwater	(Republican)	958,566	36.49%
		2,626,811	

1968

Hubert H. Humphrey	(Democrat)	1,266,804	41.14%
Richard M. Nixon *	(Republican)	1,227,844	39.87%
George C. Wallace	(American)	584,269	18.97%
		3,079,406	

1972

Richard M. Nixon *	(Republican)	2,298,896	66.23%
George McGovern	(Democrat)	1,154,289	33.25%
		3,471,281	

1976

Jimmy Carter *	(Democrat)	2,082,319	51.14%
Gerald R. Ford	(Republican)	1,953,300	47.97%
		4,071,884	

JUNETEENTH
Celebrating the Long Labor of Freedom in Texas

June 19, 1865, was already hot and sultry when Union General Gordon Granger and a regiment of United States army troops disembarked in Galveston with news that the War Between the States was over. To the large crowd that assembled around him, he announced that Confederate General Robert E. Lee had surrendered the Army of Northern Virginia to General Ulysses S. Grant two months earlier at a tiny hamlet in Virginia named Appomattox. To the slaves in the neighborhood, however, Granger brought even more earthshaking, yet welcome, news. As the anxious mob, both white and black, looked on, he declared:

"The people of Texas are informed that in accordance with a Proclamation from the Executive of the United States, all slaves are free. This involves an absolute equality of rights and rights of property between former masters and slaves, and the connection heretofore existing between them becomes that between employer and free laborer."

As Grainger finished reading his special orders, the audience looked at each other in bewilderment. They now knew that President Lincoln had signed the Emancipation Proclamation nearly two and one-half years earlier, but due primarily to little Union army activity in Texas, the announcement had never been made public in the state. The slaves in the crowd could not believe that they were actually free, yet had been held in bondage for thirty months past the President's proclamation. The white farmers immediately began planning how they would run their cotton plantations without slave labor.

As time went by and many former slaves migrated to other parts of the nation, a celebration was born commemorating the day the news of freedom was first announced in Galveston. It was called "Juneteenth" and over the years, festivities among blacks grew around the unofficial holiday. Picnics were held, along with church services, rodeos, baseball games, and other merriment. In some instances, former slaves and their children even gravitated back to their old homeplace to be with friends who had stayed behind.

Juneteenth fell from favor in the late 1800s and early 1900s, but during the civil rights disturbances of the 1960s, it gained new popularity, especially among young blacks interested in preserving their heritage. On January 1, 1980, 117 years after President Lincoln signed the Emancipation Proclamation, the state of Texas declared June 19—*Juneteenth*—an official state holiday, through the labor of a black legislator, Al Edwards, who has since made efforts to have it made a legal holiday in other states across the South. ★

Texas By The Numbers...

Lowest Elevation	**0 feet**, along the Gulf Coast
Highest Elevation	**8,749 feet** – Guadalupe Peak
Number of Peaks Above 8,000 Feet	**7**
Highest Town	**5,050 feet** – Fort Davis
State Size (Within the United States)	**2** – exceeded only by Alaska
Total Land Size	**261,914** square miles
Total Water Surface	**5,363** square miles
Longest Straight-line Distance Within State	**801 miles**, from the NW Panhandle to below Brownsville
Miles of Coastline	**624**
Length of the Rio Grande Forming the Border	**1,254** miles
Length of the Red River Forming the Border	**726** miles
Length of the Sabine River Forming the Border	**292** miles
Total Length of All Borders	**3,822** miles
Population of Largest City	**1,953,631** – Houston
Population of Smallest City	**32** – Los Ybanez
Population of Largest County	**3,087,153** – Harris
Population of Smallest County	**96** – Loving
Number of Counties	**254**
Area of Largest County	**6,204** square miles – Brewster County
Area of Smallest County	**149** square miles – Rockwall County
Record High Temperature	**120°** F, August 12, 1936, at Seymour, and June 28, 1994, at Monahans
Record Low Temperature	**-23°** F, February 12, 1899, at Tulia, and February 8, 1933, at Seminole.

> *"**If** a man has common sense, he has all the sense there is."*
>
> **Sam Rayburn,**
> Former longtime Speaker of the U.S. House of Representatives

★

In 1821, Jane Long, while waiting for her husband General James Long to return from Mexico, gave birth to the first Anglo-Saxon native Texan, Mary Jane Long, on Bolivar Peninsula. Jane is known as "The Mother of Texas."

★

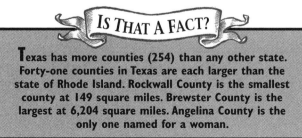

IS THAT A FACT?

Texas has more counties (254) than any other state. Forty-one counties in Texas are each larger than the state of Rhode Island. Rockwall County is the smallest county at 149 square miles. Brewster County is the largest at 6,204 square miles. Angelina County is the only one named for a woman.

"The question before you is whether it is possible for a colored man to secure and hold a position as an officer of the Army."

THE COURT-MARTIAL OF HENRY FLIPPER

On December 8, 1881, a crowd of curious onlookers convened in front of the chapel at Fort Davis, Texas. After two months of deliberations, a verdict was about to be delivered in the court-martial of Lieutenant Henry Ossian Flipper, who had been charged with embezzlement after reporting that funds were missing from the army post's commissary. However, unknown to those gathered, Flipper, who was acting officer-in-charge of the commissary, was on trial more for his skin color than for dishonesty. The preponderance of evidence indicated that he was most likely framed.

Colonel Benjamin Henry Grierson, the white commander of the all-black Tenth Cavalry to which Flipper belonged, had no doubt about his associate's innocence, writing that the young officer had displayed "efficiency and gallantry" in the field and had always discharged his duties "faithfully and in a highly satisfactory" manner.

Anxious spectators watched as Flipper, a six-foot, two-inch former slave from Georgia and the first black man ever to graduate from the U. S. Military Academy at West Point, entered the building. His accuser, the former commandant of Fort Davis, Colonel William R. "Pecos Bill" Shafter, soon followed.

After the last of the testimony, Flipper's attorney, Major Merritt Barber, summed up the true purpose of the trial in his closing arguments. "The question before you is whether it is possible for a colored man to secure and hold a position as an officer of the Army," he declared. Flipper and Barber would soon find out, as the senior officer ordered the two men to stand while he read the verdict of the court-martial panel. The twenty-five-year-old lieutenant was found innocent of the embezzlement charges, but guilty of "conduct unbecoming an officer" and so was dishonorably discharged from the Army. Despite criticism of the sentence by Robert Todd Lincoln, the U. S. Secretary of War and Abraham Lincoln's son, Flipper was cashiered out of the service.

Flipper was devastated. He had excelled in every military mission he had ever undertaken. Authorities in the nation of Liberia had been so impressed with his record at West Point that they tried to persuade him to come to their country to lead their entire army. Instead, the young lieutenant had joined Troop A, Tenth U. S. Cavalry and so became the only black officer of the all-black "Buffalo Soldiers." His regiment was one of four formed after the War Between the States to accommodate the vast number of recently freed slaves from the South who had entered military service during the last days of the conflict. The Buffalo Soldiers proved to be one of the army's most effective weapons during the Indian wars of the 1870s and 1880s.

Following Flipper's court-martial and discharge from the Army, he moved to El Paso and worked in a laundry. He took a job as civil engineer and soon became an expert on Mexican land law, eventually writing a number of authoritative books about the subject. Later, he worked in the Interior Department in Washington, D.C., helped to develop the Alaskan railroad system, and spent time as a civil engineer in the Venezuelan oil fields. On nine separate occasions during his long and fruitful career, he attempted to clear his name and set his military record straight, but each time to no avail. When he died in Atlanta, Georgia, in 1940, he was a broken and disheartened man.

During the 1970s, others interested in the Henry Flipper story tried to get his verdict overturned. Finally, on December 13, 1976, nearly one hundred years after his court-martial, the dishonorable discharge was rescinded and an honorable discharge was issued in its stead. ★

Five Frontier Forts

Old forts abound in Texas. They date from early Spanish days all the way to the post–War Between the States years, when the American Army established a number of posts, primarily as a defense against marauding Comanche, Kiowa, and Southern Cheyenne Indians. Here are five historic structures that can still be visited today.

The Alamo, located in downtown San Antonio.

Fort Concho, located within the city limits of San Angelo.

Fort Davis National Historic Site on State Highway 17 in Jeff Davis County.

Old Fort Parker State Historical Park near Groesbeck in Limestone County.

Fort Richardson State Historical Park on State Highway 199 at Jacksboro.

★ Buffalo Soldiers ★

"Buffalo Soldiers" was a name given to members of four all-black units of the United States Army that were organized following the end of the War Between the States. A large number of the soldiers of the 8th and 9th Cavalry and the 24th and 25th Infantry Regiments were former slaves, commanded by white officers. Colonel Benjamin Grierson of the 10th often praised his men for their "most gallant and zealous devotion to duty." For years, these tenacious fighters represented one of the most effective weapons in the army's arsenal during the Southwestern Indian wars of the 1870s and 1880s. The black fighters quickly earned the respect of their Indian foes, who gave them their moniker, Buffalo Solders. They went on to fight in the Spanish-American War, where they helped other elements of the U. S. Army overrun Spanish defenses in Cuba. They served in the Philippines and in 1916, they rode with one of their old officers, General John J. "Black Jack" Pershing (the name "Black Jack" came from Pershing's former duty with the all-black 10th Cavalry), into Mexico in pursuit of Pancho Villa after the bandit raided Columbus, New Mexico. During the Korean War of the early 1950s, the four regiments were integrated into the rest of the Army.

The Musical Heritage of Texas

At one time or another, many of America's most popular musicians have called Texas home, but no one, perhaps, is more identified with the Lone Star State than **Bob Wills.** Born Jim Rob Wills in the tiny village of Turkey in 1905, by the age of ten he had already mastered the fiddle, often taking his father's place in the local dance band. Before his complex life ended, Wills would be recognized as the single-most influence of the genre of music known today as "**Texas Swing.**"

Among the many occupations he could claim as a young man were insurance agent, preacher, and barber. While trying to find work around Fort Worth in 1929, he stumbled upon an opportunity to demonstrate his fiddle-playing abilities when he landed a role in a black-face minstrel show. Before long, he and the guitar player in the show had hired two others and formed a band of their own known as the Wills Fiddle Band. The group went through a number of name and personnel changes before ending up during the early '30s as the Texas Playboys.

Wills was an innovator who enjoyed mixing elements of jazz, blues, and country into his music, trying to develop a distinctive sound that folks could dance to. As one music historian has written, "It was his constant effort to put on a bigger, better show that brought about the Big Sound. He was a showman. And putting on a better show meant bringing in lots of other instruments, and more fiddles than just his own. A good show for dancing, that was the goal, not the creation of some musical revolution."

Along the way, Jim Rob Wills became simply Bob Wills and, to his growing number of listeners on radio and at live performances, his star was quickly rising on the musical scene, first in Texas and neighboring Oklahoma, then across the entire nation. He is said to have despised the "hillbilly" image that country music over in Nashville was portraying and he was quick to let anyone know that he was not a country musician. At one time or another, his band reached orchestra proportions, complete with trumpet and saxophone

TEXAS SWING

BOB WILLS

AND THE TEXAS PLAYBOYS

sections, drums, and both male and female singers that sounded as if they would be more at home with Glen Miller than with the Playboys. Although his was the music of the Great Depression and showed the strong influences of the poor, black and white, unemployed, and those "down-on-their-luck," the image he portrayed to his public was one of a big-band leader—suave, personable, and dressed to the 9's—except his suit had a western cut to it instead of a business one.

Wills and the Texas Playboys maintained their popularity for decades and year after year released a myriad of "Texas Swing" classics, "San Antonio Rose" and "Faded Love" being two of the most remembered. When he died in 1975 after an extended illness, the world was saddened with the passage of one of America's great musical legends. Bob Wills truly was the "father" of "Texas Swing." His epitaph appropriately reads, *"Deep Within My Heart Lies A Melody."* ★

Texas Hospitality

During the late 1870s, an Alabama traveler named A. B. Greenleaf found it necessary to seek overnight accommodations at the remote home of a Texas frontiersman. The man had a large family and Greenleaf was hesitant to impose upon the farmer, but since he had no other choice, he prepared for the evening meal.

When the lady of the house announced supper, "the whole retinue simultaneously bolted for the kitchen in a double-quick step," wrote the bewildered traveler later, continuing that before he could be seated, all of the home's residents "were promiscuously grabbing at the huge boiled beef bones with the voraciousness of young ducks gobbling up a bran dough." Finally taking a seat, Greenleaf watched in amazement as the meal's other participants seized the food with abandon. Having no other recourse, he, too, selected a piece of "mutilated shank" and began gnawing away.

The following morning, after a sleepless night, Greenleaf found his host and inquired about settling his account. He was told to "pay to the old umman." He found the madam in the cow pen and politely asked her what he owed for his food and lodging. "What you bin payin' tother folks es you come along?" she asked. The traveler evaded the question as best he could so as not to under estimate what the woman might have had in mind. "We'all, ez I hez the rumatiz, an' needs a little bitters, an' tha axes a dollar an' a half fur whiskey, you may give me that."

"I shelled out three eagle half dollars and exodusted [sic] with a dust," Greenleaf wrote in his reminiscences of his travels in Texas.

TWO KINDS OF COWBOYS

In 1880, a traveler with the very British-sounding name of W. Baillie Grohman wrote in a magazine published in England that "Cowboys can be divided into two classes: those hailing from the Lone Star State, Texas," and those from everywhere else. "The Texans are," he continued, "as far as true cowboyship goes, unrivalled: the best riders, hardy, and born to the business; the only drawback being their wild reputation." Grohman declared that "the bad name of Texas arises mostly from their excitable tempers, and the fact that they are mostly 'on the shoot,' – that is, very free in the use of their revolvers."

LAMAR'S FOLLY

When Texas won its independence from Mexico in 1836, its western border was defined as a line running along the channel of the Rio Grande to the river's source, and from that point, a straight line due north for three hundred miles. The real estate thus contained within the Republic's borders encompassed the entire eastern half of today's state of New Mexico, including the towns of Santa Fe and Taos.

Mirabeau B. Lamar, who succeeded Sam Houston as president of Texas in 1838, immediately set about to bring Texas into the modern age with improved roads and an expanded school system, but The Republic was suffering through bad economic times. During the three years after Lamar took office, the public debt had swelled to more than seven million dollars. Yet, blinded to the problem, Texas officials annually spent twice the Republic's yearly income of less than half a million dollars.

Lamar believed that his country's economic woes could be diminished if Texas established trade relations with the prosperous New Mexican markets. The idea was to take costly Cuban merchandise, unload on the Texas Gulf Coast, route it through Austin, then send it directly to Santa Fe, saving hundreds of miles off the traditional route from Missouri via the Santa Fe Trail.

In 1839, Lamar urged the Congress to approve an expedition to Santa Fe to explore and to confirm his trade theory. The issue simmered until April, 1841, when he advertised in the *Austin City Gazette* for armed civilian troops to escort wagons to the markets of New Mexico. Two months later, between three and four hundred men and boys, with as many horses and a score of supply vehicles,

left Austin on the first leg of the so-called Texan-Santa Fe Expedition.

In West Texas, the expedition, due to lack of provisions, eventually broke up into two groups and both elements suffered from weeks of grueling travel that quenched even the brightest fires of Lamar's enthusiasm for riches. Exhausted from hunger, thirst, and the threat of Indian attack, both parties straggled into San Miguel during the autumn days of 1841, only to be arrested by waiting Mexican soldiers, under the command of Manuel Armijo, the governor of New Mexico.

The surviving members of the Texan-Santa Fe Expedition were marched under armed guard all the way to Mexico City where they were held prisoner in Mexican jails for an extended period of time. George Wilkins Kendall, a newspaperman who had participated in the debacle and was one of the captives, wrote a book about his experience entitled, *Narrative of the Texan-Santa Fe Expedition.* ★

★ TEXAS GOVERNORS ★

1846 - Present

J. Pinckney Henderson
February 19, 1846 - December 21, 1847
George T. Wood
December 21, 1847 - December 21, 1849
Peter Hansbrough Bell
December 21, 1849 - November 23, 1853
J. W. Henderson
November 23, 1853 - December 21, 1853
Elisha M. Pease
December 21, 1853 - December 21, 1857
Hardin R. Runnels
December 21, 1857 - December 21, 1859
Sam Houston
December 21, 1859 - March 16, 1861
Edward Clark
March 16, 1861 - November 7, 1861
Francis R. Lubbock
November 7, 1861 - November 5, 1863
Pendleton Murrah
November 5, 1863 - June 17, 1865
Andrew J. Hamilton
June 17, 1865 - August 9, 1866
James W. Throckmorton
August 9, 1866 - August 8, 1867
Elisha M. Pease
August 8, 1867 - September 30, 1869
Edmund J. Davis
January 8, 1870 - January 15, 1874
Richard Coke
January 15, 1874 - December 1, 1876
Richard B. Hubbard
December 1, 1876 - January 21, 1879

Oran M. Roberts
January 21, 1879 - January 16, 1883
John Ireland
January 16, 1883 - January 18, 1887
Lawrence Sullivan Ross
January 18, 1887 - January 20, 1891
James Stephen Hogg
January 20, 1891 - January 15, 1895
Charles A. Culberson
January 15, 1895 - January 17, 1899
Joseph D. Sayers
January 17, 1899 - January 20, 1903
S.W.T. Lanham
January 20, 1903 - January 15, 1907
Thomas Mitchell Campbell
January 15, 1907 - January 17, 1911
Oscar Branch Colquitt
January 17, 1911 - January 19, 1915
James E. Ferguson
January 19, 1915 - August 25, 1917
William Pettus Hobby
August 25, 1917 - January 18, 1921
Pat Morris Neff
January 18, 1921 - January 20, 1925
Miriam A. Ferguson
January 20, 1925 - January 17, 1927
Dan Moody
January 17, 1927 - January 20, 1931
Ross S. Sterling
January 20, 1931 - January 17, 1933
Miriam A. Ferguson
January 17, 1933 - January 15, 1935

James V. Allred
January 15, 1935 - January 17, 1939
W. Lee O'Daniel
January 17, 1939 - August 4, 1941
Coke R. Stevenson
August 4, 1941 - January 21, 1947
Beauford H. Jester
January 21, 1947 - July 11, 1949
Allan Shivers
July 11, 1949 - January 15, 1957
Price Daniel
January 15, 1957 - January 15, 1963
John Connally
January 15, 1963 - January 21, 1969
Preston Smith
January 21, 1969 - January 16, 1973
Dolph Briscoe
January 16, 1973 - January 16, 1979
William P. Clements
January 16, 1979 - January 18, 1983
Mark White
January 18, 1983 - January 20, 1987
William P. Clements
January 20, 1987 - January 15, 1991
Ann W. Richards
January 15, 1991 - January 17, 1995
George W. Bush
January 17, 1995 - December 21, 2000
James Richard Perry
December 21, 2000 - present

Ann Richards

*A*nn Richards galvanized her listeners and won the hearts of millions of women at the 1988 Democratic National Convention, when she exclaimed, *"Ginger Rogers did everything that Fred Astaire did. She just did it backwards and in high heels."* In 1982, Richards, a former school teacher, had become the first woman elected to a Texas state office in half a century and, two years after her memorable keynote address to the Democrats, she was elected 45th governor of Texas.

One Riot, One Ranger

enowned Western historian Robert M. Utley has written that "of constabularies around the world, only the Royal Canadian Mounted Police compete with the Texas Rangers in nearly universal name recognition." President Lyndon B. Johnson once wrote that the Rangers were "one of the most storied, yet most truly effective, law enforcement organizations." Indeed, this small, normally efficient yet sometimes bungling group of dedicated lawmen—and lately, law-women—has, over the years, provided Texas and Texans a rich fabric both of truth and legend.

The Rangers came into being in 1823, when colonizer Stephen F. Austin mustered ten of his best qualified associates to protect the Texas frontier from Indian raids. By 1835, when the group was officially recognized by Texas officials, it had grown to about fifty-six men organized into three companies, each commanded by two lieutenants and a captain. At a salary of $1.25 per day, each individual was expected to furnish his own weapons, ammunition, supplies, equipment, and horses.

When Texans fought Santa Anna's armies for independence in 1835-36, the Rangers played a relatively small role, but a decade later, during the American war with Mexico, they displayed their martial talents by serving the U. S. Army as a fierce fighting contingent under the leadership of such legends as Samuel Walker, Ben McCulloch, W. A. A. "Bigfoot" Wallace, and others. They were so feared by the Mexican army that they soon became known as *los diablos Tejanos*, "the Texas devils."

For the remainder of the nineteenth century, the Rangers served collectively as defenders of the frontier, individually and unofficially as soldiers in the Confederate Army, and—after the Civil War—as

Some of the Rangers' Finest

★ **John Coffee "Jack" Hayes**
Born: Wilson County, Tennessee, 1817
Died: Alameda County, California, 1883

★ **Benjamin McCullough**
Born: Rutherford County, Tennessee, 1811
Died: Battle of Pea Ridge, Arkansas, 1862

★ **Samuel Walker**
Born: Prince George's County, Maryland, 1817
Died: Huamantla, Mexico, 1847

protectors from Mexican bandit and American outlaw incursions. Later, both before and during World War I, they patrolled the Mexican border for German espionage activity, helped the U. S. Army pursue Pancho Villa and his rebels, and fought illegal tequila and cattle smugglers along the Rio Grande.

Called the father of Texas, Stephen F. Austin's middle name was Fuller. ⬟

By the early 1930s, precipitated by the Great Depression and the financial and social woes hovering over America, the Texas Rangers had shrunk to a force only of about forty-five men. In 1932, when most of them threw their support for incumbent governor, Ross Sterling, against the other Democrat in the primary, Miriam A. "Ma" Ferguson, they were further decimated when "Ma" won the election and drastically cut back Ranger personnel. Eventually numbering only thirty-two men, the Rangers were no match for the flood of gangsters and other illegal activities that flooded Texas during the mid-1930s.

Salvation for the Rangers came in 1935 with the administration of Governor James Allred, who reformed state government and established the Texas Department of Public Safety. The legendary Rangers became one of the three contingents of the new department, the others being the Highway Patrol and the Headquarters Division. Qualifications for Rangers became more stringent and modern techniques of crime-fighting and detection were introduced.

The Ranger force today totals just a few more than one hundred men and women, plenty sufficient to face the task at hand if a persistent legend is believed: The story goes that when a lone Ranger rode into a dusty Texas town at the request of local authorities to put down a riot, officials were alarmed that he had no sidekicks with him. "Where are the others?" they frantically asked. "Ain't but one riot, is there?" he shot back. ★

When Texas was annexed in 1845, a resolution gave it the right to fly its flag at the same height as the national flag. That same resolution also gave Texas the right to divide into four states in addition to the original Texas. That legal right remains to this day. ⬟

★ **Leander H. McNelly**
Born: Brooke County, Virginia, 1844
Died: Washington County, Texas, 1877

★ **William A. A. "Bigfoot" Wallace**
Born: Rockbridge County, Virginia, 1817
Died: Frio County, Texas, 1899

★ **Frank Hamer**
Born: Wilson County, Texas, 1884
Died: Austin, Texas, 1955

★ TEXAS JUSTICE ★

*T*exas, like the rest of the territory lying west of the Mississippi River, saw its share of violence and outlaws during its early days when sheriffs, courts, and judges were separated by vast distances. The list of good guys and bad guys is extensive and runs the full gamut of Texas history from Republic days right down to the rip-roaring times of the Great Depression.

One of the most recognizable names in the era of outlaws and lawmen is that of **Judge Roy Bean**. Born in Kentucky around 1827, Roy's circuitous path to Texas took him first to New Orleans, Mexico, California, and New Mexico before he arrived in San Antonio during the final days of the War Between the States. There, he lived for twenty years, married a teenaged Mexican girl, sired four children, and ran a prosperous saloon on South Flores Street.

When the Southern Pacific Railroad extended its tracks from San Antonio toward El Paso in the early 1880s, Roy picked up stakes and moved to the tiny and remote village of Vinegarroon, situated on the western bank of the Pecos

River, where it was often said, "West of the Pecos there is no law." The arrival of hundreds of migrant railroad workers to the region sent lawlessness in Vinegarroon soaring, and, in 1882, Bean was appointed a justice of the peace.

Two years later he moved his operations to nearby Eagle's Nest Springs, renamed the town "Langtry" in honor of the English actress Lillie Langtry with whom he had an infatuation, and opened his combination saloon and law office.

Judge (his self-proclaimed title) Bean, his opinions, and his sometimes comical handling of the law soon became known throughout West Texas. With absolutely no legal background, he dispensed a brand of justice that would make a modern-day judge cringe. "They send me the Texas statutes, codes, and so forth every year," he once said, "but I never read them." On one occasion, when a drowned man was found in the Pecos River with a pistol and forty dollars on his person, Bean, in order to obtain the funds to bury the victim, fined the corpse forty dollars for carrying a concealed weapon.

"They send me the Texas statutes, codes, and so forth every year, but I never read them."

At another trial, the colorful judge, although he failed to come up with anything specific with which to charge the defendant, fined him two dollars and told him "get the hell out of here and never show yourself in this court again."

Bean's legendary status was assured following an incident that received national attention. In 1896, after the state of Texas had outlawed boxing, Bean invited a pair of fighters, one of whom was the well-known and popular Bob Fitzsimmons, to take part in a boxing match that he would host. Bean circumvented the law by building a pontoon bridge to an island in the middle of the Rio Grande, which constituted the international border between the United States and Mexico. There, in "no-man's" land, he held the fight, which lasted only ninety-five seconds, with Fitzsimmons walking away the winner.

Age meant little to Roy Bean, and he never anticipated retiring from the bench, nor reforming from his garrulous and unorthodox ways. When he was over seventy years old, a man came into his saloon, purchased a bottle of beer, and left for the train station without paying. The train was about to depart town when Bean, armed with a six-shooter, climbed aboard and walked down the aisle of each car looking for his former customer. According to an Associated Press dispatch dated May 27, 1901, when the judge found the man, he stuck the pistol in the surprised gent's face and demanded thirty-five cents, "or I press the button." The man gave Bean a one-dollar bill, the judge politely handed him his change, and turning, declared to the gasping passengers, "If you don't know what kind of hombre I am, I'll tell you. I'm the law west of the Pecos."

In 1903, following more than a score of years of dishing out hundreds of weird and often, bizarre, verdicts, Bean died after collapsing to the floor of his saloon and was buried in the Del Rio Cemetery. In the summer of 1904, Lillie Langtry, the woman he most admired in the world, but whom he had never met, passed through his town, where she spent thirty minutes meeting townspeople and hearing all about the legendary Bean. It "was a short visit, but an unforgettable one," she later wrote in her autobiography. A delegation of residents even offered the actress Bean's pet black bear, which he kept with him during court proceedings; refusing this, they persisted in giving her his pistol, which she hung "in a place of honor" in her English home. ★

Cynthia Ann Parker

Cynthia Ann Parker was a happy, carefree nine-year-old girl living with her family at Parker's Fort in east-central Texas in March, 1836, when the Alamo fell to Santa Anna's Mexican soldiers. Two months later, on May 19, a Comanche war party raided Parker's Fort and killed practically everyone there. For some reason, the Indians spared Cynthia Ann and her eleven-year-old brother and carried them into custody, where she grew up among her adopted people. As a young woman, she became the wife of a prominent chief and, in time, gave birth to three children, the first of whom grew up to be the renowned Comanche chief, Quanah Parker. Cynthia Ann was "rescued" many years later and, against her will, she was returned to her American kin. Unhappy in her strange new environment, she eventually died from brooding over her lost Indian children and her kinsmen among the Comanche people.

A HOROSCOPE FOR TEXANS

Some Texans are skeptical of horoscopes and the people who read and live by them. So, to allow you to fully understand all of the zodiac's signs, as well as the true meaning of each, here is the newly revised Texas Horoscope. We hope all Texans will appreciate it and, perhaps, derive a chuckle or two from it as well.

★ **OKRA** (Dec 22 - Jan 20) Okras are tough on the outside but tender on the inside. They have tremendous influence. An older Okra can look back over his or her life and see the seeds of influence everywhere. You can do something good each day if you try.

★ **CHITLIN** (Jan 21 - Feb 19) Chitlins come from humble backgrounds. A Chitlin, however, will make something of himself if he or she is motivated and has lots of seasoning. In dealing with Chitlins, be careful; they may surprise you. They can erupt like Vesuvius. Chitlins are at their best when associating with Catfish and Okra.

★ **BOLL WEEVIL** (Feb 20 - March 20) You have an overwhelming curiosity. You're dissatisfied with the surface of things, and you feel the need to bore deeply into the interior of everything. Needless to say, you are very intense and driven as if you had some inner hunger. You love to stay busy and tend to work too much. Nobody in their right mind is going to marry you, so don't worry about it.

★ **MOON PIE** (March 21 - April 20) You're the type who spends a lot of time on the front porch. It is easy to recognize the physical appearance of Moon Pies. Big and round are the key words here. You should marry anybody whom you can remotely interest in the idea. It's not going to be easy. You always have a big smile and are happy. This might be the year to think about aerobics…or, maybe not.

★ **POSSUM** (April 21 - May 21) When confronted with life's difficulties, possums have a marked tendency to withdraw and develop a don't-bother-me-about-it attitude. Sometimes they become so withdrawn, people actually think they are dead. This strategy is probably not psychologically healthy but it seems to work for possums. You are a rare breed that most folks love to watch work and play. You are a night person and mind your own business.

★ **CRAWFISH** (May 22 - June 21) Crawfish is a water sign. If you work in an office, you probably always hang around the water cooler. Crawfish prefer the beach to the mountains, the pool to the golf course, and the bathtub to the living room. They tend not to be particularly physically attractive, but they do have very, very good heads.

★ **COLLARDS** (June 22 - July 23) Collards have a genius for communication. They love to get in "the melting pot" of life and share their essence with those around them. Collards make good social workers, psychologists, and baseball managers. As far as your personal life goes, if you are Collards, stay away from Crawfish. It just won't work. Save yourself a lot of heartache.

★ **CATFISH** (July 24 - Aug 23) Catfish are traditionalists in matters of the heart, although their whiskers may cause problems for loved ones. Catfish are never easy people to understand. They run fast. They work and play hard. Even though they prefer the muddy bottoms to the clear surface of life, they are liked by most. Above all else, Catfish should stay away from Moon Pies.

★ **GRITS** (Aug 24 - Sept 23) Your highest goal is to be with others like yourself. You like to huddle together with a big crowd of other Grits. You love to travel though, so maybe you should think about joining a club. Where would you like to go? Anywhere that has cheese, gravy, bacon, butter, or eggs and a good time would be nice. You are pure in heart and should get along well with Boiled Peanuts.

★ **BOILED PEANUTS** (Sept 24 - Oct 23) You have a passionate desire to help your fellow man. Unfortunately, those who know you best—your friends and loved ones—may find that your personality is much too salty. Actually, when you come out of your shell, you are much softer than you appear. You should go right ahead and marry anybody you want to because in certain ways, you are blessed. On the road of life, you can be sure that people will always pull over and stop for you. Boiled Peanuts and Catfish—what a delicacy!

★ **BUTTER BEAN** (Oct 24 - Nov 22) Always invite a Butter Bean to a party because they get along well with everybody. You, as a Butter Bean, should be proud. You've grown on the twisted vine of life, and you feel at home no matter what the setting. You can sit next to anybody. However, you should find happiness with a Moon Pie.

★ **ARMADILLO** (Nov 23 - Dec 21) You have a tendency to develop a tough exterior, but you are actually quite gentle and kind inside. For you, a good evening is to be with old friends, a fire, some roots, fruit, worms, and insects. You are a throwback. You're not concerned with today's fashions and trends. You're almost prehistoric in your interests and behavior patterns. You probably want to marry another Armadillo, but a Possum is another, somewhat kinky, mating possibility.

Miss Texas Winners!

Year	Name	Title Held When Crowned
1936	Patricia Allen Green	Miss Corpus Christi
1937	Alice Emerick	Miss Fort Worth
1939	Charmayne Smith	Miss Dallas
1940/41	Gloria Ann Byrns	Miss Port Arthur
1942	Jo-Carroll Dennison **Miss America 1942**	Miss Tyler
1944	Joyce Courrege	Miss Orange
1945	Polly Below	Miss Galveston
1946	D. Anne Wisener	Miss University Park
1947	Luna McClain	Miss Lufkin
1948	Bonnie Jean Bland	Miss Orange
1949	Ysleta Leissner	Miss Fort Worth
1950	Margaret Sommers	Miss Dallas
1951	Glenda Holcomb	Miss West Texas
1952	Connie Hopping	Miss Littlefield
1953	Paula Lane	Miss Cleburne
1954	Yvonne Erwin	Miss Dallas
1955	June (Prichard) Williams	Miss West Texas
1956	Barbara Murry	Miss Houston
1957	Carolyn Calvert	Miss Austin
1958	Mary Nell Hendricks	Miss Arlington
1959	Marilyn Turner	Miss Fort Worth
1960	Mary Cage Moore	Miss Dallas
1961	Linda Loftis	Miss Fort Worth
1962	Penny Lee Rudd	Miss Marshall
1963	Jeanne Amacker	Miss Austin
1964	Sharon McCauley Lenda Varley	Miss Athens Miss Fort Worth
1965	Mary Lou Butler	Miss Nacogdoches
1966	Susan Logan	Miss Lubbock
1967	Molly Grubb	Miss Fort Worth
1968	Diane Hugghins Glenda Propes	Miss Nacogdoches Miss Rusk County
1969	Dana Dowell	Miss Longview
1970	Phyllis George **Miss America 1971** Bellinda Myrick	Miss Dallas Miss West Texas
1971	Janice (Bain) Cord	Miss White Settlement
1972	Mae Beth Cormany	Miss Hurst-Euless-Bedford
1973	Judy Mallett	Miss Haltom-Richland Area

Year	Name	Title Held When Crowned
1974	Shirley Cothran **Miss America 1975** Phyllis Barger	Miss Haltom-Richland Area Miss Houston
1975	Mary Ellen Richardson	Miss Waco
1976	Carmen McCollum	Miss West Texas
1977	Lori Smith	Miss Haltom-Richland Area
1978	Sandi Miller	Miss Red Bird Area
1979	Lex Ann Haughey	Miss Haltom-Richland Area
1980	Terri Eoff	Miss Lubbock
1981	Sheri Ryman	Miss Texas A&M
1982	Gloria Gilbert	Miss Palo Pinto Co.
1983	Dana Rogers	Miss San Antonio
1984	Tamara Hext	Miss Arlington
1985	Jonna Fitzgerald	Miss Greenville
1986	Stephany Samone	Miss Grand Prairie
1987	Jo Thompson	Miss Greenville
1988	Cathy Castro	Miss Duncanville
1989	Leah Kay Lyle	Miss Haltom-Richland Area
1990	Suzanne (Lawrence) Forsberg	Miss Humble/Kingwood
1991	Rhonda (Morrison) Formby	Miss Lake O' The Pines
1992	Amy Parker	Miss Tarrant Co.
1993	BaShara Chandler	Miss Northeast Texas
1994	Arian Archer	Miss Amarillo Area
1995	Carly (Jarmon) Gil	Miss Oak Cliff
1996	Michelle (Martinez) Metzger	Miss Dallas
1997	Reagan Hughes	Miss Lake O' The Pines
1998	Tatum Hubbard	Miss Arlington
1999	Yanci (Yarbrough) McGregor	Miss Hurst-Euless-Bedford
2000	Tara Watson	Miss Hurst-Euless-Bedford
2001	Stacy James	Miss Lake O' The Pines
2002	Lisa (Dalzell) Spooner	Miss Lake O' The Pines
2003	Sunni Cranfill	Miss Amarillo Area
2004	Jamie Story	Miss Arlington

Miss-ing Texas Winners No Miss Texas was crowned in 1938. In 1941, Gloria Ann Byrns, the reigning Miss Texas of 1940, retained the title for another year because of World War II. In 1943, Miss Texas was once again cancelled because of World War II.

Getaway to the
STAGECOACH INN

Whether you're looking for a quiet weekend getaway or just passing through, the Stagecoach Inn in the historic village of Salado is sure to please. Located 48 miles north of Austin on the Old Chisholm Trail, this charming country resort offers travelers a taste of Texas history. For almost 150 years, the Stagecoach Inn has been greeting travelers with Texas hospitality.

The beautiful countryside between Austin and Dallas has drawn travelers for centuries. Early Spanish and Mexican explorers frequented the area because of Salado Creek, a mineral spring that was rumored to possess "special curative powers." Later, the area was inhabited by Native Americans who hunted buffalo along the river. During the mid-1800s, the peaceful village of Salado changed forever with the arrival of the stagecoach. Located at the crossroads of the Old Chisholm Trail and the Old Military Road, Salado became a popular and busy stop both for the Pony Express and the Overland Stage Coach.

One early settler who recognized the needs of the travelers was W. B. Armstrong, who in the 1860s completed what was then known as the Shady Villa Hotel. Built on the site of a Tonkawa Indian village, the Shady Villa became a welcome stop for those traveling the long dusty trails of Texas. The Shady Villa Hotel offered travelers a hearty Texas meal and a clean bed. Long known for offering wonderful meals, the hotel employed waitresses who were usually local housewives; they would greet the weary stagecoach travelers and recite the daily bill of fare.

The Shady Villa Hotel reportedly hosted many famous and a few infamous travelers during the early years. Guests of the hotel included famous Texas patriot Sam Houston, who reportedly made one of his anti-secession speeches from the balcony. Other travelers were General George Custer, Captain Robert E. Lee, the son of General Lee, and cattle barons Shanghai Pierce and Charles Goodnight. Well known outlaws Jesse and Frank James as well as Sam Bass were also guests. The infamous did not always register under their real names and often hid in a nearby cave. Sadly, the hotel register with the names of these famous guests, as well as numerous others, was stolen in 1944.

In 1945, the Shady Villa Hotel was purchased, restored and renamed the Stagecoach Inn by Ruth and Dion Van Bibber. The Van Bibbers proudly continued the traditions started during the days of the stagecoach. In 1959, the Inn was purchased by the Van Bibber's nephew, William Bratton, who added room accommodations, a private club, and a coffee shop. Over the years Bratton expanded the property to include walking trails, ponds, and a heated mineral water spa. The year 1999 saw a new owner when Salado native Morris Foster purchased the property. Foster continues to honor the traditions, pride, and quality of service always associated with a fine meal and comfortable stay at the Stagecoach Inn.

Whether you're stopping in Salado for an afternoon or a weekend, the Stagecoach Inn will delight you. Vacationers and travelers alike will enjoy the downhome atmosphere and Texas hospitality offered at this historic inn. ★

TOP SPOTS TO VISIT IN TEXAS

As all Texans know, there are more places to see in Texas than a person can do in two or three lifetimes, but we wanted to put together a short list of some of our favorite places to spend the afternoon or a weekend. Now, we know that we have left off a bunch of really neat and cool places...but this is a start. If you have places you want us to consider for next year, drop us a note and we will try and fit in your suggestions. For the time being though, take a look at our list!

HOUSTON

1. **Downtown Houston Theater District** – Home to eight performing arts centers and covering seventeen city blocks, this revitalized district has it all. Theaters, parks, bars, and restaurants give visitors to Houston a variety of options for a night on the town.
Prestons Street, Houston, Texas 77002 713-228-8421
www.heritagesociety.org

2. **Houston Arboretum & Nature Center** – Located 4 miles west of downtown, this 155-acre nature center is a sanctuary in the middle of the most populated city in Texas. Over 5 miles of walking trails, ponds, woodlands, and meadows offer visitors to the Houston Arboretum and Nature Center a tranquil getaway from the hustle of the busy city.
4501 Woodway Drive, Houston, Texas 77024 713-681-8433

3. **Houston Zoo** – Founded in 1922 and home to over 3,500 animals, the Houston Zoo is an excellent choice for adults and children alike.
1513 N. MacGregor, Houston, Texas 77030 713-533-6500
www.houstonzoo.org

4. **NASA/Johnson Space Center/Space Center Houston** – Space Center Houston is the Official NASA Visitor's Center. The Center is open seven days a week and features interactive exhibits, live shows, and tours.
1601 NASA Parkway, Houston, Texas 77058
281-244-2100
www.spacecenter.org

5. **San Jacinto Museum of History** – A 570-foot monument marks the site where Sam Houston's army defeated Mexican General Santa Anna's forces, winning Texas' independence from Mexico. Also visit the Battleship Texas, a WWI and WWII era battleship that is permanently moored in a slip near the battlefield.
One Monument Circle, La Porte (Houston), Texas 77571-9585 281-479-2421
www.sanjacinto-museum.org

DALLAS

1. Dallas Farmer's Market – One of the oldest and largest farmer's markets in the country, the Dallas Farmer's Market features fresh produce, flowers, and crafts.
1010 South Pearl Expressway, Dallas, Texas 75201 214-939-2808
www.dallasfarmersmarket.org

2. Dallas Zoo – This nationally renowned zoo is home to many rare and endangered species from around the world. The zoo's "Wilds of Africa" was named the best African Zoo exhibit in the nation by "The Zoobook: A Guide to America's Best." 650 South R.L. Thornton Freeway, Dallas, Texas 214-670-6826
www.dallas-zoo.org

3. Sixth Floor Museum at Dealey Plaza (The Texas School Book Depository) – The Sixth Floor Museum pays tribute to the life, death, and legacy of President John F. Kennedy. Permanent and special exhibits allow visitors to relive the day Kennedy was assassinated in Dallas.
411 Elm Street, Dallas, Texas 75202 214-747-6660
www.jfk.org

4. Old City Park – This living history museum provides a glimpse of life in North Texas from 1840-1910. A working Civil War era farm, a traditional Jewish household, elegant Victorian homes, a school, a church, and commercial buildings provide examples of the life and times of those who came before us.
1717 Gano Street, Dallas, Texas 75215 214-421-5141
www.oldcitypark.org

5. West End Market Place – West End Market Place provides restaurants, boutiques, and night clubs all in a single area. Street entertainers and special events planned throughout the year offer something for everyone.
603 Munger Avenue, Dallas, Texas 75202 214-720-0170

SAN ANTONIO

1. The Alamo – Located in the center of San Antonio, The Alamo stands as a tribute to the 187 defenders who fell to General Santa Anna's Mexican army in 1836. Originally built as a mission in 1718, the Alamo is a must-see when in San Antonio.
300 Alamo Plaza, San Antonio, Texas 78299 210-225-1391
www.thealamo.org

2. The Buckhorn Saloon and Museum – Fun for all ages is waiting at this saloon and museum. The museum boasts over 4,000 items and the saloon has original furnishings dating back to the days of Teddy Roosevelt and the Rough Riders.
318 E. Houston, San Antonio, Texas 78205 210-247-4000
www.buckhornmuseum.com

3. Fort Sam Houston Museum – This museum traces the history of one of the Army's most important military installations from its presence at the Alamo in 1845 to the present.
1212 Stanley Road, San Antonio, Texas 78234 210-221-1886

4. Spanish Governor's Palace – Constructed in 1749, this adobe-walled structure served as the residence and headquarters for the local presidio captain during the Spanish rule of Texas.
105 Military Plaza, San Antonio, Texas 78205 210-224-0601

5. The Riverwalk – The Paseo de Rio, running one level below the streets of San Antonio, is edged by wonderful hotels, markets, shops, and restaurants. Scenic riverboat cruises provide the perfect view of the city. All visitors to San Antonio must experience the famed Riverwalk!
250 Nueva Street, San Antonio, Texas 78204 210-227-4262
www.thesanantonioriverwalk.com

AUSTIN

1. Austin City Limits Tour – Stand on the stage that hosted such greats as Jimmy Buffett, Rosanne Cash, Ray Charles, Leonard Cohen, B. B. King, Lyle Lovett, Willie Nelson, Roy Orbison, Bonnie Raitt, George Strait, and Tanya Tucker. A tour of Studio 6-A at station KLRU on the University of Texas at Austin campus will be entertaining for anyone who appreciates music.

2504-B Whitis, Austin, Texas 78712
512-471-4811

2. Austin Museum of Art – An excellent collection of permanent exhibits, along with impressive temporary exhibits, makes this stop a cultural must-see.
823 Congress Avenue, Austin, Texas 78701
512-495-9224
www.amoa.org

3. Texas State Capital – Built in 1888 of Texas pink granite to house the state's capital, this is one of the most unique and beautiful capitals in the country. Dominating the 46 acres on which it was built, the massive building is open for tours to the public.
11th & Congress Avenue, Austin, Texas 78711 512-305-8400 (Visitor's Center)
512-463-0063 (Tour Guide Office)
www.dot.state.tx.us

4. Governor's Mansion – Completed in 1856 as the official residence of the Governor of Texas, this dignified mansion is also home to beautiful antiques and Texas history.
1010 Colorado Street, Austin, Texas 78701 512-463-5518
www.governor.state.tx.us

5. Lyndon B. Johnson Presidential Library and Museum – This library and museum provides the visitor with insight into the life and presidency of LBJ.
2313 Red River Street, Austin, Texas 78705 512-721-0200
www.lbjlib.utexas.edu

EL PASO

1. Chamizal National Memorial – This memorial commemorates and celebrates the peaceful settlement in 1963 of a century-long boundary dispute between the United States and Mexico.
800 South San Marcial Street, El Paso, Texas 79905-4123 915-532-7273
www.nps.gov/cham/

2. Concordia Cemetery - Concordia Cemetery is the final resting place of many notorious and infamous Texans. Evidence of the wilder side of El Paso, the most visited grave is that of "The Fastest Gun in the West"— John Wesley Hardin. Admission is free and it is open 24 hours a day.
Copia Street and I-10, El Paso, Texas 915-562-7062

3. El Paso/Juarez Tours – Air conditioned rubber tired trolleys transport riders from the Civic Center in El Paso across the border into Juarez. Once in Mexico, sightseeing and shopping are on the agenda.
One Civic Center Plaza, El Paso, Texas 79901
915-544-0062
www.borderjumper.com

4. Insights – El Paso Science Center – The Insights Science Center is a hands-on museum that makes learning fun. Exhibits on solar power, motion, light illumination, electricity, space science, computers, energy, and the human body make this a fun day for all ages.
505 N. Santa Fe Street, El Paso, Texas 79901 915-534-0000
www.insightsmuseum.org

5. U.S. Army Air Defense Artillery and Fort Bliss Museum – This U.S. Army post was established in 1848 as a defense against hostile Indians and was the headquarters for the Confederate forces in the Southwest during the Civil War. The museum displays exhibits from the early days as an Army post to the current technology used in air defense and artillery.
Building 1735, Marshall Road, Fort Bliss, Texas 79916-3802 915-568-3390
www.bliss.army.mil/Museum/fort_bliss_museum.htm

FORT WORTH

1. Amon Carter Museum – The Amon Carter Museum offers visitors an opportunity to view the works of great artists such as Alexander Calder, Thomas Cole, Stuart Davis, Thomas Eakins, Winslow Homer, Georgia O'Keeffe, John Singer Sargent, and Alfred Stieglitz. Admission to the permanent exhibit is free.
3501 Camp Bowie Boulevard, Fort Worth, Texas 817-728-1933
www.cartermuseum.org

2. Billy Bob's Texas – Originally built in 1910 as an open air barn for cattle during the Fort Worth Stock Show, this world-renowned bar is best known for its Texas size dance floor, live pro bull riding, and performances by country music's biggest stars. Because it has a maximum capacity of 6,028, you should have no trouble getting in this place.
2520 Rodeo Plaza, Fort Worth, Texas 76106 817-624-7117
www.billybobstexas.com

3. National Cowgirl Museum and Hall of Fame – The only museum in the world to honor women who changed the landscape of the American west. 172 pioneers, artists and writers, tribal leaders, entertainers, social activists, modern ranchers, and rodeo cowgirls are remembered.
1720 Gendy Street, Fort Worth, Texas 76107 817-336-4475
www.cowgirl.net/halloffame.aspx

4. Stockyards Collection and Museum – Photographs and memorabilia provide insight into the thriving cattle industry of Fort Worth in the 1800s.
131 E. Exchange Avenue, Fort Worth, Texas 76106 817-625-5082

5. Texas Cowboy Hall of Fame – The Texas Cowboy Hall of Fame is located within the Stockyards and pays tribute to 58 cowboys and cowgirls who excelled in the sports of rodeo and cutting.
128 E. Exchange Avenue, Fort Worth, Texas 76106
www.texascowboyhalloffame.com

CORPUS CHRISTI

1. The Texas State Aquarium – This underwater wonderland provides visitors to the aquarium with a view of how our underwater friends live. "Touch pools" allow the curious to touch various underwater creatures. A wonderful addition to any visit to the Gulf Coast.
2710 N. Shoreline Boulevard, Corpus Christi, Texas 78402 361-881-1200
www.texasstateaquarium.org

2. Corpus Christi Museum of Science and History – The Corpus Christi Museum of Science and History brings the treasures of the Texas Gulf Coast to life. Exhibits include the history of a 1554 Spanish shipwreck and replicas of the Spanish ships *Santa Maria* and *Pinta*.
1900 N. Chaparral, Corpus Christi, Texas 78401
361-883-2862
www.ccmuseumedres.com

3. Mustang Island State Park – This 5-mile stretch of beautiful beach on the Gulf of Mexico is perfect for swimming, sunbathing, hiking, surfing, and bird watching. Camping and picnicking facilities are also available.
326 Port Aransas, Corpus Christi, Texas 78373
www.tpwd.state.tx.us/park/mustang/mustang.htm

4. Padre Island National Seashore – Padre Island is the largest undeveloped stretch of barrier island in the world. Major attractions of the island include fishing, camping, and windsurfing. Scuba diving, snorkeling, and swimming also provide entertainment for the whole family.
20301 Park Road 22, Corpus Christi, Texas 78418 361-949-8068
www.nps.gov/pais

5. Port of Corpus Christi and Harbor Bridge – Port of Corpus Christi is the fifth largest port in the country and hosts ships from around the world. A pedestrian walkway on Harbor Bridge arches over the water providing visitors a wonderful view of the harbor and city.
222 Power, Corpus Christi, Texas 78401 361-882-5633
www.portofcorpuschristi.com

LUBBOCK

1. Buddy Holly Center – A tribute to Lubbock's famous native son, the Buddy Holly Center has an extensive collection of memorabilia and numerous exhibits. The Center not only showcases the works of Holly but also other performing artists from West Texas.
1801 Avenue G, Lubbock, Texas 79401 806-767-2686
www.buddyhollycenter.org

2. Historic Depot District – This former Fort Worth to Denver Rail Road Depot is now home to microbreweries, restaurants and coffee houses. Live music and theaters round out this historic area providing an evening of fun and entertainment for all.
19th Street, Lubbock, Texas 79401

3. Llano Estancado Winery – Llano Estancado Winery opened its doors in 1976 and today is the largest premium winery in Texas. Special events are planned throughout the year and tours are given daily.
3426 East FM1585, Lubbock, Texas 79404 806-745-2258
www.llanowine.com

4. Lubbock National Historic Landmark – One of the most significant archeological sites in North America, it provides evidence of continuous human occupation from 12,000 B.C. to the present. Guests enjoy interactive exhibits, hands-on activities, hiking trails, and picnic facilities.
2401 Landmark Drive, Lubbock, Texas 79415
www.ttu.edu/~museum/lll/index.html

5. Ranching Heritage Center – This museum and historical center gives visitors a view of ranching and pioneer life from the 1780s through the 1930s.
3121 Fourth Street, Lubbock, Texas 79409 806-742-0500
www.ttu.edu/ranchingheritagecenter

LAREDO

1. Laredo Center for the Arts – Founded in 1993, the Center promotes the works, and talents of local, national, and international artists.
500 San Agustin, Laredo, Texas 956-725-1715
www.laredoartcenter.org

2. Laredo Children's Museum – This hands-on children's museum provides a fun learning experience for kids of all ages.
Washington Street, Laredo, Texas 78040
956-725-2299
www.cityoflaredo.com/Museum/museum.html

3. Nuevo Laredo, Mexico – Within walking distance of Laredo, this busy Mexican city offers visitors excellent shopping, restaurants and fine hotels. Also, seasonal bullfights, a Mexican marketplace, and wagering await those who venture across the border.
100 Convent Avenue, Laredo, Texas 78040 956-795-2200

4. Republic of the Rio Grande Building and Museum – This one-story adobe style building once served as the capitol for the Republic of the Rio Grande. Seven flags have flown over this building, which now provides a history of this period of the Rio Grande Republic from 1839 to 1841.
1005 Zaragoza Street, Laredo, Texas 78040 956-727-3480

5. San Agustin Cathedral – This now historic cathedral was first built in 1760, the chapel made of simple mud-plastered palisade construction. The present structure was built in 1872 and made a cathedral in 2001.
201 San Agustin Avenue, Laredo, Texas 78040 956-722-1382

HISTORICAL ACCOMODATIONS

The Camino Real Paso del Norte Hotel in El Paso has a Tiffany glass dome in its elegant Dome Bar. Built in 1912, the hotel's guests have included Pancho Villa, President Taft, and Colonel "Black Jack" Pershing. It is listed on the National Register of Historic Places.

AMARILLO

1. Amarillo Livestock Auction – The Amarillo Livestock Auction is one of the largest privately owned cattle auctions in the country. More than 100,000 head of cattle are sold annually at the auction, which is held every Tuesday.
100 South Manhattan, Amarillo, Texas 79104 806-373-7647

2. American Quarter Horse Heritage Center and Museum – More than 30,000 people visit this 36,500 square foot museum every year, which showcases the history and beauty of the Quarter Horse. Exhibits, memorabilia, and art are among a few of the attractions.
1600 Quarter Horse Drive, Amarillo, Texas 79104 806-376-5181
www.aqha.org

3. Cadillac Ranch – Located just off of historic "Route 66," the Cadillac Ranch features a collection of ten graffiti-covered cars half buried, nose down in the desolate north Texas sand. The Cadillacs, dating from 1948 to 1963, are meant to represent the "Golden Age" of American automobiles.
Arnot Road (west of Amarillo on I-40, between exits 60 and 62),
Amarillo, Texas 79106

4. Elkins Ranch – This ranch is a third-generation working cattle ranch located in beautiful Palo Duro Canyon. Jeep tours, chuckwagon breakfasts, and western nights are sure to entertain anyone wanting to experience the Old West.
11301 East Texas Highway 217, Canyon, Texas 79015 806-488-2100
www.theElkinsRanch.com

5. Route 66 (Old San Jacinto) – Amarillo was the largest city on the 178-mile stretch of Route 66 which ran through Texas. Many vintage Route 66 sites and memorabilia shops remain for travelers and enthusiasts.
6th Street, Amarillo, Texas 79106 806-372-8766
www.route66.com

ABILENE

1. 12th Armored Division Memorial Museum – This museum honors the "Hellcats" of the 12th Armored Division, which served in the European Theater and occupied Japan during WWII.
1289 North 2nd Street, Abilene, Texas 325-677-6515
www.12tharmoreddivision.com

2. Abilene Zoo – The Abilene Zoo is one of the five largest in the state. It is home to more than eight hundred animals representing over two hundred species.
2070 Zoo Lane, Nelson Park, Abilene, Texas 79602 325-676-6085
www.abilenetx.com/zoo/zoo_home.htm

3. Center for Contemporary Arts – Four galleries and ten studios provide continuously changing exhibits by local, national, and international artists.
220 Cypress Street, Abilene, Texas 79601 325-677-8389
www.center-arts.com

4. Grace Museum – Located in the beautifully restored historic Grace Hotel, this museum is actually home to three museums: The Arts Museum, The History Museum, and The Children's Museum.
102 Cypress Street, Abilene, Texas 79601 325-673-4587
www.thegracemuseum.org

5. Paramount Theatre – This grand theater, built in 1930 and located in the heart of Abilene's revitalized downtown, offers a variety of family entertainment in the form of films, concerts, and musical productions to name only a few.
352 Cypress Street, Abilene, Texas 325-676-9620
www.paramount-abilene.org

Did You Know?

Texas is as large as New England, New York, Pennsylvania, Ohio, and Illinois combined. Its area is 266,874 square miles, including 4,959 square miles of inland water. Its greatest east-west distance is 744 miles, while the greatest north-south distance is 737 miles. Texas ranks first in size among all the continental states.

Numbers to Know When Traveling in Texas *Texas Association of Convention and Visitors Bureaus* 361-749-0467 www.tacvb.org

Traveling Texas — Mileage Chart

	Abilene	Alpine	Amarillo	Austin	Beaumont	Big Bend	Big Spring	Brownsville	Brownwood	Bryan-Coll. Station	Childress	Corpus Christi	Dallas	Del Rio	Eagle Pass	El Paso	Fredricksburg	Fort Stockton	Fort Worth	Galveston	Harlingen	Houston	Junction	Laredo
Abilene		310	266	214	414	392	107	519	77	254	155	389	180	246	298	439	175	251	150	399	493	349	145	373
Alpine	310		397	405	637	81	203	584	327	489	407	472	483	205	260	220	329	67	452	597	558	553	268	384
Amarillo	266	397		479	635	484	221	767	342	502	116	637	360	450	505	417	430	338	337	645	742	595	380	609
Austin	214	405	479		238	474	289	325	138	100	368	192	193	232	220	577	78	337	187	207	300	162	140	232
Beaumont	414	637	635	238		639	521	437	350	160	519	288	275	433	421	814	314	575	301	78	411	86	376	398
Big Bend	392	81	484	474	639		281	636	398	559	483	524	559	253	309	329	394	136	529	651	611	603	332	434
Big Spring	107	203	221	289	521	281		569	175	361	205	440	287	231	286	333	232	143	257	494	544	449	182	406
Brownsville	519	584	767	325	437	636	569		460	382	673	159	518	379	324	803	344	564	512	374	25	352	387	200
Brownwood	77	327	342	138	350	398	175	460		191	231	330	157	231	260	493	118	259	127	336	434	286	107	330
Bryan-Coll. Station	254	489	502	100	160	559	361	382	191		387	237	164	318	306	661	178	422	167	146	356	95	237	318
Childress	155	407	116	368	519	483	205	673	231	387		544	244	382	437	483	330	347	221	529	648	479	299	528
Corpus Christi	389	472	637	192	288	524	440	159	330	237	544		377	268	217	692	214	452	372	219	134	206	258	143
Dallas	180	483	360	193	275	559	287	518	157	164	244	377		388	413	617	246	415	30	288	493	238	264	425
Del Rio	246	205	450	232	433	253	231	379	231	318	382	268	388		56	425	174	186	358	393	354	348	125	179
Eagle Pass	298	260	505	220	421	309	286	324	260	306	437	217	413	56		480	187	241	387	380	299	336	154	124
El Paso	439	220	417	577	814	329	333	803	493	661	483	692	617	425	480		501	239	587	780	778	736	440	603
Fredricksburg	175	329	430	78	314	394	232	344	118	178	330	214	246	174	187	501		262	224	279	318	235	62	217
Fort Stockton	251	67	338	337	575	136	143	564	259	422	347	452	415	186	241	239	262		385	541	539	497	201	364
Fort Worth	150	452	337	187	301	529	257	512	127	167	221	372	30	358	387	587	224	385		309	487	258	233	416
Galveston	399	597	645	207	78	651	494	374	336	146	529	219	288	393	380	780	279	541	309		348	50	341	344
Harlingen	493	558	742	300	411	611	544	25	434	356	648	134	493	354	299	778	318	539	487	348		326	362	178
Houston	349	553	595	162	86	603	449	352	286	95	479	206	238	348	336	736	235	497	258	50	326		296	313
Junction	145	268	380	140	376	332	182	387	107	237	299	258	264	125	154	440	62	201	233	341	362	296		229
Laredo	373	384	609	232	398	434	406	200	330	318	528	143	425	179	124	603	217	364	416	344	178	313	229	

In continuous operation since 1858, the Excelsior Hotel in Jefferson is the second oldest hotel in Texas—old enough to have had Ulysses S. Grant, Rutherford B. Hayes, and Oscar Wilde as guests.

The longest highway in any one state is US 83. It runs for 903 miles from Brownsville to the Panhandle.

	Lubbock	Marshall	McAllen	Mineral Wells	Midland	Nacogdoches	Odessa	Orange	Palestine	Paris	Pecos	Port Arthur	San Angelo	San Antonio	Sherman	Temple	Texarkana	Tyler	Uvalde	Van Horn	Victoria	Wichita Falls	Waco	Zapata
Abilene	162	327	482	147	109	331	167	436	273	281	240	431	89	246	227	182	358	277	244	328	335	183	141	423
Alpine	279	625	527	163	417	600	143	659	542	583	100	642	231	358	536	423	660	567	275	100	468	443	436	433
Amarillo	119	504	731	234	307	521	254	648	467	402	321	653	294	494	338	445	494	457	479	401	600	422	231	658
Austin	369	277	300	315	194	228	334	262	177	295	390	251	202	79	258	67	339	223	161	457	123	102	283	281
Beaumont	579	188	429	549	343	126	529	24	169	291	628	17	438	281	318	231	256	192	362	694	209	243	412	423
Big Bend	360	707	578	242	481	675	222	715	619	665	190	696	300	406	617	499	744	647	324	181	522	518	513	484
Big Spring	103	435	533	40	214	439	60	544	380	388	133	538	87	296	333	290	465	384	276	221	403	290	233	456
Brownsville	657	567	56	595	519	489	609	458	478	615	617	441	482	273	583	392	635	525	321	684	230	427	608	150
Brownwood	232	300	424	200	102	280	219	373	221	258	293	368	96	187	211	119	335	242	205	379	259	123	169	380
Bryan-Coll. Station	416	195	365	390	200	129	409	182	98	234	475	177	279	164	227	72	260	144	247	541	152	85	280	355
Childress	139	388	637	243	191	405	264	532	351	286	337	537	255	400	222	329	378	341	398	425	489	306	108	577
Corpus Christi	527	421	152	465	386	344	479	310	333	470	505	292	353	143	442	255	490	380	197	572	85	286	475	149
Dallas	322	147	492	327	78	161	347	288	107	103	420	292	252	271	65	127	178	97	354	508	293	92	136	474
Del Rio	332	509	323	234	334	447	247	455	408	489	239	437	157	154	442	299	566	455	71	305	264	334	387	229
Eagle Pass	387	497	268	289	363	435	302	443	396	514	294	425	212	142	471	287	558	443	66	360	240	322	429	174
El Paso	344	764	747	293	539	770	274	838	712	717	208	825	403	554	657	595	795	714	495	120	668	615	552	653
Fredricksburg	319	355	307	257	201	305	276	338	254	349	315	324	145	71	308	136	413	297	121	381	172	169	285	267
Fort Stockton	220	558	508	104	352	533	84	599	474	516	53	586	163	315	469	356	593	500	256	120	428	376	376	414
Fort Worth	292	178	487	297	48	191	317	318	132	131	390	318	222	262	84	121	208	127	332	478	287	86	113	465
Galveston	562	259	367	519	346	186	538	98	201	342	594	79	407	241	351	217	328	247	322	661	154	230	422	362
Harlingen	631	541	35	570	494	464	584	433	453	590	592	415	457	247	558	366	609	500	296	658	204	402	553	129
Houston	511	216	344	475	296	138	494	108	150	291	550	90	363	196	300	167							271	338
Junction	270	396	351	208	209	355	222	400	302	364	254	385	96	115	318	178								
Laredo	499	509	143	409	400	447	422	420	408	527	417	403	320	154	490	299								

The White Elephant S
century-old barroom,
Best 100 Bars in Ame

Texas has about 11,500 historical markers. More than 700 local history museums, 40,000 recorded archeological sites, and more than 2,000 other sites are listed in the National Register of Historic Places.

Traveling Texas — Mileage Chart

	Abilene	Alpine	Amarillo	Austin	Beaumont	Big Bend	Big Spring	Brownsville	Brownwood	Bryan-Coll. Station	Childress	Corpus Christi	Dallas	Del Rio	Eagle Pass	El Paso	Fredericksburg	Fort Stockton	Fort Worth	Galveston	Harlingen	Houston	Junction	Laredo
Lubbock	162	279	119	369	579	360	103	657	232	416	139	527	322	332	387	344	319	220	292	562	631	511	270	499
Marshall	327	625	504	277	188	707	435	567	300	195	388	421	147	509	497	764	355	558	178	259	541	216	396	509
McAllen	482	527	731	300	429	578	533	56	424	365	637	152	492	323	268	747	307	508	487	367	35	344	351	143
Midland	147	163	234	315	549	242	40	595	200	390	243	465	327	234	289	293	257	104	297	519	570	475	208	409
Mineral Wells	109	417	307	194	343	481	214	519	102	200	191	386	78	334	363	539	201	352	48	346	494	296	209	400
Nacogdoches	331	600	521	228	126	675	439	489	280	129	405	344	161	447	435	770	305	533	191	186	464	138	355	447
Odessa	167	143	254	334	529	222	60	609	219	409	264	479	347	247	302	274	276	84	317	538	584	494	222	422
Orange	436	659	648	262	24	715	544	458	373	182	532	310	288	455	443	838	338	599	318	98	433	108	400	420
Palestine	273	542	467	177	169	619	380	478	221	98	351	333	107	408	396	712	254	474	132	201	453	150	302	408
Paris	281	583	402	295	291	665	388	615	258	234	286	470	103	489	514	717	349	516	131	342	590	291	364	527
Pecos	240	100	321	390	628	190	133	617	293	475	337	505	420	239	294	208	315	53	390	594	592	550	254	417
Port Arthur	431	642	653	251	17	696	538	441	368	177	537	292	292	437	425	825	324	586	318	79	415	90	385	403
San Angelo	89	231	294	202	438	300	87	482	96	279	255	353	252	157	212	403	145	163	222	407	457	363	96	320
San Antonio	246	358	494	79	281	406	296	273	187	164	400	143	271	154	142	554	71	315	262	241	247	196	115	154
Sherman	227	536	338	258	318	617	333	583	211	227	222	442	65	442	471	657	308	469	84	351	558	300	318	490
Temple	182	423	445	67	231	499	290	392	119	72	329	255	127	299	287	595	136	356	121	217	366	167	178	299
Texarkana	358	660	494	339	256	744	465	635	335	260	378	490	178	566	558	795	413	593	208	328	609	284	441	571
Tyler	277	567	457	223	192	647	384	525	242	144	341	380	97	455	443	714	297	500	127	247	500	197	339	455
Uvalde	244	275	479	161	362	324	276	321	205	247	398	197	354	71	66	495	121	256	332	322	296	277	99	130
Van Horn	328	100	401	457	694	181	221	684	379	541	425	572	508	305	360	120	381	120	478	661	658	616	320	484
Victoria	335	468	600	123	209	522	403	230	259	152	489	85	293	264	240	668	172	428	287	154	204	124	228	189
Waco	183	443	422	102	243	518	290	427	123	85	306	286	92	334	322	615	169	376	86	230	402	180	211	334
Wichita Falls	141	436	231	283	412	513	233	608	169	280	108	475	136	387	429	552	285	376	113	422	553	371	276	489
Zapata	423	433	658	281	423	484	456	150	380	355	577	149	474	229	174	653	267	414	465	362	129	338	279	50

Numbers to Know
When Traveling in Texas

Texas Hotel and Lodging Association
800-856-4328
www.texaslodging.com

The Governor's Mansion, built in 1856, is the oldest remaining public building in downtown Austin.

	Lubbock	Marshall	McAllen	Midland	Mineral Wells	Nacogdoches	Odessa	Orange	Palestine	Paris	Pecos	Port Arthur	San Angelo	San Antonio	Sherman	Temple	Texarkana	Tyler	Uvalde	Van Horn	Victoria	Waco	Wichita Falls	Zapata
Lubbock		469	620	116	254	482	136	599	423	383	204	593	193	384	320	345	475	419	369	292	490	345	208	548
Marshall	469		558	474	225	78	494	186	101	114	568	198	395	355	167	220	71	58	438	656	339	186	280	550
McAllen	620	558		552	483	482	565	451	462	594	561	434	446	237	557	366	624	508	273	627	220	401	572	94
Midland	116	474	552		254	478	20	572	420	427	94	564	112	322	372	318	505	424	279	182	429	322	272	458
Mineral Wells	254	225	483	254		239	274	366	177	179	347	360	189	246	126	142	256	175	308	435	315	120	89	449
Nacogdoches	482	78	482	478	239		498	139	65	165	571	144	375	293	201	177	146	74	376	652	262	157	297	475
Odessa	136	494	565	20	274	498		591	439	448	73	583	131	336	393	337	525	444	292	162	448	341	292	471
Orange	599	186	451	572	366	139	591		190	297	652	19	461	303	330	254	254	204	384	718	231	266	424	444
Palestine	423	101	462	420	177	65	439	190		141	513	186	316	254	157	124	163	47	337	594	248	99	243	450
Paris	383	114	594	427	179	165	448	297	141		521	309	353	373	64	228	92	101	455	609	385	194	178	576
Pecos	204	568	561	94	347	571	73	652	513	521		639	205	368	466	409	598	517	309	88	481	414	366	467
Port Arthur	593	198	434	564	360	144	583	19	186	309	639		452	285	335	249	266	209	366	705	213	260	429	427
San Angelo	183	395	446	112	189	375	131	461	316	353	205	452		210	306	207	430	337	190	283	317	218	230	370
San Antonio	384	355	237	322	246	293	336	303	254	373	368	285	210		366	145	417	301	83	434	114	180	335	203
Sherman	320	167	557	372	126	201	393	330	157	64	466	335	603	366		192	156	127	416	554	358	157	114	539
Temple	345	220	366	318	142	177	337	254	124	228	409	249	207	145	192		278	163	228	476	178	36	231	348
Texarkana	475	71	624	505	256	146	525	254	163	92	598	266	430	417	156	278		116	499	686	408	244	270	613
Tyler	419	58	508	424	175	74	444	204	47	101	517	209	337	301	127	163	116		384	605	295	128	233	497
Uvalde	369	438	273	279	308	376	292	384	337	455	309	366	190	83	416	228	499	384		376	193	263	374	179
Van Horn	292	656	627	182	435	652	162	718	594	609	88	705	283	434	554	476	686	605	376		548	495	454	533
Victoria	490	339	220	429	315	262	448	231	248	385	481	213	317	114	358	178	408	295	193	548		202	400	213
Waco	345	186	401	322	120	157	341	266	99	194	414	260	218	180	157	36	244	128	263	495	202		199	383
Wichita Falls	208	280	572	272	89	297	292	424	243	178	366	429	230	335	114	231	270	233	374	454	400	199		538
Zapata	548	550	94	458	449	475	471	444	450	576	467	427	370	203	539	348	613	497	179	533	213	383	538	

*T*he largest body of water completely within the boundaries of Texas is Sam Rayburn Reservoir in East Texas, which covers more than 114,000 acres.

Texas has more counties (254) than any other state. Forty-one counties in Texas are each larger than the state of Rhode Island.

Historic Hotels of Texas

In a state rich in culture and history, the grand hotels of Texas reflect the pride and ingenuity of the cattle barons, beer barons, and businessmen who sought to bring a level of sophistication to the Lone Star State. During the late 1800s and early 1900s, extravagant hotels began to dot the skylines of the emerging Texas cities, making Texas one of the best choices in the country for even the most discriminating traveler.

The following hotels continue to offer travelers on business or pleasure unsurpassed luxury, service, and quality while offering a piece of Texas history.

The Adolphus Hotel – Dallas

This luxury landmark hotel in the heart of downtown Dallas was built in 1912 by beer baron Adolphus Busch. Almost one hundred years after it first opened, and millions of dollars in renovations, the Adolphus Hotel continues to be an example of grace and refinement. Guests at the Adolphus can enjoy an elegant meal in The French Room or more hearty Texas fare at the Rodeo Bar and Grill. Whatever your choice, your stay at the Adolphus will be a memorable one. This world-class hotel has been featured on *Condé Nast Traveler's Reader's Choice Gold List* as one of the "Best Places to Stay in the World."

CONTACT INFORMATION

1321 Commerce Street
Dallas, TX 75202
Tel: 214-742-8200
www.hoteladolphus.com

The Aristocrat – Dallas

The Aristocrat Hotel, located at the east end of the Central Business District, was the first hotel built by Conrad Hilton in 1925. The Aristocrat has been carefully restored to its original style and is on the National Register of Historic Places. It is also a City of Dallas Landmark and proudly displays the prestigious Texas Historical Marker.

CONTACT INFORMATION

1933 Main Street
Dallas, TX 75201
Tel: 214-741-7700
www.hotel-dallas.com

Camino Real – El Paso

Considered the "Jewel of the City," this hotel is proudly listed on the *National Register of Historic Places*. Located only six blocks from the Mexican border, Camino Real offers a combination of history and elegance. The hotel has long been known for its Tiffany cut glass dome in the lobby, stained glass windows, exquisite crystal chandeliers, and marble statuary crafted by Italian artists nearly 100 years ago. Be sure to have a cocktail in the Dome Bar, voted one of the top 12 bars in the world worth traveling for by *GQ Magazine*.

CONTACT INFORMATION

101 South El Paso Street
El Paso, TX 79901
Tel: 915-534-3000
www.caminoreal.com

Driskill Hotel – Austin

Built in 1884 by wealthy cattle baron Jesse Driskill, this historic landmark has always been the choice of discerning travelers when visiting Austin. Lovingly restored to its original glory, the Driskill has hosted six governor's inaugural balls and numerous celebrity stays. For a unique dining experience while staying at the Driskill, be sure to make reservations for the Driskill Grill Chef's Table. Seating six people and located in the middle of the kitchen, this table offers guests custom-prepared tastings from the menu and a view of the busiest spot in the hotel.

CONTACT INFORMATION

604 Brazo Street
Austin, TX 78701
Tel: 514-474-5911
www.driskillhotel.com

Hotel Galvez – Galveston Island

Christened the "Queen of the Gulf" on the day it opened in 1911, the Hotel Galvez is known as the grand dame of the island hotels. Often the host to such notable guests as Teddy Roosevelt, Howard Hughes, and Frank Sinatra, this hotel has withstood the test of time, remaining a vision of elegance rising from the beach. With gracious hospitality and historic ambiance, the Hotel Galvez is haven to Houstonians, only fifty miles away, as well as to world travelers.

CONTACT INFORMATION

2024 Seawall Boulevard
Galveston Island, TX 77550
Tel: 409-765-7721
www.galveston.com/galvez

The Mansion on Turtle Creek – Dallas

This palatial mansion, built in the 1920s for a Texas cotton magnate, was transformed in the early part of the century into an intimate hotel with the ambiance of a private residence. Whether feasting in the Mansion's elegant dining room or enjoying a cocktail poolside, every moment of a stay at the Mansion is guaranteed to provide perfection. World-renowned for its luxury, elegance, and unsurpassed attention to detail, this hotel provides a royal experience for all guests.
The recipient of numerous prestigious awards, The Mansion on Turtle Creek awaits the arrivals of the most discriminating travelers.

CONTACT INFORMATION

2821 Turtle Creek Boulevard
Dallas, TX 75219
Tel: 214-559-2100
www.mansionturtlecreek.com

The Menger Hotel – San Antonio

The oldest continuously operating hotel west of the Mississippi, the Menger was built only twenty three years after the historic battle of the Alamo. The guest book of the Menger reads like a "Who's Who" in Texas history, listing such personalities as Theodore Roosevelt, Babe Ruth, Mae West, Robert E. Lee, and Ulysses S. Grant. Visitors may be in for a haunting experience while staying at the Menger, as the hotel is rumored to be haunted by some of its previous famous guests.

CONTACT INFORMATION

204 Alamo Plaza
San Antonio, TX 78205
Tel: 210-223-4361
www.historicmenger.com

Sheraton Gunter Hotel – San Antonio

After 96 years of continuous service, the Sheraton Gunter Hotel still stands "at the Center of Everything." This elegant hotel, built in 1909, is located in the heart of San Antonio. While staying at the Gunter, be sure to catch a show at the historic Majestic Theatre, located directly across the street.

CONTACT INFORMATION

205 East Houston Street
San Antonio, TX 78205
Tel: 210-227-3241
www.gunterhotel.com

St. Anthony Wyndham Hotel – San Antonio

With the opening of the St. Anthony in 1909, Texans experienced an entirely new level of luxury. Charging rates of only $1.50 in 1915, the St. Anthony offered luxurious amenities such as illuminated closets, bedroom lights that turned off when the door was closed from the outside, as well as private bathrooms. In 1935, an antique elevator shaft was transformed into the first central air-conditioning unit. After almost one hundred years of service, the St. Anthony continues to provide travelers with timeless elegance and first class service. This hotel is conveniently located near the historic Riverwalk and other San Antonio attractions.

CONTACT INFORMATION

300 East Travis
San Antonio, TX 78205
Tel: 210-227-4392
www.wyndham.com

TRAVELIN' TEXAS

The Tarpon Inn in Port Aransas is listed on the National Register of Historic Places. Its lobby walls are covered with more than 7,000 autographed tarpon scales, including one signed by **Franklin Roosevelt**. Anglers used to leave a record of their prized catch by writing their name, hometown, date, and size of the catch on a two- to three-inch tarpon scale that was then attached to the walls. Anglers once came from all over the country to fish for tarpon, which are now scarce in these waters.

HISTORICAL MARKERS

★ There are approximately 12,800 historical markers across the state of Texas!

★ The number of markers in Texas changes monthly with the addition of new markers and the occasional removal of a marker.

★ Approximately 200 markers are added each year.

★ State of Texas historical markers were first seen dotting the Texas landscape in 1936 when the Texas Centennial Commission placed more than 900 granite markers throughout the state in celebration of the 100th anniversary of the Texas Revolution and the establishment of the Republic of Texas.

★ The Texas State Historical Survey Committee, later to become the Texas Historical Commission, was founded in 1953. The Commission took over the responsibility of caring for the markers placed in 1936.

★ The Official Texas Historical Marker program began in 1962.

★ There are three types of state historical markers: subject markers, building markers (Recorded Texas Historic Landmarks), and cemetery markers (Historic Texas Cemetery).

★ Subject markers are solely for educational and heritage tourism purposes, are usually of a local or regional significance, and generally represent topics such as church congregations, schools, communities, businesses, events, or important people dating back at least 50 years.

★ Recorded Texas Historic Landmarks are placed on properties that have been judged to be historically or architecturally significant. Buildings must be at least 50 years old and retain their original architectural integrity to receive this designation. This is the highest honor the state can bestow on a historic structure.

Does It Really Take 33 Years to Build an Airport?

The Dallas-Fort Worth Airport lies almost entirely within the city limits of Grapevine.

Once upon a time, before residents of Dallas and Fort Worth realized they lived in the same state and had more similarities than differences, officials in both cities badly wanted a new airport. In those days, rivalry between the two towns was intense and in 1940, a plan by the federal government to build and share a large, regional airport fell on deaf ears in both cities. Finally and with the help of American Airlines and Braniff Airways, a moderate-sized airport was built in Arlington, a city that was located half-way between Dallas and Fort Worth. Even though the airport was built, a disagreement about which way the terminal building should face, among other issues, doomed the project and the completed field was ceded to the city of Arlington and used during World War II as a military installation.

After the war, Fort Worth officials reclaimed the air strip, renamed it Greater Fort Worth International Airport, and began pouring money into improving it. Meanwhile, Dallas city fathers made extensive plans to improve and modernize their own airport, Love Field. When Federal authorities again suggested that the two rivals work together to inaugurate a large, cooperative, regional airport, Dallas balked. The animosity continued, and the Fort Worth airport was renamed Amon G. Carter Field in honor of the mayor, of whom it was said refused to travel to nearby Dallas unless he absolutely had to and who, rather than dine in a Dallas restaurant, preferred to carry a sack lunch from home.

Did You Know?

The Dallas-Fort Worth Airport occupies more than 30 square miles (nearly 20,000 acres) of real estate.

Twice more during the 1950s, efforts were made to finalize a joint venture, but old issues would resurface and both efforts were unsuccessful. The city of Fort Worth seemed a little more aggressive than Dallas in its desire to have an airport and officially purchased Carter Field in 1960 and once again renamed it, this time to the Greater Southwest International Airport. They sure had trouble working out a solution to the problem, but they had no trouble finding new names for airports! And even though they were insistent on having an airport of their own, Fort Worth officials sadly watched as their airport's market share of passengers dramatically fell in the late 1950s while Dallas's Love Field soared. Finally, Greater Southwest International Airport was all but abandoned.

Once again, and this time unwilling to take "No" for an answer, Federal authorities all but ordered Dallas and Fort Worth officials to work together to resolve the issue of building an airport that could accommodate the exploding air traffic in the region and that would serve the needs of both cities. Finally, heads were put together and a new spirit of co-operation prevailed and plans were laid for the present-day Dallas-Fort Worth International Airport (DFW). On January 13, 1974, an American Airlines flight from New York City became the first plane to utilize the new facilities. Today, DFW is the international headquarters of American Airlines. It occupies 30 square miles and houses three control towers, four terminals, seven runways, 100 food and beverage outlets, and 132 gates. The facility is the second largest airport in the United States and the third largest in the world. More than 52 million passengers fly in and out of DFW annually. ★

Did You Know?

DFW is the third largest airport in the world.

THE LAST PICTURE SHOW
...Or Not!

Originally, theaters of the late 1800s and early 1900s in Texas were saloons transformed for an evening to host touring vaudeville performances. The floors were dusty, the performers rough, and the cowboys often missed the spittoons, but they provided a break from the reality of life and were a welcome distraction. As times changed and technology advanced, the dusty saloons gave way to actual theaters. With Thomas Edison's brilliant invention, "moving pictures" in the early 1900s, entertainment was forever changed. Often narrated or accompanied by a piano, silent movies brought a level of entertainment to the country, and to the state of Texas, never before experienced. In the late 1920s, "talkies" came on the scene, captivating a new generation of audiences. Soon movie theaters began dotting the landscape of small towns, often becoming the social gathering point of the community. With the onset of World War II, movie theaters took on a whole new meaning, bringing newsreels of the war to every anxious citizen. The 1950s through 1970s were hard years for the movie industry. Changing cultures and more options for entertainment forced many old theaters to close their doors. Often the theaters of the grand era were left abandoned and some were even destroyed to make room for urban sprawl. A lucky few theaters survived the changes and were lovingly restored for a new generation to enjoy.

Theaters provide a historical roadmap of our country's entertainment evolution. They are a testament to changes in society and advancements in technology. Since the beginning of time, people have sought a break from difficult days and looked for entertainment in various forms. The following is a list of a few Texas theaters which—through luck and hard work—have managed to stand the test of time. If you are in the area, buy some popcorn and a drink, sit back, and enjoy the show.

The Aztec – Albany

The Aztec was built in 1927 by Frank Whitney to resemble a Spanish hacienda. With its red clay roof and stucco walls the Aztec stands in sharp contrast to the rest of the town. Once inside, patrons are transported to a different place and time, with an interior designed to resemble a Spanish courtyard. The ceiling, like that of many of the time, is a wonderful blue with twinkling stars adding to the atmosphere. The Albany, built as a movie theater, is now primarily used as a venue for the performing arts in Albany. Comfortably seating 288, this wonderful theater is a treat to visit.

The Aztec
141 South Main Street
Albany, Texas 76430
325-762-3818

The Cliftex – *Clifton*

The Queen Theatre, now known as the Cliftex, opened it doors on September 15, 1916 as the first, and at the time, only movie theater in Clifton. Renamed and relocated by 1927, the Cliftex has provided generations of Clifton residents with entertainment. Tracking the changes of the industry, the Cliftex has gone from "silent movies" to "talkies" to the first-run movies of the twenty-first century. The Cliftex has stayed in continuous operation since its opening and continues to entertain. Enjoy a movie at the Cliftex for a true old movie house experience.

The Cliftex
306 W. 5th St.
Clifton, Texas 76634
254-675-1229

The Cole – *Hallettsville*

This Spanish styled theater opened in 1929 to entertain the people of Halletsville. Originally seating 700 patrons, the Cole used an early form of air conditioning to cool the theater. Huge blocks of ice were strategically positioned and fans blew cool air onto theater goers. Completely refurbished, the Cole seats up to 200 and is a popular spot to view first run movies with an old time atmosphere.

The Cole
207 East 2nd St.
Hallettsville, Texas 77964
361-798-4569

The Gem – *Claude*

Built in 1915 and originally named the "Claudia," this picture show and vaudeville theater hosted silent movies and live performances throughout its illustrious career. Charles Goodnight, famous rancher and purveyor of the JA Ranch, made a silent movie entitled *Old Texas* using his ranch as a set. The movie *Old Texas* premiered at the Claudia in 1918. The 1963 western drama *Hud* with Paul Newman was filmed in Armstrong County and also premiered at the Gem. As have other theaters of its time, the Gem has undergone hard times and been rediscovered by the patrons of the twenty-first century. Today the Gem seats 192 theater goers and is home to numerous touring performances.

The Gem Theatre
P.O. Box 450
Claude, Texas 79019
806-226-5409

The Majestic – *Eastland*

Opened in 1920 and originally named the "Connellee," this old theater entertained a town built around the oil boom of the early nineteenth century. Showing "silent movies" and hosting live performances, the Majestic stood strong through hard times but finally closed its doors in 1986. Today, thanks to several grants and the hard work of many, the Majestic is thriving. The timeless paintings of cowboys on horseback along with the beautiful floral ceiling designs once again provide patrons with timeless ambiance. The Majestic is now home to first run movies and plays and is also used as a community civic center.

The Majestic Theatre
P.O. Box 705
Eastland, Texas 76448-0705
254-629-2102

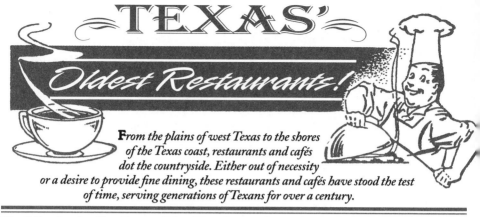

From the plains of west Texas to the shores of the Texas coast, restaurants and cafés dot the countryside. Either out of necessity or a desire to provide fine dining, these restaurants and cafés have stood the test of time, serving generations of Texans for over a century.

The following is a list of some of the oldest, best, and most interesting restaurants in Texas.

Blessing Hotel Coffee Shop – Blessing

The little town of Blessing was a bustling Texas community in the early 1900s. The Blessing Hotel, established during the town's boom in 1906, provided weary train travelers and dog race patrons a hot meal and a comfortable place to stay during their visit. Now part of a community of eight hundred people, the Blessing Hotel Coffee Shop continues to serve locals and travelers alike with timeless Texas cuisine. The coffee shop serves up classic Texas fare such as chicken fried steak, meat loaf, chopped steak, and chicken and dumplings. Served buffet style, there are plenty of breads and vegetables to choose from, guaranteeing no one leaves the Blessing Hotel Coffee Shop hungry. Also open for breakfast, the coffee shop serves up wonderful hotcakes and steaming hot coffee.

CONTACT
Blessing Hotel Coffee Shop
FM 616 & 10th
Blessing, Texas 77419
361-588-6623

★ ★ ★ ★ ★

Blue Bonnet Café – Marble Falls

Almost everyone in Texas is familiar with the Blue Bonnet Café. Serving hungry Texans their famous "home-style cooking" for over seventy five years, the Blue Bonnet Café remains the restaurant of choice for locals and tourists alike. Founded in 1929 as a local diner, the Blue Bonnet Café serves a bountiful breakfast all day long and classic meat and vegetables for lunch and dinner. Famous for their chicken fried steak, pot roast, and meatloaf, a slice of one of their wonderful pies is also recommended. The Blue Bonnet Café goes through fifty to seventy-five made-from-scratch pies per day—one hundred on Saturday! If it is a down-home Texas meal you are craving, head straight for the Blue Bonnet Café; be prepared to wait however, because they serve up to 2,000 people on Saturday and the café only seats 120.

CONTACT
Blue Bonnet Café
211 Hwy. 281
Marble Falls, Texas 78654
830-693-2344
www.bluebonnetcafe.net

Christie's Seafood Restaurant – Houston

In 1917, Turkish immigrant Theodore Christie began selling food from a stand on the Houston waterfront. Through the years, Christie responded to the needs and requests of his clientele, creating unique dishes. "Always Imitated, Never Equaled" became the restaurant's slogan as it originated such items as the Trout Sandwich, the original "Fish Stick," the Fisherman's Platter, and French Fried Shrimp. Christie's continues to provide Houstonians with the original recipes that made their fresh catches, homemade soups, dressing, and sauces famous. Definitely a Houston tradition!

CONTACT
Christie's Seafood Restaurant
6029 Westheimer Road
Houston, Texas 77057
713-978-6563
www.christies-restaurant.com

★ ★ ★ ★ ★

Fossati's Delicatessen – Victoria

Billed as "The Oldest Deli in Texas," Fossati's Delicatessen was founded in 1882 by Italian immigrant Frank Napoleon Fossati. Fossati, an Italian stone cutter who came to the United States in 1880, began his career as a restaurateur selling chili and sandwiches from a stand on Main Street. Today Frank Fossati's descendants proudly serve food prepared from the original recipes that made Fossati's a success. Soups made from scratch, sandwiches piled high, and Fossati's famous Italian spaghetti continue the traditions of this original Italian deli.

CONTACT
Fossati's Delicatessen
302 Main Street
Victoria, Texas 77901
361-576-3354

★ ★ ★ ★ ★

Gaido's Seafood Restaurant – Galveston

Gaido's Seafood Restaurant has been a Galveston tradition since 1911. This landmark restaurant was opened almost one hundred years ago by Italian immigrant San Jacinto Gaido. Now run by his great-grandchildren, Gaido's continues the tradition of excellence by providing diners with the freshest catch cooked to order. Gaido's serves oysters, shrimp, scallops, snapper, and more to more than 350,000 loyal patrons a year. Obviously, a stop in Galveston would not be complete without a wonderful meal at Gaido's.

CONTACT
Gaido's Seafood Restaurant
3800 Seawall Boulevard
Galveston, Texas 77550
409-762-9625
www.galveston.com/gaidos

James Coney Island – Houston

Since 1923, James Coney Island has been serving Houstonians the best hotdogs and onion rings in Texas. A Houston institution

CONTACT
James Coney Island
5745 Westheimer
Houston, Texas 77057
713-785-9333
www.jamesconeyisland.com

founded by Greek immigrants James and Tom Papadakis, JCI brings the tastes of the East Coast to Texas. Their trademark James Coney Island hotdog consists of a custom-made grilled wiener stuffed inside a specially baked and steamed bun, topped with mustard, chili sauce, and onions. There are a variety of options at JCI but the original is still the favorite. James Coney Island remains strong serving more than 7.5 million hot dogs annually at 24 locations in the Houston area.

★ ★ ★ ★ ★

OST Restaurant – Bandera

The OST Restaurant (which stands for Old Spanish Trail) can be found in Bandera, the self-proclaimed "Cowboy Capital of the World." Open since 1921, OST brings out the cowboy in everyone with wagon wheel chandeliers, a spur collection big enough to outfit the entire cavalry, and a saddle bar. During the week the clientele stays true to its heritage, mostly local cowboys and ranch hands. On the weekends, a different look comes to the OST when bikers from across the nation travel through town. The OST is host to many different types of people, but the menu remains constant with solid Texas

fare ranging from classic chicken fried steak to a selection of Tex-Mex entrees. The OST is also known for its breakfast buffet, which is guaranteed to be fast and filling. For a taste of the Old West, drop by the OST for some genuine Texas samplings.

CONTACT
OST Restaurant
305 Main Street
Bandera, Texas 78003
830-796-3836

★ ★ ★ ★ ★

Po-Po Restaurant – Boerne

Located in the Texas Hill Country, this wonderfully colorful restaurant was

CONTACT
Po-Po Restaurant
829 FM 289
Boerne, Texas 78006
830-537-4194
www.poporestaurant.com

first established as a dance hall in 1929 by rancher/dairyman Edwin Nelson. Operating as a restaurant since 1932, the Po-Po Restaurant has been a popular destination for families in San Antonio and residents of the Hill Country for more than seventy five years. Over 1,700 plates adorn the walls of the Po-Po Restaurant from the travels of the owners. The Po-Po Restaurant specializes in hand-cut steaks, fried shrimp, fried chicken, and its famous burgers.

Stagecoach Inn – Salado

Founded in the 1860s, the Stagecoach Inn is one of the oldest restaurants in Texas. Built on an old Tonkawa Indian village site by early settler W. B. Armstrong, the Inn was a welcome sight for stagecoach travelers along the Chisholm Trail. Having hosted such famous travelers as Sam Houston, General George Custer, the James Brothers, and Sam Bass, the Inn has carved its place in history. The Inn continues a tradition of the stagecoach days with waitresses reciting the daily bill of fare. Meals are a fixed price and generally include original recipes for prime rib, fried chicken, and baked ham. Be sure not to fill up on the hush puppies because dessert comes with the meal!

CONTACT
The Stagecoach Inn
1 Main Street
Salado, Texas 76571
800-732-8994
http://touringtexas.com/stage

★ ★ ★ ★ ★

Wunsche Bros. Café and Saloon – Spring

Charlie and Willie Wunsche built the Wunsche Bros. Hotel and Saloon in 1902 to accommodate railroad employees in the switchyard town of Spring. Serving up hearty Texas fare to workers on the Houston and Great Northern Railroad, the café established a reputation for providing a hot meal and a strong drink. The Wunsche Bros. Café and Saloon, now completely refurbished, once again serves the home-cooked dishes that satisfied the railroad workers so many years ago. Currently owned by Brenda and Scott Mitchell, this wonderful café offers diners such classic Texas plates as chicken fried steak, a half-pound hearty hamburger, and their mouthwatering trademark chocolate whiskey cake. Spring is now a thriving community outside Houston with specialty shops and charming retail stores. If you stop in Spring, be sure to make time for the Wunsche Bros. Café and Saloon.

CONTACT
Wunsche Bros. Café and Saloon
103 Midway Street
Spring, Texas 77383
281-350-1902
www.wunschebroscafe.com

Websites to Know
When Traveling in Texas

★ *Texas Road Information – TxDOT Expressway*
www.dot.state.tx.us/hcr/main.htm

★ *Texas State Travel Guide*
www.traveltexas.com

★ *National Park Service*
www.nps.gov

Ten Places of Historical Interest

It is impossible to define the ten most historic sites in Texas. The state is filled with so much history and abounds with so many places steeped in traditions— first of the Republic and later the state—that to list all of the important places would take many pages. Here, in no particular order, are ten sites that rank high on anyone's list as foundation stones of Texas history and heritage.

The Texas Historical Commission is devoted to the identification and preservation of Texas' architectural, archeological, and cultural landmarks. To learn more about the historic sites of Texas and the Texas Historical Commission, please contact:

**Texas Historical Commission
P.O. Box 12276
Austin, Texas 78711-2276
512-463-6100
www.thc.state.tx.us**

★ The Alamo

Located in downtown San Antonio, the Alamo was the site of the Mexican army's massive effort in March 1836 to retake the mission and the city from their Anglo defenders. Although Santa Anna's army conquered the ancient mission and decimated all of its guardians, the victory was short-lived. "Remember the Alamo" became the clarion call of Texans everywhere as they took up arms under General Sam Houston and defeated their foe at San Jacinto the following month.

★2 The King Ranch

Covering 826,000 acres, an area larger than the state of Rhode Island, this is the largest ranch within the continental United States. It was started in 1853 by a Rio Grande steamboat captain, Richard King. In 1915, the famed Santa Gertrudis breed of cattle was developed here and, a short time later, oil was discovered on the property, income from which saved the ranch from financial ruin. King Ranch is open to visitors and is located off Route 141, near Kingsville.

★3 The Texas School Book Depository Building

Assassin Lee Harvey Oswald peered out of a window on the sixth floor of this structure on November 22, 1963, as he fired shots that killed President John F. Kennedy and wounded Governor John B. Connally. The Depository Building and nearby Dealey Plaza, containing the John F. Kennedy Memorial, are both open to the public and are located at the corner of Houston and Elm Streets in downtown Dallas.

★4 Fort Davis National Historic Site

Built in 1854, Fort Davis, following the War Between the States, became home to the all-black 10th U. S. Cavalry, called by the Indians, "Buffalo Soldiers." The fort was the site of the court-martial of Lieutenant Henry Ossian Flipper, the first black graduate of West Point. Found guilty on trumped-up charges of "conduct unbecoming an officer," Flipper was exonerated in 1976 when his dishonorable discharge was rescinded and his guilty verdict overturned. It is located on State Route 17, north of the town of Fort Davis.

★5 Texas State Capitol Complex

Completed in 1888, the Texas State Capitol is located at 100 East 11th Street in Austin. Built in the Renaissance Revival style, the structure is several feet taller than the national capitol in Washington, D. C. Across the street is the Governor's Mansion, built between 1854 and 1856. Inside, exhibits include Sam Houston's bed and Stephen F. Austin's desk. The Texas State Library, located east of the Capitol on Brazos Street between 12th and 13th Streets, houses a copy of the Texas Declaration of Independence, as well as a panoramic mural depicting the phases of Texas history.

☆Fort Worth Stockyards Historical District

Fort Worth was still a rowdy cowtown in the 1880s when a few entrepreneurs teamed up to develop a large stockyard and railroad facilities north of town. Several meat-packing plants soon made the area home and within a few years, Fort Worth became the second largest livestock market in America. Today, the area is accented by restored buildings now housing such authentic reminders of yesteryear as the Booger Saloon, Cowtown Coliseum, the Livestock Exchange Building, and the Stockyards Hotel. The District is located along Exchange Avenue and neighboring streets.

☆Fredericksburg

Located at the junction of US Highways 87 and 290 is the town of Fredericksburg. The surrounding area was first permanently settled by Germans during the 1840s, and today the Teutonic influence is still felt in the town's several "old-country" restaurants. Admiral Chester Nimitz, the U. S. naval commander in the South Pacific during World War II, was born here in 1885. His grandfather's hotel is now a state historical park commemorating both Nimitz and the war in the Pacific. The site is located at 340 East Main Street.

☆Palo Duro Canyon State Park

Once the domain of prehistoric bison hunters and, later, the Comanche Indians, Palo Duro Canyon stretches for 120 miles along State Route 217 in the Panhandle. Later, Comancheros and American buffalo hunters frequented the area that eventually became the ranch of famed cattleman Charles Goodnight. The nearby town of Canyon houses the Panhandle-Plains Historical Museum, the state's oldest such tax-supported facility, where murals by Harold Bugbee and Ben Carlton Mead tell the story of Texas.

☆Galveston

The city of Galveston is almost like a living architectural museum. Facing the Gulf of Mexico, the town was almost obliterated in the great hurricane of 1900, but, thankfully, enough homes and commercial buildings were spared to allow a present-day visitor to revel in the beauty of the place. Many of the buildings are museum homes and open to the public, but a good overview of the town can be had by simply walking up one street and down another. The Rosenberg Library at 2310 Sealy houses an impressive rare book collection, as well as vast research materials pertaining to the region.

☆Washington-on-the-Brazos

The village of Washington was the first and last capital of the Republic of Texas and it was here, on March 2, 1836, that the Texas Declaration of Independence was signed by fifty-nine men who vowed to shake the bonds of Mexican domination. Today, a state park dominates the area, which features the Star of the Republic Museum and Independence Hall. Washington is located on State Route 6, northwest of Houston.

Did You Know?

Throughout its history, six different flags have flown over Texas, but governments have actually changed eight times: Spain (1519-1685); France (1685-1690); Spain (1690-1821); Mexico (1821-1836); Republic of Texas (1836-1845); United States (1845-1861); Confederate States of America (1861-1865); and United States (1865-present). Texas joined the Union for the first time on December 29, 1845. It's the only state to enter statehood by treaty instead of territorial annexation.

An Open Letter from the Great State of Texas,
Chamber of Commerce, to All You Yankees Visitin' Amongst Us

THINGS TO REMEMBER WHEN IN TEXAS

Never order a bottle of pop or a can of soda in Texas. In Texas, everything is called Coke, even if you want a Dr Pepper, Sprite, or Pepsi. After ordering a Coke, you will then be asked what kind.

If you forget a Texan's name, you may call him (or her) "Bubba." You have a 75 percent chance of being right.

Just because you can drive on snow and ice does not mean that we can. Stay home the two days of the year it snows.

If you run your car into a ditch during a freak snow storm, don't panic. Four men in the cab of a four-wheel drive truck with a 12-pack of beer and a tow chain will be along shortly. Don't try to help them; just stay out of their way. This is what they live for.

Don't be surprised to find movie rentals and bait in the same store, a convenience appreciated by many Texans. It is important, however, not to buy food at the convenience store.

We believe that everything tastes better when fried in bacon grease, so if you have any issues with pig products, you will starve here.

When speaking in Texas, remember that "y'all" is singular, "all y'all" is plural, and "all y'all's" is plural possessive.

There is nothing sillier than a Yankee imitating a Texas accent, unless it is a Texan imitating a Yankee accent.

Get used to hearing, "You ain't from around here, are you?"

People walk and talk slower in Texas—be patient.

Don't worry that you don't understand anyone—they don't understand you either.

The first Texas expression picked up by a transplanted Yankee is usually the adjective "big ol'." This can be used in a number of ways such as he's got a "big ol' truck," he's a pretty "big ol' boy," or she has a "big ol' ass on her."

The proper pronunciations you learned in school are no longer proper.

Be advised: The "He needed killin'" defense is valid in Texas.

If attending a funeral in Texas, remember, we stay until the last shovel of dirt is thrown on and the tent is torn down.

If you hear a Texan exclaim, "Hey, y'all, watch this!" stay out of his way. These are likely the last words he will ever say.

Texans do not use turn signals, and they ignore those who do. In fact, if you see a signal blinking on a car with a Texas license plate, you may rest assured that it was on when the car was purchased.

If there is the prediction of the slightest chance of even the most minuscule accumulation of snow, your presence is required at the local grocery store. It does not matter if you need anything from the store, it is just something you're supposed to do.

Satellite dishes are very popular in Texas. When you purchase one, it is to be positioned directly in front of your home or trailer. This is logical, bearing in mind that the dish cost considerably more than the home or trailer and should, therefore, be displayed.

In Texas churches you will hear the hymn, "All Glory, Laud and Honor." You will also hear expressions such as, "Laud, have mercy," Good Laud," and "Laudy, Laudy, Laudy."

As you are cursing the person driving 15 mph in a 55 mph zone, directly in the middle of the road, remember, many folks learned to drive on a model of vehicle known as John Deere, and this is the proper speed and lane position for that vehicle.

You can ask a Texan for directions, but unless you already know the positions of key hills, trees, and rocks, you're better off trying to find it yourself.

In Texas, "You can just kiss my ass" is a perfectly acceptable way to end an argument.

Always take your hat off when you say the name "Tom Landry."

Sincerely,

The Chamber

TEXAS HIGHWAY TRIVIA

TxDOT: The Texas Department of Transportation was established in 1917 to administer federal highway funds.

Size of the road network: There are more than one-quarter million miles, the largest in the nation.

Acres of right-of-way in the state highway system: There are 1.3 million acres of right-of-way.

Adopt-a-Highway Program: The Adopt-a-Highway program was established in 1985. There are more than 4,000 volunteer groups participating in the Adopt-a-Highway program and more than 8,000 miles of highway have been adopted.

The first road built: The first road built by the highway department in Texas began in 1918 and was completed in 1920. The 20-mile section stretched between Falfurrias and Encino in Brooks County. This section is along the same corridor as the present-day US 281.

The shortest highway: The shortest highway in Texas is Loop 168 in downtown Tenaha in Shelby County. The road is 0.074 miles long, or approximately 391 feet.

The longest highway: The longest highway in Texas is US 83, which stretches from the Oklahoma state line near Perryton to the Mexican border at Brownsville. It is 899 miles long.

The highest highway: The highest highway in Texas is 6,791 feet above sea level. The highest point is at the end of a spur from Texas 118 to the McDonald Observatory on Mount Locke in the Davis Mountains of West Texas.

The highest bridge: The highest bridge is the Rainbow Bridge near Port Arthur. There is 177 feet of clearance between the water and the roadway.

The longest bridge: The longest bridge is the Queen Isabella Causeway between Port Isabel and South Padre Island. It is 2.37 miles long.

Number of bridges: There are 30,000 bridges in the state of Texas, totaling 6,000 acres.

The only tunnel: The only tunnel in the state highway system is the 4,110-foot tunnel beneath the Houston Ship Channel between Baytown and LaPorte.

Centerline miles: There are more than 79,000 centerline miles in the state-maintained system.

Amount of wildflower seeds used yearly by TxDOT: The Texas Department of Transportation sows more than 60,000 pounds of wildflower seeds every year.

Number of vehicles registered in Texas: There are more than 18.7 million motor vehicles registered in the state of Texas.

Average miles driven on Texas highways: Approximately 457 million miles per day are driven on Texas highways.

Busiest highway in Texas: The busiest highway in Texas is US 59 in southwest Houston, west of Loop 610. Over 370,000 vehicles use this stretch of highway daily.

Amount of paint used to stripe highways: About 1.6 million gallons a year of white and yellow paint are used to stripe the highways of Texas.

CORNDOG...ANYONE?

FIRST PRIZE

The origin of the State Fair of Texas dates all the way back to 1886, when a small group of Dallas businessmen chartered the Dallas State Fair and Exposition as a private corporation, with James B. Simpson as the first president. Arguments between the parties ensued and after failing to reach a compromise over where to locate the fairgrounds, some of the new organization's directors, led by C. A. Keating, bolted and formed a second outfit called the Texas State Fair and Exposition. Both fairs opened to the public in late October 1886, and drew significant crowds, but directors of both boards soon realized that competition between the two rival institutions would eventually doom them both. During the following year, a merger was hammered out combining the two events into the Texas State Fair and Dallas Exposition. The newly organized fair was thereafter held on the grounds of present-day Fair Park, a 277-acre site located east of downtown. Before long, people clamored at the gates to view the outstanding displays of farm equipment, the state's best produce, finest livestock, horse races, and public appearances by the leading figures of the day, including the black educator Booker T. Washington, perennial presidential candidate William Jennings Bryan, fiery temperance leader Carry Nation, and world-renowned band director John Philip Sousa.

The Fair fell on financial hard times in 1903 when the Texas legislature outlawed gambling on horses. Selling the fairgrounds to the city of Dallas the following year, the Fair's directors retained the right to have the event at the site on an annual basis. The board reorganized the exposition, renaming it the *State Fair of Texas* and,

Dallas hosts the largest state fair in the U.S. with attendance well over 3 million. Big Tex, a cowboy with a 5 foot tall, 75-gallon hat, greets visitors at the gate.

There is not another rivalry in the country that holds the passions that permeate the annual clash between the University of Texas Longhorns and the University of Oklahoma Sooners in the Annual "Red River Shootout" that is held in conjunction with the Fair. These two teams first met in 1900, and even though both teams enter every season with aspirations for a national championship, more often than not a win in this brawl comes higher on their priority list. While Oklahoma has had the better of the Longhorns of late, Texas still leads the all time series 55-39-5.

for the next few years, unprecedented numbers attended the fall attraction. President William Howard Taft visited the Fair in 1905 and soon-to-be president Woodrow Wilson held several thousand onlookers spellbound with a speech in 1911. By World War I, more than a million people per year paid to experience the wonder and beauty of the Fair.

During WW1, the Fair was cancelled and the fairgrounds were converted into an army base. Back in business following the Armistice in 1918, the event added new structures, including the Music Hall. In 1929, the Texas-Oklahoma football game became an annual event. The following year saw the dedication of what soon became known as the Cotton Bowl, built on the site of the old racetrack.

In 1936, the Fair hosted the Texas Centennial Exposition, a six-month-long event that drew more than six million visitors, including President Franklin D. Roosevelt who spoke to 40,000 eager listeners in the Cotton Bowl. January 1, 1937 ushered in the world-famous "Cotton Bowl Classic," pitting Texas Christian University against Marquette. Amidst 17,000 cheering Texans, TCU won the contest 16-6.

The State Fair of Texas By the Numbers

The year of the Fair's origin	1886
Size of the Fairgrounds	277 acres
Approximate number of livestock entries	8,000
Number of food service outlets	200
Approximate food and ride revenues	$25,000,000
Duration of the Fair	24 days
Hours of operation	10 A.M.-10 P.M.
Height of the Ferris wheel	212 feet
Exhibit space	370,000 square ft.
Number of amusement rides	75
Annual economic contribution to Dallas	$350,000,000

Following World War II, the Fair continued to grow, adding new attractions, exhibits, and events. The Fair commemorated its one hundredth birthday in 1986 with a total attendance of nearly four million visitors, a record high for state fairs anywhere, and the Fair was designated a National Historic Landmark the same year. Today, for twenty-four days in September and October, the State Fair of Texas packs visitors in like no other fair in North America. The affair truly is the "granddaddy of all state fairs." ★

4-H: An integral part of the Fair

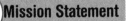

Mission Statement

The first County Extension Agent in Texas was appointed in 1906, eight years before the organization of the Texas Agricultural Extension Service. Two years later, T.M. Marks, county agricultural agent, organized the first boys' "Corn Club" in Jack County. Marks found that he was more successful teaching new production technology to the youth than to the adults. Within a matter of years, "pig clubs," "beef calf clubs" (Coleman County, 1910), and girls' "tomato clubs" (Milam County, 1912) were also initiated. The stage was set for the rapid expansion of educational programs directed to rural youth. Within a span of ninety-one years, 4-H enrollment in Texas had grown from the original twenty-five corn club members in Jack County in 1908 to more than three quarters of a million in the late 1990s!

Prepare youth to meet the challenges of childhood, adolescence, and adulthood, through a coordinated, long-term, progressive series of educational experiences that enhance life skills and develop social, emotional, physical, and cognitive competencies.

4-H PLEDGE

I pledge:

My head to clearer thinking, My heart to greater loyalty, My hands to larger service, My health to better living, For my club, my community, my country, and my world.

The Texas Corn Dog

What would the fair be without the Corn Dog? Introduced at the **1942 Texas State Fair** by **Neil Fletcher**, the corn dog has become a part of American carnival culture and a mainstay in school cafeterias. Originally made without sticks, the corn dog is the beloved food choice of adults and children alike at fairs nationwide.

— *Make yours at home!* —

6 cups cornmeal
3 cups all-purpose flour
2 ½ teaspoons baking soda
1 ½ teaspoons salt
hotdogs

2 tablespoons sugar
3 cups buttermilk
2 ½ cups water
2 eggs

Mix dry ingredients in a large bowl. Add buttermilk and water, and beat in eggs. Insert sticks in the hot dogs and dip in batter to coat. Fry in hot grease until browned.

NOW THAT'S A NICE LITTLE SPREAD YOU HAVE THERE...

Texas and large ranches are synonymous. Over time, raising cattle became a profitable business, so entrepreneurs began to assemble huge spreads across the state that have, over time, reached almost legendary status.

In 1853, Richard King, a former steamboat captain, acquired a 15,500-acre Spanish land grant in Nueces County. That purchase was the genesis of what eventually became a 1.25 million-acre ranch where he and his family developed the world-famous Santa Gertrudis cattle breed by crossing Brahman and short-horn stock. By the late twentieth century, the **King Ranch** controlled more than 12 million acres in the United States, Australia, Brazil, Morocco, Argentina, and Venezuela.

Charles Goodnight, who in 1866 with his business partner, Oliver Loving, blazed a cattle trail from Fort Belknap, Texas, to Denver, Colorado, returned ten years later to Texas, where he established a new ranch and developed new strains of cattle. With an Irish immigrant named John Adair,

he helped amass almost one million acres in the Panhandle on a spread that eventually supported nearly one hundred thousand cattle. The resultant **JA Ranch** became one of the largest and most famous in all of North America.

During the 1870s, Abel H. ("Shanghai") Pierce amassed a large ranch, eventually totaling nearly 250,000 acres, in Wharton County. Called the **Pierce-Sullivan Pasture Company**, Pierce and his nephew, Abel Pierce Borden, were instrumental in successfully introducing tick-resistant Brahman cattle from India to the Gulf Coast of Texas. Pierce descendants still operate the ranch, now totaling around 32,000 acres.

H. H. Campbell and A. M. Britton founded the forerunner of the **Matador Ranch** in Motley County in 1879 when they purchased range rights to a large expanse of prairie from an old buffalo hunter. Three years later and after introducing

eight thousand head of cattle on the property, they sold out to the **Matador Land and Cattle Company**, a Scottish-held consortium that invested more than two million dollars in the property. Rapidly growing in size to nearly three-quarters of a million acres of combined deeded and leased lands, the ranch spread over several Panhandle counties and supported one hundred thousand cattle by 1891. The Matador was eventually purchased by an American enterprise and broken up into smaller parcels even though the parent ranch is still functional today.

When the **XIT Ranch** was at its peak shortly following its organization in 1879, it was the largest ranch in the world, consisting of more than three million acres stretching across ten counties. Some say that the XIT stands for "ten counties in Texas." the ranch was assembled by the Texas legislature created the XIT Ranch by appropriating land to finance the design and construction of the State Capitol building in Austin.

In the 1880s the XIT Ranch in Dalhart was the largest ranch in the world under a single fence. Its 3,000,000 acres of land were corralled by a fence that stretched for 6,000 miles. The ranch was created by the Texas legislature and purchased by northern investors as part of the legislature's plan to finance a new State Capitol building in Austin.

★ Texas cowhands always assembled quickly around the chuck wagon when it was time to serve up the sowbelly and beans. The typical cook on a Texas spread wielded subtle but formidable power, and the men working these spreads scrambled to stay in his favor.

The wire that divided the West

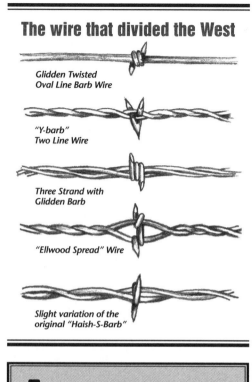

Glidden Twisted
Oval Line Barb Wire

"Y-barb"
Two Line Wire

Three Strand with
Glidden Barb

"Ellwood Spread" Wire

Slight variation of the
original "Haish-S-Barb"

As part of the agreement with the Legislature, the Chicago consortium responsible for building the capitol received the property piecemeal as each section of the structure was completed. When fully functional, the ranch supported 160,000 head of cattle, 1,000 horses, and 150 working cowboys. Over the years, the inflated price of land and the deflated price of cattle caused most of the real estate to be sold off. Today, little remains of this once-magnificent ranch.

The **Four Sixes Ranch** had its beginning in 1898 when Samuel Burnett purchased the 140,000-acre **8 Ranch** from the Louisville Land and Cattle Company. Four years later, he expanded his operations with the acquisition of the 110,000-acre **Dixon Creek Ranch** from the Cunard Line. Eventually growing to more than 300,000 acres, the present-day ranch, located in three Panhandle counties, is operated by Burnett's great-granddaughter, Anne Windfohr Marion. ★

The King Ranch, located in south Texas, is bigger than the state of Rhode Island and largest of its kind in the world. It covers 825,000 acres and stretches over four counties: Nueces, Kenedy, Kleberg, and Willacy. Established in 1853 by former riverboat captain Richard King, it still operates as a working ranch.

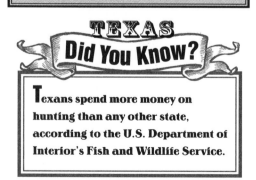

Did You Know?

Texans spend more money on hunting than any other state, according to the U.S. Department of Interior's Fish and Wildlife Service.

SHANGHAI PIERCE

Abel Head (Shanghai) Pierce was born in Rhode Island in 1834 and as a young man gravitated to Texas where he amassed a cattle empire of nearly 250,000 acres. He was instrumental in the importation of Brahman cattle, a breed which he believed might be helpful in developing a tick-resistant livestock strain. It is said that he acquired his nickname, "Shanghai," after a friend commented that his new set of oversized spurs "made him look like a Shanghai rooster." Pierce died in 1900 and is buried in Hawley, Texas.

A GUIDE TO WATCHING WILDLIFE

The state of Texas is an animal lover's paradise. Birds and other wildlife provide the perfect environment for amateur and seasoned wildlife enthusiasts to view nature in its own habitat. The following tips and guidelines will provide those who appreciate the animal world with hours of entertainment.

Be Prepared
- Take along a good field guide to help track and identify animals. Do not forget a pencil or pen to draw or record sightings.
- Binoculars are a necessity for wildlife watching. Beginners may borrow binoculars or buy an inexpensive pair.
- If photography is part of the outing then a good camera with at least a 400 mm lens will be necessary.

Blend In
- Walk quietly and slowly. Be careful not to snap twigs or cause noise that will startle animals.
- Use the natural protection of the environment as camouflage. Hide behind trees, shrubs, and rocks to view wildlife.

Tips To Remember
- Be courteous to other wildlife watchers.
- Move like molasses: slow, smooth, and steady.
- Respect the environment and the animals. Remember, you are in their world.

The Birds of Texas

By Bill Thompson, III
Editor, Bird Watcher's Digest

The list of birds found in Texas is as big or bigger than all of the Lone Star State's other attributes. More than 600 bird species have been seen at least once in Texas—more than any other state—which is not surprising given the fact that Texas contains such a wide variety of habitat types across its broad expanse. From the northeastern piney woods to the western desert canyons and from the rolling gulf-coast dunes to the tropical richness of the Rio Grande Valley, Texas is a paradise both for birds and bird watchers.

The birdlife of Texas includes species of both the East and the West. As you might expect, east Texas has many birds found in the eastern U.S. while west Texas includes many distinctly western birds. Adding to this avian richness is the fact that Texas is at the confluence of three major migration flyways—the "paths in the sky" that birds follow when migrating south in the fall and north in the spring. Millions of birds pass through the state each year, some stopping to spend the winter, and some staying to breed in the spring and summer.

Among the highlights of the birds of Texas are the annual spring "fallouts" of warblers, orioles, buntings, tanagers, and other brilliant songbirds as they land in woodlands along the Gulf Coast in early spring. Thousands of bird watchers are there to see them and, on a day of heavy migration, the birds literally seem to "fall out" of the sky into the trees. Tired from having flown across the Gulf of Mexico, these birds are focused on resting and feeding and they seem to ignore the oohs and ahhs of the admiring bird watchers. High Island, north of Galveston, is one of the best known of the spring migration hotspots, drawing bird watchers from all over the world each April seeking the feathered wonders.

Summer in Texas is for breeding birds and backyard bird watchers do their best to provide housing, food, water, and bird-friendly habitat in hopes of attracting a nesting pair of cardinals, wrens, hummingbirds, or even the gorgeous painted bunting—perhaps the most stunningly plumaged bird in

The Bird Lady of Texas

Conger "Connie" Hagar was one of the first Texans to bring national attention to the state's rich diversity of birds. Her reports of spring migration around her Rockport home were so incredible that other ornithologists did not believe them. One particularly dubious ornithologist asked Connie, while sitting in her living room, how she could possibly have seen a certain rare bird species. She replied, "Sir, if you will look out the window behind you, I believe you will see one!"

Connie Hagar reported an incredible total of more than 500 species in the Rockport area during her lifetime. She died in 1973 and is buried in Rockport Cemetery, overlooking Aransas Bay and the area now known as the Conger Hagar Wildlife Sanctuary.

North America. Orange halves impaled on a tree branch often attract tanagers or orioles in summer, but perhaps the busiest place in any Texas backyard is the birdbath where thirsty birds come to drink and bathe.

Thousands of hummingbirds migrate along the Texas Gulf Coast in fall, often crowding around hummingbird nectar feeders and draining them in short order. Meanwhile, songbirds are streaming southward through Texas, many headed for Central or even South America. High overhead in September and October, hawks of many species are soaring southward, seeking warmer climes for winter.

In winter, Texas is home to huge flocks of ducks, geese, cranes, herons, egrets, and other water-loving birds. Many hawks and other raptors winter in Texas, wherever the hunting is best. Driving along the highways and farm roads it's easy to spot these winter visitors as they perch atop the power poles and fence posts, waiting and watching for an unlucky mammal to show itself.

No matter what the season, Texas is blessed with an abundance of birds and there are countless places in which to encounter and enjoy them in the backyard—or beyond! ★

The Tallest Bird

North America's tallest bird is the whooping crane, a mostly white bird with black wingtips and a red crown, standing more than four feet tall. The whooping crane is an endangered species and the world's entire wild population numbers about 200 birds. Nearly all of these birds spend the winter along the Texas coast near Aransas National Wildlife Refuge. In spring, they migrate thousands of miles to nest in the remote wet prairies of northwestern Canada.

Listen to the Mockingbird

The state bird of Texas is the northern mockingbird, a bird known not for its flashy plumage but for its ability to imitate the sounds it hears. An adult male mockingbird will have a vocal repertoire between 50 to 200 different songs and sounds. They are experts at imitating other birds, but will also imitate sirens, telephones, whistles, and other noises. The mockingbird is also known for singing at night, especially during the spring and early summer when the moon is full.

Hit the Birding Trail

Texas was the first state in the U.S. to develop a specific bird watching trail. The Great Texas Coastal Birding Trail traverses 43 Texas counties and highlights more than 308 bird and wildlife viewing sites. Since the trail's completion in 2000, hundreds of thousands of birders have visited portions of the trail and all of this nature tourism has had a Texas-sized economic impact on the state.

THE TEXAS CATTLE DRIVE

The image is burned into the mind of the American public. Hot dusty trails...cold, rainy nights...weathered hats pulled low over craggy faces...and hundreds, perhaps thousands, of cattle...moving slowly, prodded on by a group of men who worked the herd for money, but also for the freedom that the trail provided.

It was on these long, lonely trails where the American cowboy became famous in the years immediately following the Civil War. Even before the War, cattle had been in Texas since the first settlers from Tennessee, Kentucky, and other southern states emigrated into Texas following Mexico's independence from Spain in 1821. In those early years, ranching was certainly not a big business, and cattle were raised primarily for domestic use. The few attempts at cattle drives out of Texas by early entrepreneurs prior to the Civil War were almost futile and usually ended up in some kind of disaster that ended in the loss of their investment or in the loss of life.

The Texas rancher of the mid- to late 1800s was certainly not scared of hard work, and he was almost always willing to take a gamble on a risky business venture if there was the possibility of a large return. But the reality is that the Texas cattle industry was not born through the hard work of Texas ranchers or cowboys. Instead,

In the 1930s and as his health began to fail, King Ranch owner Robert J. Kleberg turned operations of the ranch over to two of his five children. Richard Mifflin (Mr. Dick) Kleberg, Sr., who served as a seven-term member of the U. S. Congress, concentrated on the legal and financial aspects of the ranch. Another son, Robert Justus (Mr. Bob) Kleberg, acted as head of the ranch's operations and continued as president and CEO for over fifty years.

It was during these years that the King Ranch made its name in animal husbandry. When Robert and his ranch hands began crossbreeding Brahman bulls, native to India, with British Shorthorn stock, the result was the Santa Gertrudis. Recognized as the first American breed of beef cattle, the new breed turned out to be the first recognized in the world in more than a century. Even today, the Santa Gertrudis is recognized throughout the world as one of the greatest breeds of cattle that can sustain arid climates while retaining a taste that appeals to appetites.

the industry grew when very few people were home because when the rough-and-tumble young Texans answered the call to fight in a war that began in South Carolina, wild cattle overran the small, unattended ranches of Texas and quickly multiplied into tens of thousands.

When the war finally ended and young Texans returned home, they found ranches that had barely survived years of neglect. The war had not only taken its toll on Texas by taking the lives of thousands of young men, but the economy of the state was literally in shambles. Facing an almost insurmountable battle back to economic stability, the Texans of the 1860s rolled up their sleeves, tightened their belts and began the long road back. This road revolved around the one resource that had survived and thrived during the war—cattle.

The war devastated the economy of Texas. In fact, almost every area of the country was trying to rebuild from the ravages of war, and part of this recovery was the consistent availability of food to feed the population that was growing as well. It became clear to a few aggressive businessmen that the herds of cattle roaming throughout the state were the solution to the economic crisis in Texas and the food shortages of the East. The problem was that Texas was a very long way from these population centers and there were no railroads running through Texas at the time. So, the only way to get the herds to market was to "drive" them, on hoof, to the nearest railhead. There, they could be loaded into freight cars and

they could be loaded into freight cars and shipped to market for processing.

Joseph G. McCoy, an Illinois-born rancher, first formulated the revolutionary idea that made the mass-transportation-of-cattle concept tenable. By 1867, the rail lines reached only to Abilene, Kansas, so McCoy established the town as a temporary holding area for the tens of thousands of cattle that he hoped would eventually be driven the several hundred miles north out of Texas. He purchased 250 acres of nearby prairie and supervised the construction of stockyards, offices, a hotel, and holding pens—all strategically placed near the railroad—in anticipation of the herds of cattle that would soon be trekking through downtown Abilene.

Some thirty-five thousand cattle were processed in Abilene during the summer of 1867, and the first train pulling twenty cars full of Texas longhorns left town in September headed for the Chicago stockyards. McCoy did not make much money on this initial experiment, but he did prove that the long-range transportation of beef on the hoof could be accomplished economically with the help of the rapidly expanding rail system. This was great news for the struggling economy of Texas and helped determine the fate of the nation as a whole and the fortunes of hundreds of future cattlemen. The era of the great cattle drives had begun, and with it the advent of what was to become an American icon—the cowboy.

As railroad construction progressed westward, the cattle trails that accommodated the railhead towns shifted

TEXAS Did You Know?

Huge herds of cattle were slaughtered in Rockport after the Civil War to provide Easterners with hides for leather goods, tallow for candles and soap, bones for fertilizer, and horns for buttons and combs. Meat was considered a by-product and much of it was thrown away.

as well. In time, as the popularity of the Northwest grew, Texas cattle were driven there to take advantage of the rich grazing lands to be found in Montana. Before long, the entire region was full of cowboys who had worked their way up the Texas Trail.

"The Texas Trail was no mere cowpath," wrote one historian in 1892, emphasizing rather that "It was the course of empire." Indeed, a cattle empire was exactly what the trail promoted during the 1870s and 1880s. With its beginnings in South Texas, the trail headed northward and passed through Fort Worth, Texas; Camp Supply, Oklahoma; Dodge City, Kansas; Ogallala, Nebraska; Fort Robertson, Nebraska; and across parts of present-day South Dakota and Wyoming, before terminating in central Montana. Before the great cattle drives were over, replaced by more modern modes of transportation, millions of Texas longhorn cattle had made the long trek, watched over by countless thousands of nameless cowboys.

As difficult as the work was, many young men became cowboys to make a living for themselves and their families, but they also came because the trail was a place of freedom and full of adventure. Figures vary, but it is estimated that between twenty-five and thirty-five thousand men worked on the open range of the late 1800s, driving between six to ten million cows and more than a million horses from Texas to Kansas, Nebraska, Colorado, Wyoming, and the rich grasslands of Montana. To be a cowboy during the late 1800s was to live a life that was drastically different from

any other in the United States. A man had to be resourceful, hardy, healthy, an expert horseman, a good shot with both pistol and rifle, and, above all else, a cool-headed, yet decisive, manager of his own time and abilities. It was not an easy life. Cowboys spent months on the trail, living out of saddlebags, putting up with the intense heat and the unbearable cold, sharing questionable grub with other cowboys and dealing with animals on the trail—all for thirty dollars a month. It took a special breed of man.

Larry McMurtry's Pulitzer prize-winning novel, *Lonesome Dove*, was inspired by the life of *Oliver Loving*, the Dean of Texas Trail Drivers.

Although the Texas cowboy's role in the winning of the American West was brief, it was an extremely important one. In time, as the railroad reached more and more communities, the need for the long and extensive cattle drives to get the herds to market dwindled. Finally, when the open range was no more and wire fencing crossed the face of the grasslands, the writing was on the wall for the cattle drive. Fortunately, by then, the cattle drive's place in history was assured. We believe that the spirit that was born along these dusty trails and in the heart and soul of the men who road over them still lives on in the hearts of Texans today. ★

The horse was introduced to American Indians by the Spaniards (probably in Texas) after 1500.

EAGLE LAKE
Where Snow Covers the Ground

Eagle Lake, named for a Karankawa Indian legend that tells of a brave who bested his rival by crossing the lake and returning with an eagle for an Indian maiden, is known today as the Goose Hunting Capital of the World. During the annual migratory waterfowl hunting season, hunters bag thousands of snow, blue, and speckle bellied geese as well as other migratory waterfowl. These geese and ducks flock to the area to feast on the abundant rice harvest that exceeds a million bushels annually, but Eagle Lake's history stretches back to the time when the vast prairies were covered with tall grasses and wildflowers. The Indians who lived in this area fished in the lake, ate the alligators, and used the grease from them to ward off the mosquitoes. Surely, they lived a life that included hunting and harvesting the waterfowl that attracts hunters today from all over the world.

Most of these hunters come to the Eagle Lake area to hunt snow geese. These white fronted geese migrate long distances from their summer breeding grounds in the Arctic. In fact, these geese fly so high during their migration that they can barely be seen by the naked eye. But even at that altitude, they can often be identified because they fly in such large groups and because they fly in a formation that looks like a curved line that constantly moves back and forth...much like a wave hitting the shore along the Gulf Coast.

Interestingly, some old-time hunters call these birds "Wavies," but that name does not come from the shape that they make as they fly south. Instead, the word is derived from the Chippewa name for the species "Wewe."

While the residents of the Eagle Lake area love the snow goose, these geese are becoming increasingly unpopular with farmers, ranchers, and biologists. The problem is twofold: First, the snow goose population is exploding and secondly, the snow goose's eating habits,

> **S**now goose hunting in the eastern United States was stopped in 1916 because of low population levels. Hunting was allowed again in 1975 after populations had increased. Populations have been growing so large that the geese are destroying nesting habitat. Hunting has not slowed the dramatic increases in population size.

unlike other migratory waterfowl, destroy the area in which they feed.

Snow geese nest in huge colonies in the Arctic during the spring and summer, and most of the geese that winter along the Texas coast nest in the Hudson Bay region. This group of birds is called the mid-continent population of snow geese. It is interesting to note that prior to the development of the Midwest and prairie to provide the country with agricultural products, snow geese flew nonstop from the Arctic breeding grounds to the Gulf Coast wintering grounds. Obviously, this was a long, hard trip and the survival rate of birds was not high. But the planting of agricultural foods along their flyway provided the birds the opportunity to stop for extended periods and increased their survival rate. This population explosion has expanded the birds' wintering range to include Louisiana, Arkansas, Mississippi, Missouri, Oklahoma, and Kansas.

In the Arctic, snow geese feed on grasses by grazing, but they also feed with a technique known as grubbing, where they pull up plants to feed on the roots and rhizomes. This technique destroys the entire plant, and the Arctic ecosystem cannot repair itself quickly enough to support itself. The development of the agricultural areas of the Midwest is a fairly recent development and the increase in snow goose populations has put even more stress on the Arctic ecosystem. The plants in the Arctic coastal marshes have not changed over the years and are adapted to light to moderate grazing by geese. The loss of vegetation under heavy grazing by these new large populations of geese and the grubbing technique has led to high evaporation rates and increased soil salinity, which prevents plants from reestablishing themselves.

Snow goose populations are monitored through surveys conducted in winter, and the mid-continent population has tripled in size since 1970 and now totals almost 3.5 million birds. These figures seem to be much higher than the population before the Midwest was developed agriculturally. But the wintering population of Texas birds has remained relatively stable during this time, averaging between 750,000 and 1 million birds, meaning that most of the birds in the population increase winter in the states between the Arctic and Texas. Wildlife conservationists believe that the mid-continent population should be between 1 and 1.5 million birds for the health of the birds and the ecosystem. However, since the early 1980s, the population has remained much higher than this figure, and it continues to increase. Hunting regulations along the flyway have been liberalized over the years, but hunting has not slowed the population increase. ★

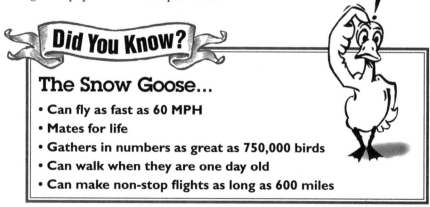

Did You Know?

The Snow Goose...

- **Can fly as fast as 60 MPH**
- **Mates for life**
- **Gathers in numbers as great as 750,000 birds**
- **Can walk when they are one day old**
- **Can make non-stop flights as long as 600 miles**

Places to Hunt Snow Geese Near Eagle Lake

BLUE GOOSE HUNTING CLUB
John Fields
9800 Hwy. 90-A
P.O. Drawer M
Altair, TX 77412
Phone: 979.234.3597
Fax: 979.234.5188
e-mail: bluegoose@elc.net
Web Site: www.elc.net/bluegoose

LARRY GORE'S
Eagle Lake and Katy Prairie
Outfitters
P.O. Box 129
Katy, TX 77492
Phone: 281-391-6100
e-mail: elkpo@pdq.net

PRAIRIE WATERFOWL HUNTS
Davis Waddell & Harlan Boettcher
1014 Quail Loop
Eagle Lake, TX 77434
Phone: 979.335.6012 (Harlan)
e-mail: boettcher@ev1.net

TAILFEATHERS GUIDE SERVICE
Mike (Duck) Fisher
P.O. Box 426
Eagle Lake, TX 77434
Phone: 979.732.2997
Cell: 979.732.7549
Web Site:
www.tailfeathersguideservice.com

TIM KELLEY'S
WATERFOWL OUTFITTERS UNLIMITED
& THE EAGLE LAKE LODGE
Tim Kelley
P.O. Box 195
Eagle Lake, TX 77434
Phone: 979.234.3819
888-TX-LODGE
Cell Phone: 832-528-1447
email: waterfowl@elc.net
Web Site:
www.WaterfowlOutfittersUnlimited.com

B & D ELLIS GOOSE HUNTING
GUIDE SERVICE
David Ellis and Brian Ellis
800 Campbell
Eagle Lake, TX 77434
Phone: 979.234.2314

Source: *Eagle Lake Chamber of Commerce Web Site*

Did You Know?

Parent geese stay with their young through the first winter. Families travel together on both the southbound and northbound migrations, separating only after they return to the Arctic breeding grounds.

Texas is a favorite spot for migrating birds. According to the Parks and Wildlife Department, 618 different species (the largest number of any state) have been seen and recorded in here.

Is It Pronounced Ro-dee-o or Ro-day-o?

For years people have argued over the correct pronunciation of the word, *rodeo.* Derived from the Spanish, *rodear* (ro-day-ar), which means to encompass or to encircle, early Mexican cattlemen used the word to simply mean the rounding up of the animal. American cowboys used the pronunciation, *ro-dee-o,* for the sport, while calling the act of rounding up cattle a *ro-day-o.* Today, the latter usage has grown practically obsolete, except among some old-timers and shoppers in Beverly Hills.

Domestic cattle were introduced into North America in the sixteenth century by Spanish conquistadors in Mexico, and gradually, as the northern reaches of New Spain (today's Southwest) were explored, the cattle moved northward as well and multiplied to the extent that they became big business there. *Vaqueros,* or Mexican cowboys, developed many of the skills and equipment of today's working American counterpart.

When fencing was introduced in the 1880s, the cowboy's work was simplified, since ranches now were self contained and the intense work of covering the vast acreage of the open range ended. With a degree of leisure time on his hands, the cowboy started performing some of his routine chores at sporting events and in so-called Wild West Shows, like the one organized by William F. (Buffalo Bill) Cody in 1882. Annual competitions became commonplace, and one of the events held at Pecos, Texas in 1883 became the first rodeo to award prizes to the victorious cowboys.

As sporting rodeos became increasingly popular and, as competition among cowboys intensified, several governing associations were organized to monitor the sport, define procedures and rules, and to qualify judges. The forerunner of the most prominent of these, today's Professional Rodeo Cowboys Association (PRCA), was formed in 1939 as the Cowboys Turtle Association. Reorganized in Houston in 1945 with famed calf roper and Bandera native, Toots Mansfield, as its first president, the PRCA opened offices in Fort Worth. This new group sanctioned for inclusion in its events bull riding, steer wrestling, saddle bronc riding, bareback riding, calf roping, and team roping.

The gals got in on the action, too. Although in the early days of rodeos women sometimes competed with men in such events as bronc riding, they primarily favored trick

Texas is the nation's leading cattle producer with 14.8 million head.

roping, and relay races. The Women's Professional Rodeo Association (WPRA) was founded in San Angelo in 1948 to promote more varied women's participation in the sport following a PRCA decision to sanction barrel racing as the only women's event in its offerings. Today, WPRA all-women rodeos offer team roping, bareback bronc riding, barrel racing, steer riding, and tie-down and breakaway calf roping.

Youth rodeo had its origins in Texas as well when the National Intercollegiate Rodeo Association (NIRA) was chartered in 1949, with Charlie Rankin from Texas A&M as its first president. That same year, Harley May from Sul Ross State University at Alpine won the first-ever NIRA all-around national championship. Two years later, Midland's Jo Gregory Knox was awarded the first NIRA women's all-around championship.

A list of rodeo champions from Texas reads like a "Who's Who" of the sport. Beginning with Bill Pickett, the black cowboy who "invented" bulldogging, to more modern figures like Toots Mansfield, Harry Tompkins, Don Gay, Dick Griffith, and Ty Murray, Texans of both sexes have done their state proud when it comes to demonstrating cowboy (and cowgirl) skills.

Today, three of the nation's largest and most successful rodeos are held in Texas: the Fort Worth Southwestern Exposition and Livestock Show and Rodeo, the Houston Livestock Show and Rodeo, and the San Antonio Livestock Exposition Rodeo. ★

STATS

PRCA Career Earnings Leaders (Through 2003)
1. Joe Beaver (TD, TR, SR), $2,362,361
2. Fred Whitfield (TD, SR), $2,163,199
3. Dan Mortensen (SB, BR) $2,127,816
4. Roy Cooper (TD, SR, TR, SW), $2,074,080

Highest Single-Year Earnings
$297,896, Ty Murray in 1993

Most Money Won at a Rodeo
$124,821, Ty Murray at 1993 NFR

Youngest World Champion
Jim Rodriguez Jr., 1959 team roper at age 18

Oldest World Champion
Ike Rude, 1953 steer roper at age 59

Most World Titles

Overall Titles:
17, Guy Allen

All-Around:
7, Ty Murray

Bareback Riding:
5 (tie), Joe Alexander, Bruce Ford

Steer Wrestling:
6, Homer Pettigrew

Steer Roping:
17, Guy Allen

Team Roping:
7 (tie), Jake Barnes/Clay O'Brien Cooper and Speed Williams/Rich Skelton

Saddle Bronc Riding:
6 (tie), Casey Tibbs and Dan Mortensen

Tie-down Roping:
8, Dean Oliver

Bull Riding:
8, Don Gay

Source PRCA.com

Did You Know?

Stephenville resident *Ty Murray*, the seven-time *PRCA World All-Around Champion*, is a founding member and original shareholder of the *Professional Bull Riders, Inc. (the PBR)*.

THE HISTORY OF CATTLE BRANDS

Ever since humans first understood the principle of private property, they have placed some kind of identifying mark on their possessions. The Egyptians were branding cattle, for instance, as far back as 2,000 B.C. and in our own country's dark days when human slavery was prevalent, brand markings were frequently used on men, women, and children.

The practice of branding cattle was already widespread in Europe in the fifteenth century when Columbus "discovered" America and, years later, when Spanish conquistadors landed in Mexico, they brought brand-marked cattle with them. It was only a matter of time before the cattle moved northward with the adventurous Spanish who often maintained large herds with them as they explored far and wide across New Spain. Later, Mexican vaqueros inherited the idea and, from them, Texas cowboys adopted the procedure that proved particularly valuable for claiming the thousands of free-roaming, feral cattle grazing the Texas landscape after the Civil War.

In the early days, the only permanent way to mark a cow was to burn the brand into the hide, usually on the left hip, which fortunately did no harm to the animal. Cattle were also sometimes identified by earmarks, a unique design that was cut into one or both ears. In more modern times, when the ownership of cattle is no longer questioned as it was in the days of the open range where animals belonging to many cowmen were difficult to segregate, tattoos or metal tags in the animal's ear have been used.

The number of brand marks utilized over the years was as numerous as the owners who needed a way to protect their cattle and the design of the marks was as varied as the vivid imaginations of the men who created them. For some of the classic ranches in Texas, the brand was synonymous with the name of the spread itself. Thus the Four Sixes Ranch in the Panhandle literally displayed four 6s. The huge XIT Ranch in the Panhandle used the XIT as its brand and some pundits say that both the brand and the name of the ranch signified "ten counties in Texas," which is the size of the territory over which the ranch spread. On the other hand, the primary King Ranch brand was a running W. One important rule was always followed when devising brands: the design of the mark should be difficult, if not impossible, to alter. Many are the tales of stolen cattle that had their marks "re-branded" with a similar, yet slightly different, brand.

Branding was done during the spring roundup. Then, cowboys would ride far and wide collecting the newborn calves and their

> The largest cattle auction in Texas is held at Western Stockyards in Amarillo. They sell more than 600,000 head of cattle annually.

mothers, many of them never before branded. Then, according to our cowboy-president **Theodore Roosevelt**,

"A fire is built, the irons heated, and a dozen men dismount to, as it is called, 'wrestle' the calves. The best two ropers go in on their horses to catch the latter; one man keeps tally, a couple put on the brands, and the others seize, throw, and hold the little unfortunates. A first-class roper invariably catches the calf by both hind feet, and then, having taken a twist with his lariat around the horn of the saddle, drags the bawling little creature, extended at full length, up to the fire, where it is held before it can make a struggle... If there are seventy or eighty calves in a corral, the scene is one of the greatest confusion. The ropers, spurring and checking the fierce little horses, drag the calves up so quickly that a dozen men can hardly hold them; the men with the irons, blackened with soot, run to and fro; the calf-wrestlers, grimy with blood, dust and seat, work like beavers; while... the tallyman shouts out the number and sex of each calf. The dust rises in clouds, and the shouts, cheers, curses, and laughter of the men unite with the lowing of the cows and the frantic bleating of the calves to make a perfect babel."

As the number of brands increased in any particular state or territory, the job of maintaining them became quite laborious. In some jurisdictions, an elected official was responsible for recording and keeping up with the marks and their ownership. Brand marks were often published in a brand book, which was simply a directory of brands distributed by the local cattlemen's association. ★

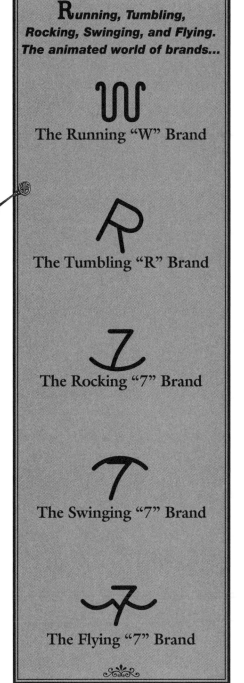

Running, Tumbling, Rocking, Swinging, and Flying. The animated world of brands...

The Running "W" Brand

The Tumbling "R" Brand

The Rocking "7" Brand

The Swinging "7" Brand

The Flying "7" Brand

ROSS PEROT
An American Phenomenon

Way back in 1981, when a reporter for the *Dallas Morning News* asked Ross Perot what he wanted placed on his tombstone, the wiry Texan replied, *"Made more money faster. Lost more money in one day. Led the biggest jailbreak in history. He died."* In a nutshell, these few

> **"If someone as blessed as I am is not willing to clean out the barn, who will?"**

words describe the life and times of H. Ross Perot, one of the most interesting characters ever to emerge from Texas.

> The "H" in H. Ross Perot is for "Henry."

Born in Texarkana in 1930, Perot was educated in local public schools and later delivered newspapers and sold Christmas cards and magazines. In 1949, he received an appointment to the United States Naval Academy, graduating four years later as class president and chairman of the honor committee. Following a four-year stint of active duty aboard an aircraft carrier and a destroyer, he left the Navy and went to work for IBM as a computer hardware salesman.

In 1962, Perot founded Electronic Data Systems (EDS), a data processing company that soon grew to become one of the nation's leading software and facilities management concerns. Before Perot sold EDS to General Motors Corporation in 1984 for $2.5 billion, the company employed seventy thousand people and had made him a billionaire.

During President Richard Nixon's first administration, Perot was called upon to make a study of Americans taken prisoner of war during the Vietnam conflict. By Perot's own later admission, the attempt was a guise to alleviate Americans' fear that nothing was being done to bring the POWs home. For the next few years, he continued working with the U. S. government in a variety of advisory roles. When two of his EDS employees were taken hostage in Iran in 1979, he personally directed and financed a rescue mission that freed the two men and made Perot a national celebrity. Novelist Ken Follett's book, *On Wings of Eagles*, as well as a television movie starring Richard Crenna as Perot, were based upon the daring episode.

Although he was restricted from participating in data processing endeavors for three years following the EDS sell-out to General Motors, Perot, nevertheless, organized a new company, Perot Systems, two years later. During these years, he purchased a rare copy of the *Magna Carta* and placed it on permanent loan to the National Archives in Washington, D. C.

When George Bush ran for president in 1988, Perot refused to endorse him after he learned that Bush had established his Texas residency simply by renting a hotel suite in Houston. When President Bush ran again in 1992 against Bill Clinton, Perot announced his own candidacy for chief executive. During the campaign, he spent $57 million of his own money and garnered nineteen percent of the vote, the highest number cast for a third party candidate since Theodore Roosevelt led the Bull Moose Party in 1912.

In the 1996 elections, as the candidate for the Independence Party, which he had created, Perot received eight percent of the total votes cast. In the 2000 elections, supporters of his party, now renamed the Reform Party, were torn between him and contenders Pat Buchanan, John Hagelin, and Jesse Ventura. Perot eventually threw his support behind George W. Bush.

In 2004, *Forbes Magazine* named Ross Perot the 73rd wealthiest American with a net worth of $3.8 billion. ★

Texas is the largest petroleum producing state in the U.S. If Texas was an independent nation, it would rank as the world's fifth largest petroleum producing country.

GEORGE STRAKE hit oil in Conroe on June 4, 1932 and started the Conroe Field—which is still in production today. Strake is considered Houston's first **million-dollar oil man.**

TOP 10 TEXAS EXPORTS

Rank	Description by Category	ANNUAL 2001	ANNUAL 2002	ANNUAL 2003	% 2002-03 Inc/Dec
	Total All Industries	94,995,266,011.00	95,396,196,650.00	98,846,082,565.00	3.62
1	COMPUTER AND ELECTRONIC PRODUCTS	25,688,465,150.00	26,707,013,008.00	28,378,198,276.00	6.26
2	CHEMICALS	14,600,389,671.00	15,002,401,622.00	17,125,246,559.00	14.15
3	MACHINERY, EXCEPT ELECTRICAL	12,821,159,976.00	12,602,234,219.00	11,407,672,253.00	-9.48
4	TRANSPORTATION EQUIPMENT	11,258,080,827.00	10,507,662,862.00	9,902,791,603.00	-5.76
5	PETROLEUM AND COAL PRODUCTS	3,704,992,583.00	3,594,678,668.00	4,701,403,193.00	30.79
6	ELECTRICAL EQUIPMENT, APPLIANCES, AND COMPONENTS	4,816,803,917.00	4,604,995,237.00	4,642,580,101.00	0.82
7	FABRICATED METAL PRODUCTS, NESOI	3,198,787,601.00	2,935,686,823.00	3,073,005,139.00	4.68
8	FOOD AND KINDRED PRODUCTS	2,594,319,728.00	2,490,043,699.00	2,755,198,756.00	10.65
9	AGRICULTURAL PRODUCTS	1,932,511,564.00	2,158,417,340.00	2,617,771,450.00	21.28
10	PLASTICS AND RUBBER PRODUCTS	2,763,242,222.00	2,714,788,230.00	2,518,904,196.00	-7.22

The 20 Richest Texans

Texas Rank	National Rank	Name	Net Worth ($mil)	Age	Residence	Source
1	4	Walton, Alice L.	18,000	55	Fort Worth, TX	Wal-Mart
2	9	Dell, Michael	14,200	39	Austin, TX	Dell
3	40	Duncan, Dan L.	4,200	71	Houston, TX	Natural Gas
3	40	Perot, Henry Ross & family	4,200	74	Dallas, TX	Computer Services
4	54	Rowling, Robert	3,500	51	Dallas, TX	Oil & Gas, Hotels, Investments
5	65	Bass, Robert Muse	2,900	56	Fort Worth, TX	Oil, Investments
6	92	Hunt, Ray Lee	2,300	61	Dallas, TX	Inheritance, Oil, Real Estate
7	97	Butt, Charles C.	2,200	66	San Antonio, TX	Supermarkets
8	106	Rainwater, Richard Edward	2,000	60	Fort Worth, TX	Real Estate, Energy, Insurance
8	106	Simmons, Harold Clark	2,000	73	Dallas, TX	Investments
9	124	Mitchell, George Phydias	1,800	85	Houston, TX	Mitchell Energy
9	124	Sarofim, Fayez Shalaby	1,800	75	Houston, TX	Finance
10	142	Bass, Lee Marshall	1,700	48	Fort Worth, TX	Oil, Investments
11	152	Kinder, Richard	1,600	60	Houston, TX	Pipelines
11	152	Marshall, E. Pierce	1,600	65	Dallas, TX	Investments
12	165	McNair, Robert C.	1,500	66	Houston, TX	Energy
13	203	Ford, Gerald J.	1,400	60	Dallas, TX	Banking
14	203	Ueltschi, Albert Lee	1,400	87	Irving, TX	FlightSafety International
15	215	Bass, Sid Richardson	1,300	61	Fort Worth, TX	Oil, Investments
15	215	Cuban, Mark	1,300	46	Dallas, TX	Broadcast.com
15	215	Goldsbury, Christopher	1,300	61	San Antonio, TX	Salsa
15	215	Jamail, Joseph Dahr Jr.	1,300	78	Houston, TX	Lawsuits
15	215	McLane, Robert Drayton Jr.	1,300	68	Temple, TX	Wal-Mart, Logistics
16	234	McCombs, Billy Joe "Red"	1,200	76	San Antonio, TX	Radio, Cars, Oil
17	260	Mays, L. Lowry	1,100	69	San Antonio, TX	Clear Channel
17	260	Troutt, Kenny A.	1,100	56	Dallas, TX	Excel Communications
18	278	Bass, Edward Perry	1,000	59	Fort Worth, TX	Oil, Investments
18	278	Jones, Jerral W.	1,000	61	Dallas, TX	Dallas Cowboys, Oil & Gas
18	278	Marion, Anne Windfohr	1,000	65	Fort Worth, TX	Inheritance, Oil
19	314	Wyly, Samuel	990	69	Dallas, TX	Investments
20	340	Bass, Perry Richardson	900	89	Fort Worth, TX	Oil, Investments

Source: www.forbes.com (2004 statistics)

According to the 1850 census, Texas had a population of 213,000. By 1900 that figure had grown to an amazing 3,000,000!

The 20 LARGEST
Privately Owned Texas Companies

Texas Rank	National Rank	Company Name	Industry	Revenues ($mil)	Number of Employees
1	10	H. E. Butt Grocery	Retail (Grocery)	115,002	60,000
2	40	Gulf States Toyota	Auto & Truck Manufacturers	3,835	3,150
3	71	Grocers Supply	Retail (Grocery)	2,729	9,500
4	89	Hunt Consolidated/Hunt Oil	Oil & Gas - Integrated	2,250	2,900
5	91	Glazer's Wholesale Drug	Beverages (Alcoholic)	22,002	5,500
6	122	Sammons Enterprises	Conglomerates	1,971	3,250
7	123	US Oncology	Healthcare Facilities	1,966	8,100
8	128	Brookshire Grocery	Retail (Grocery)	1,944	12,000
9	131	Dr Pepper/7 Up Bottling Group	Beverages (Non-Alcoholic)	1,900	8,900
10	141	Mary Kay	Personal & Household Products	1,800	3,600
11	153	Builders FirstSource	Construction - Supplies & Fixtures	1,675	6,500
12	156	Dresser	Oil Well Services & Equipment	1,657	8,300
13	176	Ben E. Keith	Retail (Grocery)	1,515	2,800
14	212	Goodman Manufacturing	Appliance & Tool	1,300	3,800
15	214	Republic Beverage	Beverages (Alcoholic)	1,300	2,400
16	218	National Waterworks	Misc. Fabricated Products	1,278	1,450
17	231	Vought Aircraft Industries	Aerospace & Defense	1,209	6,000
18	234	Truman Arnold Cos.	Oil & Gas Operations	1,205	500
19	235	Austin Industries	Construction Services	1,203	6,000
20	269	GSC Enterprises	Retail (Grocery)	1,073	1,050

Source www.forbes.com

> "I realised that the computer market was very inefficient. The mark-ups were incredibly high over the cost of materials and the service was very poor."
> **Michael Dell**

Michael Dell founded Dell Computer Corporation (now Dell, Inc.) in 1984 on the premise that customization of computer products, along with direct sales and delivery, offered the best choices to a rapidly growing constituency often bewildered by ever-changing computer technology. Today, the company calls Round Rock, Texas, its home where it oversees nearly 45,000 employees worldwide and fifty billion dollars in revenues annually.

DAISY BRADFORD
East Texas' Richest Lady

What would East Texas be without oil? Not many Texans can remember a time when the brushy landscape of East Texas was home to cattle ranches and dirt farms, but that was how it was in the early 1920s. Days were simple for the ranchers and farmers who worked the land, and few could foresee the changes that would come in the decade to follow. Although oil production in the 1920s had been successful for years in other areas of Texas, East Texas was never considered to be a prospective or prosperous area, but as other areas of Texas, Oklahoma, and Arkansas were getting crowded with derricks, a few curious wildcatters and adventuresome fortune hunters decided to head east and take their chances on a gusher.

One of those who headed east was 70 year old wildcatter Marion "Dad" Joiner. Joiner, realizing that his age and appearance could give him an advantage over the other wildcatters who were trying to buy leases and rights throughout the area, presented himself as a kind and honest gentleman, but in reality, he was a ruthless businessman who played loose when it came to honesty and integrity. Joiner controlled several mineral leases and thousands of acres of East Texas scrub land. The problem was that these leases and the rights to this acreage was really not worth very much, so Joiner decided to sell stock certificates in these leases to individuals for a minimal investment. Playing on the public's desire for a quick buck during the Great Depression, Joiner sent misleading reports to his investors and promoted his enterprise to the public. "The oil will be flowing soon!"

Even though he was making a pretty good buck selling interests in his leases, Joiner eventually had to drill a well or two to keep his investors from taking a rope to his neck. One of the leases that Joiner had the rights to belonged to Rusk County's Daisy Bradford, so figuring that any dry hole was as good as another, Joiner began to drill on Daisy's property. The first two holes were dry as a West Texas August and neither well produced any evidence of oil so both were closed. Investors were anxious and angry, so in an attempt to save his own neck,

Tol Barret drilled the first oil well in Texas, just after the Civil War, in Nacogdoches. It only produced ten barrels, so it was quickly abandoned.

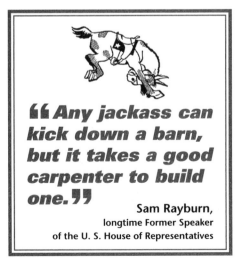

H.L. Hunt acquired the East Texas field discovery well in a history-making deal with C.M. "Dad" Joiner.

Joiner returned to Rusk County on May 8, 1929, and began drilling the Daisy Bradford No. 3. After two days of drilling and at a depth of 1,200 feet, some evidence of oil was seen. Shocked at the news, Joiner raced to Rusk County where on October 3, 1930, at approximately 3,592 feet, the Daisy Bradford No. 3 flowed live oil and gas. "Black Gold Fever" had hit East Texas with a vengeance.

The discovery of oil on Daisy Bradford's property brought money and hordes of people to East Texas. One of those people was independent oilman H. L. Hunt. Hunt, who had drilled a successful well in Arkansas in the early 1920s, was a man with a nose for money and a man who liked to take a chance. Hunt made Joiner an offer he couldn't refuse...and bought the well and the surrounding leases for $30,000.

That $30,000 investment by Hunt was, to say the least, prudent because it is still pumping crude today, over seventy-five years later! From Daisy Bradford's fields in Rusk County, one of the world's great oil companies took form, and by 1932 Hunt had nine hundred wells pumping in East Texas alone. With this success, Hunt grew his company to include pipelines, offshore drilling, refining, and real estate. You never know when history is going to be made, but the story of how Joiner and Hunt hooked up is not uncommon in Texas history. One man was of questionable character and took advantage of hard working men and women while the other was a hard-working risk taker who lived life to its fullest. But above all...he also knew a good deal when he saw one! ★

> **❝Any jackass can kick down a barn, but it takes a good carpenter to build one.❞**
> **Sam Rayburn,**
> longtime Former Speaker
> of the U. S. House of Representatives

THE SAGA OF Southwest Airlines

Had it not been for the fierce tenacity of two San Antonio businessmen, millions of Americans would have been deprived of doing business for the past thirty-odd years with one of the nation's largest and most successful business ventures. Southwest Airlines was the brainchild of licensed pilot Rollin King who held an M.B.A. from Harvard University and was a partner in a local investment firm. In 1964, King acquired a tiny local air taxi carrier called Wild Goose Flying Service, which flew between San Antonio and a few small southwest Texas towns. Three years later, King toyed with the idea of expanding Wild Goose to accommodate Dallas, Houston, and San Antonio. When he met over a meal with his friend, attorney Herb

Kelleher, and explained his idea by drawing a triangle connecting the three communities on a paper napkin, Kelleher had reservations about the rationale of such a limited undertaking in the highly competitive world of passenger airlines.

It didn't take long for King to convince his friend of the project's potential and, by March 15, 1967, the enterprise was incorporated as Air Southwest. Eight months later, papers were filed with the Texas Aeronautics Commission that would allow the company to begin operations among its "triangle" cities. In mid-February, 1968, the Commission gave its approval for the infant company to begin business.

Southwest Airlines By The Numbers

Number of Daily Flights	2,900+
Number of States Served	31
Number of Cities Served	59
Number of Airports Served	60
Number of Passengers Served (2003)	65,700,000
Net Income (2003)	$442,000,000
Total Operating Revenue	$5,900,000,000
Number of Employees	32,000+
Average Number of Flights per Plane per Day	7
Average Number of Hours Flown per Plane per Day	12
Average Aircraft Trip Length	81 miles
Number of Cans of Soda, Juices, and Water Served (2003)	52,600,000
Number of Bags of Peanuts Served (2003)	85,000,000
Number of Gallons of Jet Fuel Purchased (2003)	1,100,000,000
Average Cost of Ticket	$87.90

Southwest Airlines has 415 airplanes in its fleet at an average age of 9.2 years.

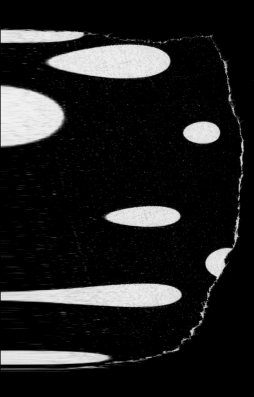

King, Kelleher, and the several investors that they had recruited knew that success would not come for their fledgling airline. Within twenty-four hours of the Commission's favorable ruling—even before the euphoria of the decision had worn off—a restraining order submitted by Braniff, Continental, and Trans-Texas Airlines was served on King prohibiting his planes from ever getting off the ground. Only after nearly three long years of legal entanglement, when the United States Supreme Court ultimately ruled that Air Southwest had a legal right to fly within the boundaries of Texas, did the airline begin to once again make plans to place its first plane in the air.

In 1971, Air Southwest changed its name to Southwest Airlines, hired a new president, Marion Lamar Muse, and looked with dismay at its unpaid bills of $133,000 and its savings account of $148. Another capital campaign got underway and, within four months, three Boeing 737-200 aircraft had been acquired, airport space at Houston, San Antonio, and Dallas had been negotiated, a massive advertising campaign had begun, and scores of pilots, crew members, and mechanics had been hired and trained.

As final plans were being laid to get Southwest's maiden flight into the air, a fresh batch of legal maneuverings by Braniff and Texas International again brought operations to a halt. Finally, on June 18, 1971, following a Texas Supreme Court decision to void an injunction filed by the two competitors that would forbid Southwest from commencing business, the first Southwest flight lifted from the tarmac at Dallas's Love Field with President Muse aboard. Southwest Airlines was finally in business.

Since those harried and frustrating days of the early 1970s, Southwest Airlines has become a major player in air travel in the United States. The company's stock was listed on the New York Stock Exchange in 1977, the same year it carried its five millionth passenger and, two years later, flights began from Dallas to New Orleans, the first city outside Texas to be added to the growing network of Southwest's service. In 2004, the airline announced its thirty-first consecutive year of profitability, a feat unheard of among its competitors. ★

Federal Tomfoolery

In 1979, when the tenacious upstart Southwest Airlines announced it would commence business outside the borders of Texas, veteran Congressman Jim Wright muscled legislation through the U. S. Congress that was ostensibly designed to protect the then five-year-old Dallas-Fort Worth International Airport. In order to force as much business through DFW as possible, the so-called *Wright Amendment* prohibited any full-size commercial airplane from flying out of Love Field whose destination was not an adjacent state. Alabama, Mississippi, and Kansas were added to the exclusive list in 1997.

Over the years, DFW has grown to five times the size of Love Field, yet the Wright Amendment is still on the books, although in September, 2004, several Tennessee congressmen challenged the law and introduced a bill to allow direct flights from Love Field to Nashville. Soon afterward, when Delta announced that it would close most of its DFW gates, Southwest Airlines reentered the fracas and called for the repeal of the law as well. As this book goes to press, the argument continues.

❄ Largest 50 Companies in Texas ❄

The following is a ranking of the 50 largest companies based in the state of Texas. The rank of the company is determined by a composite of sales, profits, assets, and market value.

Rank in Texas	National Rank	Company Name	Category	Sales ($bil)	Profits ($bil)	Assets ($bil)	Market Value ($bil)
1	4	Exxon Mobil	Oil & gas operations	222.88	20.96	166.99	277.02
2	33	SBC Communications	Telecommunications services	39.16	5.97	100.17	82.93
3	38	ConocoPhillips	Oil & gas operations	90.49	4.83	81.95	46.72
4	113	Dell	Technology hardware & equipment	41.44	2.65	19.31	88.46
5	204	Kimberly-Clark	Household & personal products	13.99	1.6	16.41	30.59
6	208	Clear Channel Communications	Media	8.85	1.14	28.17	27.86
7	214	Marathon Oil	Oil & gas operations	36.68	1.32	19.06	10.39
8	233	Texas Instruments	Semiconductors	9.83	1.2	15.51	53.25
9	255	Waste Management	Business services & supplies	11.57	0.72	20.66	16.87
10	270	Burlington Santa Fe	Transportation	9.29	0.78	26.94	12.03
11	305	Sysco	Food markets	27.54	0.84	7.31	24.28
12	333	Valero Energy	Oil & gas operations	34.51	0.58	15.25	6.7
13	339	Anadarko Petroleum	Oil & gas operations	5.12	1.25	20.55	12.92
14	343	JC Penney	Retailing	32.34	0.34	18.6	7.71
15	393	Centex	Construction	10.44	0.74	15.58	6.17
16	441	Apache	Oil & gas operations	4.2	1.1	12.42	12.82
17	465	Burlington Resources	Oil & gas operations	4.07	1.03	12.58	11.12
18	502	Southwest Airlines	Transportation	5.84	0.44	9.88	11.49
19	512	DR Horton	Construction	9.19	0.7	7.17	7.07
20	625	CenterPoint Energy	Utilities	9.36	0.29	20.06	3.16
21	645	Dean Foods	Food, drink & tobacco	9.18	0.36	6.99	5.33
22	647	Electronic Data Systems	Software & services	21.48	-0.27	18.28	9.98
23	650	Halliburton	Oil & gas operations	16.27	-0.81	15.47	13.86
24	683	TXU	Utilities	10.77	-4.09	30.77	7.89
25	769	El Paso Corporation	Oil & gas operations	7.93	-3.22	42.68	5.14
26	776	Baker Hughes	Oil & gas operations	5.29	0.13	6.3	12.12
27	786	AdvancePCS	Healthcare equipment & services	15.02	0.2	3.76	6.01
28	810	Temple-Inland	Materials	4.64	0.16	21.35	3.41
29	824	Affiliated Computer	Software & services	4.03	0.5	3.86	6.76
30	867	Kinder Morgan	Utilities	1.1	0.38	9.98	7.43
31	902	Cooper Industries	Capital goods	4.06	0.27	4.9	5.24
32	927	AMR	Transportation	17.15	-1.65	29.94	2.42
33	988	Radio Shack	Retailing	4.66	0.28	2.22	5.43
34	1,040	Reliant Resources	Utilities	11.23	-2	16.62	2.37
35	1,099	EOG Resources	Oil & gas operations	1.82	0.44	4.75	5.07
36	1,101	Transocean	Oil & gas operations	2.43	0.02	11.66	9.26
37	1,217	Weatherford Intl.	Oil & gas operations	2.45	0.13	4.93	5.73
38	1,235	BJ Services	Oil & gas operations	2.27	0.22	2.84	6.79
39	1,239	GlobalSantaFe	Oil & gas operations	1.91	0.13	6.13	6.79
40	1,257	Continental Airlines	Transportation	8.87	0.04	10.65	0.97
41	1,272	Dynegy	Oil & gas operations	5.81	-0.47	13.84	1.62
42	1,290	Pioneer Natural Resources	Oil & gas operations	1.3	0.4	3.95	3.68
43	1,298	XTO Energy	Oil & gas operations	1.19	0.29	3.61	5.22
44	1,310	Smith International	Oil & gas operations	3.59	0.12	3.1	5.05
45	1,323	Brinker International	Hotels, restaurants & leisure	3.47	0.18	2.02	3.53
46	1,345	Triad Hospitals	Healthcare equipment & services	3.81	0.13	4.48	2.65
47	1,382	Lyondell Chemical	Chemicals	3.8	-0.3	7.63	3.03
48	1,399	Whole Foods Market	Food markets	3.34	0.12	1.28	4.51
49	1,462	Michaels Stores	Retailing	3	0.16	1.76	3.22
50	1,493	Noble Corp	Oil & gas operations	0.99	0.17	3.19	5.32

TEXAS
WEATHER EXTREMES

The weather of Texas is as diverse as its landscape. From the harsh winters of the Panhandle to the hurricanes of the Gulf Coast, pioneers, farmers, and ranchers have braved the extreme Texas weather to settle the Lone Star *State. With centuries of flooding, drought, heat waves, and snowstorms to face, early settlers and modern Texans have always persevered. History has proven that you can't beat Mother Nature, you can only be prepared.*

Drought

Although much has been made of the Dust Bowl drought from 1932 to 1939, the worst drought in Texas history spanned a seven year period from 1950 to 1957. During these difficult years, Texans endured unbearable heat with little or no rainfall; just 0.02 inches of rainfall fell statewide during October 1952. After droughts in the 1880s, 1920s, 1930s, and 1950s, Texans began to expect a twenty year drought cycle. Fortunately the cycle was broken in the 1970s, although Texas still experienced a few dry years in the late 1990s and early 2000s.

Heat

Long known for its sweltering heat, Texas has endured its fair share of exceptional heat waves. The record high for the state was set in Seymour on August 12, 1936; it was tied on July 27, 1994, in Monahans. The financial impact of a drought and heat wave was realized in 1998, when over $2 billion in agricultural losses was recorded for Texas and Oklahoma. The deadliest summer attributed to heat was the summer of 1980, with over 70 deaths in Texas alone. During that summer, extreme heat brought ten consecutive days of temperatures higher than 110 degrees in Wichita Falls.

Hail

The worst recorded hailstorm in Texas history occurred on May 5, 1995, in the Dallas-Fort Worth area. As the sun was setting on the annual May Festival in Worth, a super cell and strong squall combined to produce the "perfect st Baseball-sized hail fell on the city ca one death and numerous injuries. squall line moved through Dallas, rains caused flash flooding resultin deaths of 19 persons, 109 injured, estimated $2 billion in damage.

Through the years, a number hailstorms have brought destruc state. On May 16, 1917, hail fell deep in Ballinger and reportedly days to clear. In August 1979, a in the High Plains destroyed 15 acres of crops and damaged 55 Damage from this storm was to be $200 million. A hailstor 5, 2003, in the north-central of Texas produced hail up to in diameter causing an estim million in damages.

Flash Floods

Flash floods, usually caused by sudden rainfall over a wide area, are the most dangerous type of floods. Saturated soil and inadequate drainage make flash floods a significant threat to life and property. One of the most memorable flash floods occurred in August 1882. Heavy thunderstorms fell upstream of the town of Ben Ficklin, the county seat of Tom Green County. During the night, the river flooded the town, killing 45 people. The town was completely destroyed, and the citizens decided not to rebuild the town in the flood-prone area. Instead, the county seat was moved to San Angelo, which might not exist had it not been for the flood of 1882.

Record Rainfall

Although Texas is sometimes considered dry and arid, it is also a state of extreme rainfall. Because of its proximity to the Gulf of Mexico, Texas bears the brunt of many storms with a direct feed of tropical moisture. Texas holds the all-time record for rainfall in a 24 hour period. Tropical Storm Claudette, which made landfall in July 1979, dropped a remarkable 40 inches of rain in 24 hours on Alvin, Texas. An unofficial site, but confirmed by the National Weather Service, recorded 43 inches of rain in twenty-four hours. Claudette went on to cause $750 million in property and crop damage across southeast Texas.

Ice

Because of the conveniences of electricity, automobiles, and air travel, ice storms are more destructive to modern society than they were in the past. Ice storms were rarely recorded prior to the advent of electricity because the effects were not as far reaching. The most expensive and deadly ice storms on record in Texas both occurred in December 2000, in northeast Texas. Striking just two weeks

apart, the storms inflicted an estimated $300 million of damage in Texas and Oklahoma, with 27 deaths recorded in the two states. In many areas of Texas, power was out so long that the water supplies were affected.

Cold

Texas is a state of extremes and extreme cold hit the state with a vengeance in 1899. On February 12, 1889, the temperature for over half of Texas was below 0 degrees. Galveston Bay reportedly was covered with ice and the Texas state record for cold temperature was set in Tulia, which had a temperature of minus 23 degrees. Other cold days in Texas history were noted in December, 1989, when Amarillo experienced 261 consecutive hours below freezing. In January 1930, the temperature in Galveston plummeted to a record 13 degrees.

Snow

The Texas Panhandle, with its northern location and lower winter temperatures is usually hit the hardest by winter precipitation. The winter of 1956 was no exception when the biggest single snowstorm recorded in Texas hit the town of Hale. In February of that year, 33 inches of snow covered the town, resulting in twenty deaths. Another devastating storm hit the Panhandle in February 1971. Drifts of up to 20 feet were reported in Texas and Oklahoma. Despite military airdrops of hay, 13,000 head of cattle were lost. Another big snow in Texas history was a blizzard recorded in the Panhandle from February 1 to February 7, 1964. The storm produced 25 inches of snow in the town of Borger and 30 mph winds produced

Average annual precipitation in Texas ranges from 60 inches at Caddo Lake to 8.8 inches in El Paso.

drifts that reached ten feet. The few snowplows in San Antonio proved inadequate on January 12 and January 13, 1985, when 13.5 inches of snow fell in that southern city.

Dust Storms

On April 14, 1935, a perfect combination of dry weather and strong winds produced a day in Texas weather history known as "Black Sunday." Within an hour, day switched to night, visibility dropped to one mile, and life in the towns and cities on the plains of Texas came to a screeching halt. The Black Sunday dust storm came upon the state suddenly and left hundreds dead and millions of dollars in destruction. Although other months may be drier, dust storms are most likely to hit in springtime. In springtime the fields are still bare, the temperatures are rising, and the winds are strong.

Tornadoes

One of the most devastating weather events to affect the state of Texas is the deadly tornado. Tornadoes and Texas are sadly sometimes synonymous in people's minds. A tie for the record of deadliest tornado in Texas history exists between the one which occurred in Waco on May 11, 1953, and the tornado of 1902, in Goliad. Both tornadoes killed 114 people each.

The coastline of Texas stretches 624 miles along the Gulf of Mexico and contains more than 600 historic shipwrecks.

Since the beginning of recorded history, Indian tribes have roamed the plains, forests, and deserts of Texas. Beginning with the Paleo Indians in 10,000 B.C., hundreds of different Indian tribes and bands have called Texas home. The following is a short list of some of the streams, rivers, mountain ranges, towns, and counties that derive their name from some of these bands.

Apache Mountains – These mountains, which are located in Culberson County, are located in the area that was the last stronghold of the Apache Indians in Texas.

Bedias – A town that is located in Grimes County is named after the Bidai Indians, a Caddoan group whose name meant "brushwood."

Caddo Lake – A lake that is in Marion and Harrison counties named for the Caddo Indians.

Cherokee County – This county is named for the Cherokee Indians who lived under the leadership of Chief Bowles in East Texas in the early 19th century.

Comanche County – This county is named for the most famous tribe of Plains Indians, the Comanches.

Delaware Bend – This town in Cooke County is named after the Delaware Indians, who were closely associated with the Cherokees in East Texas.

Nacogdoches County – This county is named after the Nacogdoche Indians.

Seminole – The Seminole Indian tribe came north from Florida and lived with the Cherokees in East Texas. This town, in Gaines County, was named after them.

Shawnee Creek – This small creek is named after the Shawnee Indians, who settled on the upper Sabine River in the 1820s.

Tehuacana – Named after the Tawakoni Indians, who lived in this area until the 1840s; this town is in Limestone County.

Waco – Named after the Waco Indians, a Wichita group, that entered Texas in the early 18th century and occupied this region.

Wichita County – Named after the Wichita Indians. Other place names derived from this group are Wichita Falls and the Wichita River.

The Weather Man

For the past twenty-four hours, Isaac M. Cline, the forecaster in charge of the Galveston weather station, had been watching the barometer closely.

It was Friday, September 7, 1900. Beginning with an abnormal reading of 29.974 the previous morning, the mercury in the barometer had been steadily dropping. This morning, the instrument was registering 29.678.

On Thursday, weather forecaster Isaac M. Cline had noted in his log that the weather was unusually hot for that time of the year. In fact, the temperature had peaked at 90.9 degrees. On Friday, the weather station would record an even warmer high of 91.1 degrees, and Cline knew that these conditions were what gave birth to hurricanes. But as Cline worried about the barometer and the temperature, he also noticed that the sky was fairly clear except for some high-flying stratocumulus clouds. To further complicate things, Cline noted that the wind was only blowing at about ten miles an hour from the north with an occasional gust up to twenty miles an hour. According to Cline's report, none of the usual hurricane signs were present, especially the brick dust-colored sky that normally accompanied such storms in the region.

When Cline and his brother, Joseph, a weather observer assigned to the same office, reported for work early on Saturday morning September 8, they read with interest an item from that morning's newspaper. According to the article, a vicious storm was raging in the Gulf of Mexico offshore from Mississippi and Louisiana. Details were sketchy, but it was reported that considerable damage had been done to shipping in the area. As they read on, a second article caught the brothers' attention. Filed just before the newspaper went to press early Saturday morning, it reported that no updated information about the storm was available and that it might have "changed its course or spent its force before reaching Texas."

> During a **24-hour period in 1979**, tropical storm **Claudette** dropped **43 inches of rain** on the town of **Alvin**, located 20 miles south of Houston. This set a U.S. 24-hour rainfall record, but no one was applauding.

In 1900, there was very little way to inform the general public of news quickly let alone instantly. Before most Galveston residents had read their morning papers, the weather conditions had changed dramatically, so Isaac Cline began to warn city residents who lived nearest the Gulf to prepare for the worst. At 6:30, the forecaster wired his concern to the central weather bureau in Washington, D. C., declaring that frequent and unusually heavy swells had already overflowed portions of Galveston. At 7 A.M., when the Cline brothers collected the early weather statistics, the sky was cloudy, the wind was up to a steady twenty-three miles an hour, and the barometer was continuing its plunge. By 7:45, a steady rain had begun, and although Isaac and his brother now suspected that a severe hurricane was imminent, he could not have known that within hours the most destructive storm in North American history would hit Galveston head on.

Throughout the morning the angry waters continued to lash the southern part of town, which was the primary residential section. The business district, with its sturdier brick structures, was more protected from the oncoming storm by the shield of houses that lay between it and the Gulf. Wind velocity increased, and, at 5:15 P.M., the weather station's instruments on top of the Levy Building blew away. The Clines could only guess at wind speed after that, but they later reported it reached at least 120 miles an hour during the worst part of the storm. Although the station's rain gauge had been destroyed as well, later estimates suggest that at least ten inches of rain fell on Galveston on September 8.

With little else to do because his instruments had been destroyed by the storm, Isaac and Joseph went out into the

The Great Rainmaking Experiment

In mid-October, 1891, several Duval County farmers gathered in the small village of San Diego to witness a strange experiment. They had been persuaded to invest in a rain-making scheme that would test whether a series of loud explosions could trigger precipitation. The weather had been hot and dry for weeks, and the experiment was begun beneath a crystal-clear sky. Yet, following hours of noisy detonations, rain actually did begin to fall and totaled nearly one-half inch before the skies turned clear again. Coincidence or science? The happy farmers were ready to fund more experiments, but modern technology has since proven that loud noises have no effect on rainfall.

"Bum-ism"

"The thing that decides the size of your funeral is the weather."

"Bum" Phillips
Former Houston Oilers Coach

deadly storm to find their families. After struggling through the torrential rain and howling wind, they finally reached their families. Just as they arrived home at a little after 5:00 P.M., Isaac Cline, along with his wife, three daughters, and brother Joseph, were inside their home when it was washed from its foundations and carried into the Gulf of Mexico. Miraculously, all of the family except Isaac's wife survived the harrowing ordeal.

Six thousand residents of the city were killed on this fateful day in 1900. Most of the residential section of Galveston was destroyed while the majority of the business district was spared. General Thomas Scurry, commander of the Texas National Guard, which was dispatched to the city to prevent looting, later declared that "at least one-seventh of its population [had been] killed, and more than fifteen thousand of its surviving citizens made absolutely destitute...Three-fourths of its estimated valuation has been totally destroyed." Before the storm hit, Galveston's wealth in proportion to its population had been surpassed only by Providence, Rhode Island. Now, according to General Scurry, "there is scarcely a city in America poorer..."

Within hours, the fourth largest city in Texas had been reduced to a pile of rubble. Property damage in present-day terms ran into the hundreds of millions of dollars. However, out of tragedy sometimes comes triumph. City fathers vowed that their town would never again suffer such destruction, so they passed ordinances requiring that all of Galveston Island be elevated several feet by importing millions of tons of sand and gravel. Many places in the downtown area were raised as much as 17 feet and a modern sea wall was built that would protect the city from future abnormal tides. ★

Wind Chill Chart

								Temperature (°F)										
Calm	40	35	30	25	20	15	10	5	0	-5	-10	-15	-20	-25	-30	-35	-40	-45
5	36	31	25	19	13	7	1	-5	-11	-16	-22	-28	-34	-40	-46	-52	-57	-63
10	34	27	21	15	9	3	-4	-10	-16	-22	-28	-35	-41	-47	-53	-59	-66	-72
15	32	25	19	13	6	0	-7	-13	-19	-26	-32	-39	-45	-51	-58	-64	-71	-77
20	30	24	17	11	4	-2	-9	-15	-22	-29	-35	-42	-48	-55	-61	-68	-74	-81
Wind 25	29	23	16	9	3	-4	-11	-17	-24	-31	-37	-44	-51	-58	-64	-71	-78	-84
(mph) 30	28	22	15	8	1	-5	-12	-19	-26	-33	-39	-46	-53	-60	-67	-73	-80	-87
35	28	21	14	7	0	-7	-14	-21	-27	-34	-41	-48	-55	-62	-69	-76	-82	-89
40	27	20	13	6	-1	-8	-15	-22	-29	-36	-43	-50	-57	-64	-71	-78	-84	-91
45	26	19	12	5	-2	-9	-16	-23	-30	-37	-44	-51	-58	-65	-72	-79	-86	-93
50	26	19	12	4	-3	-10	-17	-24	-31	-38	-45	-52	-60	-67	-74	-81	-88	-95
55	25	18	11	4	-3	-11	-18	-25	-32	-39	-46	-54	-61	-68	-75	-82	-89	-97
60	25	17	10	3	-4	-11	-19	-26	-33	-40	-48	-55	-62	-69	-76	-84	-91	-98

Source: NOAA

As you know, it can get really hot in Texas. *Thank God for that, because most Yankees can't take the heat!* If you are not sure whether someone is truly a native son or daughter of Texas, here is a list of little known facts that every Texan should know.

YOU KNOW SOMEONE IS A NATIVE IF...

- They can stay out in 110 degree heat in a pair of jeans and boots.
- They eat hot chilies to cool off their mouth.
- They know how to make "instant" sun tea.
- They know that a seat belt makes a pretty good branding iron.
- They get chilly on August nights when the temperature drops below 95.
- They know that in July it takes only two fingers to drive your car.
- They know that you can get a sunburn through your truck window.
- They know the best parking place is determined by shade instead of distance.
- They know that hot water comes out of both taps.
- They know asphalt has a liquid state.

In Texas the temperature has reached the 120 degree mark on two different occasions. On August 12, 1936, the town of Seymour hit the high mark and on July 27, 1994, it was time for Monahans to sizzle.

Heat Index

Temperature (F) versus Relative Humidity (%)

F	90%	80%	70%	60%	50%	40%
80	85	84	82	81	80	79
85	101	96	92	90	86	84
90	121	113	105	99	94	90
95		133	122	113	105	98
100			142	129	118	109
105				148	133	121
110						135

Heat Index	Possible Heat Disorder
80 F - 90 F	*Fatigue possible with prolonged exposure and physical activity.*
90 F - 105 F	*Sunstroke, heat cramps, and heat exhaustion possible.*
105 F - 130 F	*Sunstroke, heat cramps, and heat exhaustion likely, and heat stroke possible.*
130 F or greater	*Heat stroke likely with continued exposure.*

 An average of 123 tornados touch down in Texas each year. From 1951 to 1993, 5,281 tornados were recorded.

TEXAS HURRICANES AND TROPICAL STORMS

Galveston Hurricane of 1527

The Galveston Hurricane of 1527 is the first recorded hurricane along the Texas coastline. The storm took two hundred lives, and a merchant fleet on Galveston Island was completely destroyed. This hurricane is unique because it occurred in November. Since then, only one other hurricane has ever struck during the month of November (1839).

Galveston Hurricane of 1818

The Galveston Hurricane of 1818 was described as a storm of extraordinary violence, destroying all but six buildings on Galveston Island.

110 miles per hour during the storm's peak, and the storm surge was near fifteen feet. Texas justice was swift in these days as 15 looters were killed by angry locals when they were caught pillaging from the dead. In the Gulf, the steamer *Paisana*, carrying $200,000, was lost between Brazos Santiago and Galveston.

The Indianola Hurricane of 1886

Once again, Indianola suffered from the wrath of Mother Nature during the hurricane of 1886. At the time, this hurricane was considered the worst storm to reach the interior of South Texas. High winds and a storm surge of 15 feet overtook the town

The Great Galveston Hurricane of 1900

The Great Galveston Hurricane stands as one of the worst natural disasters in the United States. In 1900, Galveston had a population of 30,000 and was the most significant port in Texas. The majority of the town's structures were of wood frame and built just above sea level. Word of the hurricane's magnitude reached Galveston by telegraph and sailors returning from sea, so some residents moved inland for safety from the storm. Sadly though, few heeded the warnings and decided to ride out the storm. The storm smashed homes and left their occupants to drown in the resulting flood. Winds, gusting to over 125 miles per hour, drove sea water into the city of Galveston, covering most of the town to a depth of 15 feet. When the storm finally subsided, it had destroyed 2,600 homes. Three fourths of the city (a total of twelve square blocks) was completely obliterated. The Great Galveston Hurricane left 6,000 to 8,000 dead and damage was estimated at fifty million dollars.

HURRICANE CATEGORIES

Category	Windspeed	Surge	Minimum Pressure
1	75-95 m.p.h.	4-5 ft.	greater than 28.93 in.
2	96-110 m.p.h.	6-8 ft.	28.48 - 28.90 in.
3	111-130 m.p.h.	9-12 ft.	27.85 - 28.45 in.
4	131-155 m.p.h.	13-18 ft.	27.13 - 27.85
5	over 156 m.p.h.	over 18 ft.	less than 27.13 in.

The notorious pirate Jean Lafitte, (who was occupying Galveston at the time), moved into the hull of a damaged ship so that his home could be used as a hospital for the French colonists.

The Indianola Hurricane of 1875

The Indianola Hurricane of 1875 brought devastating rain and wind to the town, washing away three-fourths of the buildings and killing 176 people. Wind gusts were estimated at

and left all the homes uninhabitable. Before the hurricane, south Texas was suffering from a terrible drought. Water was being sold for ten cents a bucket in Galveston... twice the cost of beer! Ironically, the storm did relieve the extreme drought in the area. Prior to this hurricane, Indianola had been Texas' leading port of call. Because of the devastation, Galveston succeeded Indianola as the new Texas port of call—which it remains to this day.

The Galveston Hurricane of 1915

In 1915 Galveston once again found itself at the center of a devastating hurricane. With the memory of the hurricane of 1900 still fresh in their minds, many residents wisely fled inland. Storm surges reached 15.3 feet, and the water level in the Galveston business district reached 5 feet. Despite the warnings, 275 people died and damage was estimated at fifty million dollars.

The Corpus Christi Hurricane of 1919

Corpus Christi received a direct hit in 1919 from a hurricane with wind speeds of 110 miles per hour and storm surges of 16 feet. Bodies and wreckage were strewn along the beaches, and many of the over three hundred who died were buried in mass graves near White Point. The damage from this hurricane was estimated at twenty million dollars.

Hurricane Carla 1961

Hurricane Carla is remembered as one of the most powerful tropical systems to affect the Texas coastline. Carla made landfall between Port O'Connor and Port Lavaca with winds gusting to175 miles per hour. The storm spewed tornadoes inland and produced a 22-foot storm surge. Fortunately, a quarter of a million people were evacuated inland to safety, contributing to the low death toll of only thirty four. Four hundred million dollars in damage was estimated throughout Texas.

Hurricane Beulah 1967

Hurricane Beulah was the third largest hurricane on record at the time to hit the U.S. mainland, behind Carla and a hurricane that struck New England in 1938. Beulah made landfall in Brownsville and brought torrential rains and strong winds. Wind gusts reached 136 miles per hour in Port Brownsville and the storm surge on Padre Island reached 20 feet. An incredible one hundred fifteen tornadoes were spawned by the system—the most ever known to be generated by a hurricane. Fifteen Texans died as a result of the hurricane and damages were estimated at one hundred million dollars.

Hurricane Alicia 1983

Hurricane Alicia made landfall in Galveston bringing storm surges of 12.1 feet along the Galveston Bay. Seventeen tornadoes were spawned from Alicia, and claimed seventeen lives. Damage included erosion of 5,200 feet of Galveston Island's coast and a huge crude oil spill near Texas City. Alicia did bring some good fortune— it relieved the parched areas of the drought as it headed north toward Oklahoma. Damage from Hurricane Alicia was estimated at more than three billion dollars.

Tropical Storm Allison 2001

In 2001, Galveston once again bore the brunt of high winds and torrential rainfall with Allison. Record rainfall brought catastrophic flooding across the state. Forty three people lost their lives in Tropical Storm Allison, and the flooding damage alone in Houston was estimated at two billion dollars. Though classified as a tropical storm, not as a hurricane, Allison was one of the most costly storms to hit the United States. Damage from Allison in Texas was estimated at four billion dollars.

The phonetic alphabet was used beginning in 1950 by the United States military to name Atlantic Ocean storms. The intent was to end confusion when multiple storms were present. In 1954, the use of women's names became the standard for naming hurricanes. Today, both men's and women's names are used to name hurricanes.

THE MOST DEADLY STORMS IN TEXAS

Year	Name	Category	Lowest Pressure (MB)	Wind Gust	Storm Surge	Landfall	Deaths	Estimated Damage
1527		1				Upper Coast	200	
1818		2 or 3				Galveston		
1875		4		110 m.p.h.	15 ft.	Indianola	176	
1886		2	29.03 in.	80 m.p.h.	15 ft.	Indianola	30	$2 Million
1900		4 or 5	27.46 in.	125 m.p.h.	15 ft.	Galveston	6000 - 8000	$50 Million
1915		4	28.14 in.	120 m.p.h.	15.3 ft.	Galveston	275	$50 Million
1919		4	28.65 in.	110 m.p.h.	16 ft.	Corpus Christi	300 +	$20 Million
1961	Carla	4	27.39 in.	175 m.p.h.	22 ft.	Port Lavaca	34	$400 Million
1967	Beulah	3	28.07 in.	136 m.p.h.	20 ft.	Brownsville	15	$100 Million
1983	Alicia	3	28.39 in.	102 m.p.h.	12.1 ft.	Galveston	17	$3 Billion
2001	Allison	Trop. Storm	30.11 in.	45 m.p.h.	2 ft.	Galveston	43	$4 Billion

When the Sky Went Dark

In the spring of 1935, when the southern Great Plains was engulfed in the fury of the Dust Bowl, the now-famous balladeer Woody Guthrie sat on his front porch in Pampa, Texas, took up his pen, and wrote,

"On the 14th day of April of 1935, there struck the worst of dust storms that ever filled the sky. You could see that dust storm comin', the cloud looked deathlike black, and through our mighty nation, it left a dreadful track."

In a few verses of a folk melody, Guthrie accurately described what has been called one of America's most devastating natural disasters of all time.

The indirect cause of the Dust Bowl dates to the pre-World War I year of 1914, when Turkish naval forces closed the Dardanelles to shipping, thus cutting off millions of tons of Russian wheat to the United States and Western Europe. In an effort to fill the vacuum, farmers in the American Midwest opened millions of acres of marginal, poorly watered land to the plow and, within a short time, had increased their own wheat yield by three hundred percent. But, the stakes were high. When a severe drought hit the vast region during the late 1920s, the stage was set for disaster as the poor and worn-out soil awaited the inevitable.

The hardest hit areas were the Panhandles of Texas and Oklahoma, eastern New Mexico and Colorado, and western Kansas. From the mid-1930s until 1940, winds blowing up to fifty miles per hour howled daily across the desolate landscape that supported little or no life. When he heard a loud commotion, one child went outside the protection of his meager house to see his grandmother "hanging on to a fence post," the victim of "wind blowin' so hard she looked like a pennant in a breeze." By 1932, the parched land of the region, unwatered for month upon month, had yielded the last of its grass cover to the drought, leaving the thirsting soil

> ...winds blowing up to fifty miles per hour howled daily across the desolate landscape that supported little or no life.

with no protection from the ever-present winds. Cities hundreds of miles eastward were affected as dust blowing across the continent covered the sun, blotted out natural light, and left films of soil on furniture, in yards, and along roadways. Even President Franklin D. Roosevelt complained about the dust that had settled on his desk in the White House. Nearly forty percent of Texas Panhandle farmers deserted their land and began the long search for new livelihoods.

The woes of the Dust Bowl, coupled with the simultaneous sufferings of the Great Depression, drove many Texans, as well as refugees from the other affected areas, to California. They were collectively called "Okies," whether or not they hailed from Oklahoma. John Steinbeck, the American novelist, won the Pulitzer Prize in 1940 for his book, *The Grapes of Wrath*, which graphically depicted the plight of an Okie family caught up in the midst of the Dust Bowl and its aftermath.

In time, the tired and persecuted land partially recovered from the ravages of the Dust Bowl, but the lessons learned were hard ones. Out of the misery and suffering of thousands of Americans came the bitter lesson that the nation's natural resources are limited and precious and that it's best not to tamper with Mother Nature's ways. ★

Fujita Tornado Damage Scale

The Fujita Scale, developed in 1971 by Theodore Fujita, is the system used by the National Weather Service to rank the intensity of tornadoes. The intensity level is determined by estimating the damage caused by the tornado after it has passed over a man-made structure.

SCALE	WIND ESTIMATE (MPH)	TYPICAL DAMAGE
F0	< 73	Light damage. Some damage to chimneys; branches broken off trees; shallow-rooted trees pushed over; sign boards damaged.
F1	73-112	Moderate damage. Peels surface off roofs; mobile homes pushed off foundations or overturned; moving autos blown off roads.
F2	113-157	Considerable damage. Roofs torn off frame houses; mobile homes demolished; boxcars overturned; large trees snapped or uprooted; light-object missiles generated; cars lifted off ground.
F3	158-206	Severe damage. Roofs and some walls torn off well-constructed houses; trains overturned; most trees in forest uprooted; heavy cars lifted off the ground and thrown.
F4	207-260	Devastating damage. Well-constructed houses leveled; structures with weak foundations blown away some distance; cars thrown and large missiles generated.
F5	261-318	Incredible damage. Strong frame houses leveled off foundations and swept away; automobile-sized missiles fly through the air in excess of 100 meters (109 yards); tree debarked; incredible phenomena will occur.

DAY OF YEAR	DAY OF WEEK	DAY OF MONTH	RISE	SET	LENGTH OF DAY	TIDES AM	TIDES PM	MOON PHASE	NORMAL HIGH TEMP	On this date in January...
1	Sun	1	7 49	5 55	H M 10 06	1 24 H 10 39 L	7 30 H 10 34 L	●	56°	New Year's Day; Confederate troops recapture Galveston. (1863); Longhorns defeat Navy 28-6 winning National Championship. (1963)
2	Mon	2	7 49	5 56	10 07	2 29 H 11 30 L	8 07 H 11 37 L	●	56°	New Year's Day observed; last day of Chanukah. (Jewish)
3	Tues	3	7 49	5 57	10 08	3 42 H	12 22 L 8 35 H	●	56°	Stephen Austin receives a grant land in Texas from the government of Mexico. (1823); Mexican government imprisons Stephen Austin for insurrection in Mexico City. (1834)
4	Wed	4	7 50	5 58	10 08	1 09 H 5 25 H	1 15 L 8 57 H	●	56°	The population of San Antonio is 149. (1784)
5	Thurs	5	7 50	5 58	10 08	2 49 L 7 48 H	2 12 L 9 15 H	◐	56°	Davy Crockett arrives in Texas in time to fight at the Alamo. (1836)
6	Fri	6	7 50	5 59	10 09	4 04 L 10 21 H	3 26 L 9 30 H	◑	56°	The Texas Rangers consists of only 25 men, all of them deployed either from Harlingen, Ysleta, Austin, or Amarillo. (1910)
7	Sat	7	7 50	6 00	10 10	5 01 L	12 45 H 5 35 L 9 40 H	◑	56°	Legendary Texas Ranger W.W.A. "Bigfoot" Wallace dies. (1899)
8	Sun	8	7 50	6 01	10 11	5 50 L	2 28 H	◑	56°	First all female State Supreme Court appointed in Texas. (1925)
9	Mon	9	7 50	6 02	10 12	6 36 L	3 33 H	◑	56°	Outlaw gang led by Bonnie and Clyde holds Texas State Motorcycle Policeman, Thomas Persell, hostage. (1933)
10	Tues	10	7 50	6 02	10 12	7 20 L	4 22 H	○	56°	Oil is discovered at Spindletop, near Beaumont. (1901)
11	Wed	11	7 50	6 03	10 13	8 03 L	5 06 H	○	56°	Pancho Villa drives 4,500 Mexican Federal soldiers and civilians across the Rio Grande to refuge in Presidio, Texas. (1914)
12	Thurs	12	7 50	6 04	10 14	8 43 L	5 47 H	○	56°	Tex Ritter is born. (1906)
13	Fri	13	7 50	6 05	10 15	9 22 L	6 24 H 10 20 L	○	56°	The French explorer, La Salle, leaves Matagorda Bay on foot for Canada. (1687)
14	Sat	14	7 49	6 06	10 17	12 37 H 9 59 L	6 55 H 9 37 L	○	56°	Photographer Erwin E. Smith advertises his portfolio, "Pictures of the West," in **Scribner's Magazine,** a project that was never completed. (1921)
15	Sun	15	7 49	6 07	10 18	1 29 H 10 33 L	7 17 H 9 58 L	○	56°	Cowboys defeat Broncos 27-10 in Super Bowl XII. (1978)
16	Mon	16	7 49	6 08	10 19	2 10 H 11 04 L	7 36 H 10 52 L	○	56°	Martin Luther King Day; Cowboys defeat Dolphins 24-3 in Super Bowl VI. (1972)

Add one hour for Daylight Saving Time, if and when in use.

January 2006 — *January is named for Janus, the Roman god of doors and gateways.*

January is the first month of the year in the Gregorian calendar and one of seven months with 31 days. The Romans considered the winter to be a monthless period and therefore the original Roman calendar consisted only of 10 months, starting with March. In 700 B.C.,

King Numa Pomilius added the months of January and February to the Roman calendar making it equal to a standard lunar calendar with 354 days. A superstition against even numbers brought the addition of a day to January, thus making the Roman year 355 days long.

DAY OF YEAR	DAY OF WEEK	DAY OF MONTH	RISE	SET	LENGTH OF DAY	TIDES AM	TIDES PM	MOON PHASE	NORMAL HIGH TEMP	On this date in January...
					H M					
17	Tues	17	7 49	6 09	10 20	2 49 H 11 34 L	7 52 H	◑	56°	Mexico permits Moses Austin and 300 American families to settle in Texas. (1821) Armed Democrats seize the Texas government ending Radical Reconstruction. (1874)
18	Wed	18	7 49	6 09	10 20	12 06 L 3 36 H	12 02 L 8 08 H	◑	57°	Cowboys lose to Steelers 21-17, in Super Bowl X. (1976)
19	Thurs	19	7 48	6 10	10 22	1 32 L 5 11 H	12 30 L 8 20 H	◑	57°	Troop C, 4th U.S. Cavalry, clashes with Indians near the Nueces River. (1867)
20	Fri	20	7 48	6 11	10 23	2 43 L 7 51 H	12 59 L 8 25 H	◑	57°	James Hogg becomes the first native Texan to be governor of Texas. (1891)
21	Sat	21	7 48	6 12	10 24	3 28 L 10 26 H	1 31 L 8 16 H	◑	57°	Cowboys lose to Steelers 35-31, in Super Bowl XIII. (1979)
22	Sun	22	7 47	6 13	10 26	4 06 L	7 03 H	◐	57°	Archer, Hardin, Kimble, Mason, Menard, Stephens, and Zapata Counties are founded. (1858)
23	Mon	23	7 47	6 14	10 27	4 45 L	2 18 H	◐	57°	During the fight for Mexican independence, rebels jail the Spanish governor in the Alamo. (1811)
24	Tues	24	7 46	6 15	10 29	5 28 L	3 00 H	◕	58°	Dallas Texans established, formerly the NY Yanks. (1952)
25	Wed	25	7 46	6 16	10 30	6 16 L	3 41 H	◕	58°	U.S. House of Representatives votes to admit Texas to the Union. (1845)
26	Thurs	26	7 45	6 17	10 32	7 07 L	4 23 H	◕	58°	Company A, 2nd U.S. Cavalry, skirmishes with Commanches on Kickapoo Creek. (1860)
27	Fri	27	7 45	6 18	10 33	7 59 L	5 04 H 8 33 L 11 24 H	◕	58°	Tom Landry hired as Dallas football coach. (1959)
28	Sat	28	7 44	6 19	10 35	8 52 L	5 40 H 8 48 L	●	58°	Cowboys defeat Steelers 27-17 in Super Bowl XXX. (1996)
29	Sun	29	7 44	6 20	10 36	12 56 H 9 43 L	6 09 H 9 31 L	●	59°	Famed El Paso artist and writer, Tom Lea, dies at the age of 93. (2001)
30	Mon	30	7 43	6 21	10 38	2 16 H 10 34 L	6 34 H 10 28 L	●	59°	Cowboys defeat Bills 13-3 in Super Bowl XXVIII. (1994)
31	Tues	31	7 43	6 22	10 39	3 38 H 11 24 L	6 54 H 11 34 L	●	59°	Nolan Ryan is born. (1947); Cowboys defeat Bills 52-17 in Super Bowl XXVII. (1993)

● New Moon   ◐ First Quarter   ○ Full Moon   ◑ Last Quarter

Atmospheric and Astronomical data provided by NOAA, National Ocean Service and U.S. Naval Observatory.

On this date in February...

DAY OF YEAR	DAY OF WEEK	DAY OF MONTH	RISE	SET	LENGTH OF DAY	TIDES AM	TIDES PM	MOON PHASE	NORMAL HIGH TEMP	On this date in February...
32	Wed	1	7 42	6 22	H M 10 40	5 09 H	12 13 L 7 12 H	●	59°	Texas Convention votes to secede from the Union. (1861); Texas Instruments requests patent of Integrated Circuit. (1959)
33	Thurs	2	7 41	6 23	10 42	12 44 L 6 53 H	1 06 L 7 27 H	●	60°	Treaty of Guadalupe Hidalgo ends Mexican War; United States acquires Texas, California, New Mexico, and Arizona for $15 million. (1848)
34	Fri	3	7 41	6 24	10 43	1 54 L 8 52 H	2 07 L 7 39 H	◗	60°	Buddy Holly dies. (1959)
35	Sat	4	7 40	6 25	10 45	3 02 L 11 05 H	4 03 L 7 39 H	◗	60°	Mexican government changes name of La Bahia to Goliad. (1829)
36	Sun	5	7 39	6 26	10 47	4 07 L	1 16 H	◖	60°	Roger Staubach is born. (1942)
37	Mon	6	7 38	6 27	10 49	5 08 L	2 40 H	◖	61°	Railroad bridge completed between Virginia Point and Galveston Island. (1860)
38	Tues	7	7 38	6 28	10 50	6 08 L	3 38 H	◖	61°	Seguin incorporated. (1853); Cowboy and western author Charles Siringo is born. (1855)
39	Wed	8	7 37	6 29	10 52	7 03 L	4 27 H	○	61°	Record low temperature ties previous record in Seminole of -23 degrees. (1933)
40	Thurs	9	7 36	6 30	10 54	7 54 L	5 10 H	○	62°	Eric Dickerson is born. (1960); Herschel Evans dies. (1939)
41	Fri	10	7 35	6 31	10 56	8 38 L	5 41 H 9 52 L	○	62°	Alamo survivor Madam Condelaria dies. (1899)
42	Sat	11	7 34	6 31	10 57	12 26 H 9 16 L	5 54 H 9 15 L	○	62°	First Texas railroad, the Buffalo Bayou, Brazo & Company Railway, chartered. (1850)
43	Sun	12	7 33	6 32	10 59	1 24 H 9 48 L	5 57 H 9 28 L	○	62°	Record low temperature set in Tulia of -23 degrees. (1899); Tom Landry dies. (2000)
44	Mon	13	7 32	6 33	11 01	2 18 H 10 16 L	6 03 H 10 08 L	○	63°	Texas Ranger M.T. (Lone Wolf) Gonzaullos dies. (1977)
45	Tues	14	7 32	6 34	11 02	3 12 H 10 42 L	6 12 H 10 54 L	○	63°	Valentine's Day
46	Wed	15	7 31	6 35	11 04	4 14 H 11 07 L	6 22 H 11 40 L	○	63°	Citizens of Texas adopt Constitution of 1876. (1876)
47	Thurs	16	7 30	6 36	11 06	5 26 H 11 34 L	6 30 H	○	63°	Arthur Jerome Drossaerts is named first Archbishop of Catholic Diocese of San Antonio. (1927)

Add one hour for Daylight Saving Time, if and when in use.

February 2006

February was named for the Roman god Februus, the god of purification.

February is the second month of the year in the Gregorian calendar and the shortest month. During leap years, years divisible by 4, the month of February has 29 days. In years which are not leap years, the month of February has 28 days. The month of February was added to the Roman calendar around 700 B.C. by Numa Pompilius to make the year consistent with the standard lunar year. Once added to the calendar, February was considered the last month of the year, with March being the first month of the year.

DAY OF YEAR	DAY OF WEEK	DAY OF MONTH	RISE	SET	LENGTH OF DAY (H M)	TIDES AM	TIDES PM	MOON PHASE	NORMAL HIGH TEMP	On this date in February...
48	Fri	17	7 29	6 37	11 08	12 22 L 6 52 H	12 04 L 6 30 H	◗	64°	H.L. Hunt is born. (1889); League of United Latin American Citizens founded. (1929)
49	Sat	18	7 28	6 37	11 09	1 04 L 8 30 H		◖	64°	World War II hero Dolly Shea graduates from flight nurse school. (1943)
50	Sun	19	7 27	6 38	11 11	1 48 L 10 21 H		◖	64°	Texas government formally installed in Austin. (1846)
51	Mon	20	7 26	6 39	11 13	2 37 L	4 24 H	◖	64°	President's Day; Former slave, Walter Moses Burton, wins seat in Texas Senate. (1874)
52	Tues	21	7 25	6 40	11 15	3 34 L	2 07 H	◖	65°	Dalhart becomes county seat of Dallam County. (1902)
53	Wed	22	7 23	6 41	11 18	4 38 L	3 01 H	◖	65°	President John Quincy Adams signs treaty renouncing U.S. claim to Texas. (1819)
54	Thurs	23	7 22	6 41	11 19	5 44 L	3 39 H	◗	65°	Voters in Texas approve secession from Union by popular referendum. (1861)
55	Fri	24	7 21	6 42	11 21	6 48 L	4 08 H 7 43 L 9 59 H	◗	66°	Colonel William Barret Travis sends for additional troops to defend Alamo. (1836); Texas League ends baseball games for duration of World War II. (1943)
56	Sat	25	7 20	6 43	11 23	7 48 L	4 29 H 7 51 L	●	66°	LaSalle and followers become lost searching for Mississippi River after leaving fort in East Texas. (1687)
57	Sun	26	7 19	6 44	11 25	12 16 H 8 44 L	4 47 H 8 35 L	●	66°	Civil Rights activist Herman Sweatt applies for admission to University of Texas Law School. (1946)
58	Mon	27	7 18	6 45	11 27	1 48 H 9 37 L	5 02 H 9 27 L	●	66°	Governor John Connally is born. (1917)
59	Tues	28	7 17	6 45	11 28	3 12 H 10 27 L	5 17 H 10 21 L	●	67°	Dr Pepper becomes a privately owned company. (1984)

● New Moon   ◖ First Quarter   ○ Full Moon   ◗ Last Quarter

Atmospheric and Astronomical data provided by NOAA, National Ocean Service and U.S. Naval Observatory.

DAY OF YEAR	DAY OF WEEK	DAY OF MONTH	☼ RISE	☼ SET	LENGTH OF DAY	TIDES AM	TIDES PM	MOON PHASE	NORMAL HIGH TEMP	On this date in March...
					H M					
60	Wed	1	7 16	6 46	11 30	4 37 H 11 18 L	5 32 H 11 16 L	●	67°	President John Tyler signs resolution annexing Texas. (1845)
61	Thurs	2	7 15	6 47	11 32	6 04 H	12 12 L 5 44 H	◑	67°	Sam Houston is born. (1793); Republic of Texas declares independence from Mexico. (1836)
62	Fri	3	7 13	6 48	11 35	12 12 L 7 36 H	1 13 L 5 52 H	◐	67°	Republic of Texas officially recognized by President Andrew Jackson and Congress. (1837)
63	Sat	4	7 12	6 48	11 36	1 08 L 9 17 H	2 51 L 5 41 H	◐	68°	Batson-Old oilfield in Hardin County reaches peak production with 150,000 barrels. (1904)
64	Sun	5	7 11	6 49	11 38	2 09 L 11 08 H	11 08 H	◐	68°	Samuel Colt manufactures first pistol, a .34-caliber "Texas" model. (1836)
65	Mon	6	7 10	6 50	11 40	3 14 L	1 02 H	◑	68°	The Alamo falls to General Santa Anna. (1836)
66	Tues	7	7 09	6 51	11 42	4 26 L	2 26 H	◑	69°	Texas legislature declares the bluebonnet the state flower. (1901)
67	Wed	8	7 07	6 51	11 44	5 39 L	3 26 H	◑	69°	George Glenn, a black traildriver, is born into slavery. (1850)
68	Thurs	9	7 06	6 52	11 46	6 47 L	4 11 H	◑	69°	The Roman Expedition enters Texas. (1707)
69	Fri	10	7 05	6 53	11 48	7 43 L	4 36 H 9 25 L 11 54 H	◖	69°	Sam Houston retreats from Gonzales to avoid Mexican army. (1836)
70	Sat	11	7 04	6 54	11 50	8 28 L	4 38 H 9 08 L	○	70°	State's first all-black public college, Alta Vista Agricultural College, opens. (1878)
71	Sun	12	7 02	6 54	11 52	1 06 H 9 03 L	4 33 H 9 10 L	○	70°	1,600 dockworkers strike. (1920)
72	Mon	13	7 01	6 55	11 54	2 08 H 9 32 L	4 33 H 9 30 L	○	70°	Forte Inge is established in Uvalde County. (1849)
73	Tues	14	7 00	6 56	11 56	3 07 H 9 57 L	4 37 H 9 59 L	○	70°	27 people killed, 15 injured when a truck of migrant workers collides with a train outside of McAllen. (1940); Jack Ruby convicted of murder of Lee Harvey Oswald. (1964)
74	Wed	15	6 59	6 56	11 57	4 07 H 10 23 L	4 43 H 10 30 L	○	71°	Jazz trumpeter Harry James is born. (1916)
75	Thurs	16	6 57	6 57	12 00	5 09 H 10 52 L	4 47 H 11 01 L	○	71°	Sam Houston is ousted as governor of Texas following his refusal to advocate secession. (1861)

Add one hour for Daylight Saving Time, if and when in use.

March 2006 · *March is named for Mars, the Roman god of war.*

March is the third month of the Gregorian calendar, and one of seven months with 31 days. Until 45 BC when Julius Caesar reformed the Roman calendar, March was considered the first month of the new year. Many countries, including France and England, did not accept January as the beginning of the new year for centuries. France adopted the Gregorian calendar in 1564 and Great Britain, in 1752. Because March is named for the Roman god of war, March was considered a lucky time to begin a war.

DAY OF YEAR	DAY OF WEEK	DAY OF MONTH	RISE	SET	LENGTH OF DAY	TIDES AM	TIDES PM	MOON PHASE	NORMAL HIGH TEMP	On this date in March...
76	Fri	17	6 56	6 58	12 02	6 13 H / 11 25 L	4 44 H / 11 34 L	◔	71°	Slavery abolished in Texas. (1836); First law school in Texas established at Austin College. (1855); Sammy Baugh born. (1914)
77	Sat	18	6 55	6 59	12 04	7 21 H	12 03 L / 4 24 H	◔	71°	Gas explosion in a school in New London kills 294 people. (1937)
78	Sun	19	6 53	6 59	12 06	12 10 L / 8 35 H	12 46 L / 3 45 H	◑	72°	Cherokee leader John Dunn Hunter arrives in Mexico City to negotiate a settlement in Texas. (1826)
79	Mon	20	6 52	7 00	12 08	12 52 L / 10 00 H		◑	72°	Aguayo expedition enters Texas. (1721)
80	Tues	21	6 51	7 01	12 10	1 44 L / 11 43 H		◑	72°	Rebecca Fisher, former Indian captive, dies. (1926)
81	Wed	22	6 50	7 01	12 11	2 47 L	1 49 H	◑	72°	Texas Navy seizes mercantile brig Durango. (1836)
82	Thurs	23	6 48	7 02	12 14	4 02 L	2 41 H	◐	73°	Joan Crawford is born (1908); Fort Worth Stockyards incorporated. (1893)
83	Fri	24	6 47	7 03	12 16	5 19 L	2 55 H	◐	73°	Mexican legislature passes State Colonization Law offering settlers land. (1825)
84	Sat	25	6 46	7 03	12 17	6 31 L	3 06 H / 7 21 L / 11 24 H	●	73°	17 Texans executed in Black Bean Episode. (1843)
85	Sun	26	6 45	7 04	12 19	7 36 L	3 17 H / 7 51 L	●	74°	Battleship Texas takes part in battle of Okinawa in WWII. (1945)
86	Mon	27	6 43	7 05	12 22	1 13 H / 8 35 L	3 29 H / 8 34 L	●	74°	James Fannin and 400 Texans executed at Goliad. (1836)
87	Tues	28	6 42	7 05	12 23	2 42 H / 9 30 L	3 41 H / 9 19 L	●	74°	Texas Confederate troops defeated at Battle of Glorieta Pass in N.M. (1862)
88	Wed	29	6 41	7 06	12 25	4 02 H / 10 25 L	3 53 H / 10 05 L	●	74°	Earl Campbell is born. (1955); Sam Rayburn Reservoir fills with water. (1965)
89	Thurs	30	6 39	7 07	12 28	5 20 H / 11 23 L	4 03 H / 10 51 L	●	75°	Texas is the last Confederate state readmitted to the Union. (1870)
90	Fri	31	6 38	7 07	12 29	6 36 H / 11 38 L	12 28 L / 4 08 H	●	75°	300 cowboys go on strike when open range ranching is closed. (1883)

● New Moon   ◑ First Quarter   ○ Full Moon   ◐ Last Quarter

Atmospheric and Astronomical data provided by NOAA, National Ocean Service and U.S. Naval Observatory.

DAY OF YEAR	DAY OF WEEK	DAY OF MONTH	☀ RISE	☀ SET	LENGTH OF DAY	TIDES AM	TIDES PM	MOON PHASE	NORMAL HIGH TEMP	On this date in April...
91	Sat	1	6 37	7 08	H M 12 31	7 53 H		●	75°	Debbie Reynolds is born. (1932)
92	Sun	2	6 36	7 09	12 33	12 28 L 9 14 H		●	75°	Slave smuggler and forger Monroe Edwards is convicted of forgery. (1840)
93	Mon	3	6 34	7 09	12 35	1 23 L 10 46 H		●	76°	"Bigfoot" Wallace is born. (1817)
94	Tues	4	6 33	7 10	12 37	2 26 L	12 31 H	◐	76°	Sarah Ann Horn is captured by Comanche Indians. (1836)
95	Wed	5	6 32	7 11	12 39	3 41 L	1 58 H	◑	76°	Kelly Field in San Antonio opens. (1917)
96	Thurs	6	6 31	7 12	12 41	5 03 L	2 47 H	◑	76°	Mexico forbids further immigration into Texas by U.S. settlers. (1830)
97	Fri	7	6 29	7 12	12 43	6 18 L	3 06 H	◑	77°	Texas Oil Company (Texaco) is formed. (1902)
98	Sat	8	6 28	7 13	12 45	7 17 L	3 04 H 8 41 L	○	77°	Lady Bird Johnson dedicates Padre Island National Seashore. (1968)
99	Sun	9	6 27	7 14	12 47	12 30 H 8 02 L	3 00 H 8 41 L	◯	77°	Tornadoes strike West Texas and Oklahoma killing 169 people. (1947); Houston Astros play NY Yankees in first game at the Astrodome. (1965)
100	Mon	10	6 26	7 14	12 48	1 45 H 8 39 L	2 59 H 8 50 L	○	77°	Don Meredith is born. (1938)
101	Tues	11	6 24	7 15	12 51	2 51 H 9 12 L	3 01 H 9 08 L	○	78°	Majestic Theatre opens in downtown Dallas. (1921)
102	Wed	12	6 23	7 16	12 53	3 50 H 9 44 L	3 04 H 9 30 L	○	78°	Texas becomes a U.S. territory. (1844)
103	Thurs	13	6 22	7 16	12 54	4 45 H 10 19 L	3 04 H 9 55 L	○	78°	First day of Passover (Jewish)
104	Fri	14	6 21	7 17	12 56	5 38 H 10 59 L	2 56 H 10 24 L	○	78°	Good Friday (Christian); Spanish Governor Coahuila discovers and names Guadalupe River. (1689)
105	Sat	15	6 20	7 18	12 58	6 31 H 11 44 L	2 32 H 10 56 L	○	79°	Mexican government issues empresario contracts encouraging settlement of Texas. (1825)
106	Sun	16	6 18	7 18	13 00	7 27 H	11 34 L	○	79°	Easter Sunday (Christian); Cargo ship explodes in harbor of Texas City killing 522 people. (1947)

Add one hour for Daylight Saving Time, if and when in use.

April 2006 — *April is derived from the Latin word* **aprilis.**

April is derived from the Latin word *aprilis* with its origin either from the Latin word *aperire*, meaning "to open" or the Etruscan name *Apru* for Aphrodite.

April is the fourth month of the Gregorian calendar, and one of four months with 30 days. April was originally the second month of the year in the Roman calendar and consisted of only 29 days. In 45 B.C., Julius Caesar reformed the Roman calendar by adding one day to the month of April and starting the new year in January.

DAY OF YEAR	DAY OF WEEK	DAY OF MONTH	RISE	SET	LENGTH OF DAY	TIDES AM	TIDES PM	MOON PHASE	NORMAL HIGH TEMP	On this date in April...
107	Mon	17	6 17	7 19	13 02	8 31 H		◯	79°	State legislature approves bill organizing Texas Agriculture and Mechanical College. (1871)
108	Tues	18	6 16	7 20	13 04	12 20 L 9 47 H		◔	79°	Juan Seguín resigns as mayor of San Antonio. (1842)
109	Wed	19	6 15	7 20	13 05	1 14 L 11 18 H		◔	80°	Last day of Passover (Jewish); Kiowa Chief White Horse surrenders. (1875)
110	Thurs	20	6 14	7 21	13 07	2 19 L	12 40 H	◑	80°	Society for Protection of German Immigrants is organized. (1842)
111	Fri	21	6 13	7 22	13 09	3 34 L	1 12 H	◑	80°	Texas wins independence from Mexico at the Battle of San Jacinto. (1836); George W. Bush and Edward W. Rose become CEOs of Texas Rangers. (1989)
112	Sat	22	6 12	7 23	13 11	4 54 L	1 27 H 7 20 L 10 23 H	◐	80°	Spanish explorer Alonso De León discovers ruins of French settlement on Texas coast. (1689)
113	Sun	23	6 11	7 23	13 12	6 11 L	1 39 H 7 15 L	◐	81°	Roy Orbison is born. (1936)
114	Mon	24	6 10	7 24	13 14	12 37 H 7 22 L	1 50 H 7 45 L	◐	81°	Magnolia Petroleum Company is founded. (1911)
115	Tues	25	6 08	7 25	13 17	2 12 H 8 29 L	2 01 H 8 23 L	◐	81°	Convention of Limits is signed by United States and Republic of Texas. (1838)
116	Wed	26	6 07	7 25	13 18	3 31 H 9 34 L	2 12 H 9 02 L	◕	82°	U.S. War Department orders land surveys for Indian reservations. (1854)
117	Thurs	27	6 06	7 26	13 20	4 42 H 10 41 L	2 20 H 9 43 L	●	82°	Tornadoes kill seven in Hemming. (1907)
118	Fri	28	6 05	7 27	13 22	5 47 H 11 55 L	2 21 H 10 25 L	●	82°	Southwest Texas Sacred Harp Singing Convention is organized. (1900)
119	Sat	29	6 04	7 27	13 23	6 49 H	11 09 L	●	82°	32 camels arrive in Indianola as part of the Texas Camel Expedition. (1856)
120	Sun	30	6 03	7 28	13 25	7 52 H	11 56 L	●	83°	Willie Nelson is born. (1933)

● New Moon　◐ First Quarter　◯ Full Moon　◑ Last Quarter

Atmospheric and Astronomical data provided by NOAA, National Ocean Service and U.S. Naval Observatory.

The Great State of Texas Almanac　**107**

DAY OF YEAR	DAY OF WEEK	DAY OF MONTH	RISE	SET	LENGTH OF DAY	TIDES AM	TIDES PM	MOON PHASE	NORMAL HIGH TEMP	On this date in May...
121	Mon	1	6 03	7 29	H M 13 26	8 59 H		●	83°	Dallas Mavericks become twenty-third member of the NBA. (1980)
122	Tues	2	6 02	7 30	13 28	12 46 L 10 19 H		●	83°	John Jones is appointed to lead Frontier Battalion of Texas Rangers. (1874)
123	Wed	3	6 01	7 30	13 29	1 43 L 11 50 H		●	84°	Surgeon Dr. Denton Cooley performs first heart transplant in U. S. at Houston's St. Luke's Hospital. (1968)
124	Thurs	4	6 00	7 31	13 31	2 49 L	12 53 H	◑	84°	Pope Pius IX establishes Catholic Diocese of Galveston. (1847)
125	Fri	5	5 59	7 32	13 33	4 03 L	1 13 H	◑	84°	Cinco de Mayo. Mexican troops defeat French forces, ending Spanish rule. (1862)
126	Sat	6	5 58	7 32	13 34	5 19 L	1 16 H 8 06 L 11 27 H	◐	84°	Oldest Missionary Baptist Church in Texas is organized. (1838)
127	Sun	7	5 57	7 33	13 36	6 25 L	1 17 H 7 58 L	◐	85°	Suffrage advocate Anna Pennybacker is born. (1861)
128	Mon	8	5 56	7 34	13 38	1 10 H 7 22 L	1 18 H 8 02 L	◐	85°	First major battle of the Mexican War fought at Palo Alto. (1846); Galveston hurricane kills 6,000 people. (1900)
129	Tues	9	5 56	7 35	13 39	2 26 H 8 14 L	1 20 H 8 13 L	◐	85°	Jefferson Davis captured by Union troops. (1865)
130	Wed	10	5 55	7 35	13 40	3 27 H 9 05 L	1 19 H 8 31 L	○	85°	Joan Crawford dies. (1977)
131	Thurs	11	5 54	7 36	13 42	4 18 H 9 59 L	1 13 H 8 54 L	○	86°	Tornado in Waco kills 114, causes $39 million in damage. (1953)
132	Fri	12	5 53	7 37	13 44	5 04 H	9 22 L	○	86°	The song "Eyes of Texas" is sung for the first time at a minstral show at the University of Texas. (1903)
133	Sat	13	5 52	7 37	13 45	5 48 H	9 54 L	○	86°	Last battle of Civil War fought at Palmito Ranch. (1865); Fiddler Bob Wills dies. (1975)
134	Sun	14	5 52	7 38	13 46	6 35 H	10 32 L	○	86°	Mother's Day; Capital building in Austin dedicated. (1888)
135	Mon	15	5 51	7 39	13 48	7 28 H	11 15 L	○	87°	Tornado kills 78 in Texas. (1896)
136	Tues	16	5 50	7 39	13 49	8 28 H		○	87°	The Capitol building in Austin opens. (1888)

Add one hour for Daylight Saving Time, if and when in use.

May 2006 — *May was most likely named for the Roman goddess of fertility.*

May was most likely named for the Roman goddess of fertility, Bona Dea, whose festival was held at this time of the year. May is the fifth month of the Gregorian calendar, and one of seven months with 31 days contained in it.

No other month begins on the same day as May.
May's flower is the lily of the valley.
May's birthstone is the emerald.
The signs of the zodiac during the month of May are Taurus and Gemini.

DAY OF YEAR	DAY OF WEEK	DAY OF MONTH	RISE	SET	LENGTH OF DAY	TIDES AM	TIDES PM	MOON PHASE	NORMAL HIGH TEMP	On this date in May...
					H M					
137	Wed	17	5 50	7 40	13 50	12 04 L 9 36 H		◗	87°	1,200 prisoners leave Confederate prison, Camp Ford. (1865)
138	Thurs	18	5 49	7 41	13 52	12 59 L 10 39 H		◗	87°	George Strait is born. (1952)
139	Fri	19	5 49	7 42	13 53	2 00 L 11 18 H		◗	88°	Comanche warriors raid Fort Parker, taking five captives including Cynthia Ann Parker. (1836)
140	Sat	20	5 48	7 42	13 54	3 08 L 11 41 H	6 46 L 9 13 H	◑	88°	Amarillo becomes Potter County seat. (1893)
141	Sun	21	5 47	7 43	13 56	4 25 L 11 56 H	6 28 L 11 58 H	◑	88°	Physician Abbe Alzu Ledbetter is born. (1844)
142	Mon	22	5 47	7 44	13 57	5 51 L	12 08 H 6 54 L	◑	88°	Tornadoes kill 30 people in Texas. (1987)
143	Tues	23	5 46	7 44	13 58	1 45 H 7 20 L	12 18 H 7 28 L	◑	89°	Bonnie Parker and Clyde Barrow killed. (1934)
144	Wed	24	5 46	7 45	13 59	3 06 H 8 47 L	12 26 H 8 05 L	●	89°	24 defendants stand trial in Stockade Case. (1869)
145	Thurs	25	5 46	7 45	13 59	4 11 H 10 13 L	12 28 H 8 43 L	●	89°	Texas Division of the United Daughters of the Confederacy meets for the first time. (1896)
146	Fri	26	5 45	7 46	14 01	5 08 H	9 23 L	●	89°	Conflict between union workers and ranchers leads to unionization of farm workers. (1975)
147	Sat	27	5 45	7 47	14 02	6 00 H	10 04 L	●	89°	First printed reference made to Chisolm Trail in **Kansas Daily Commonwealth.** (1870)
148	Sun	28	5 44	7 47	14 03	6 51 H	10 47 L	●	90°	U.S. Border Patrol established. (1924); Tornado in Jarrell kills 28. (1997)
149	Mon	29	5 44	7 48	14 04	7 45 H	11 31 L	●	90°	*Memorial Day*
150	Tues	30	5 44	7 48	14 04	8 43 H		●	90°	El Chico restaurant founder Adelaida Cuellor is born in Mexico. (1871)
151	Wed	31	5 43	7 49	14 06	12 17 L 9 46 H		◐	90°	First wedding in an aircraft flying over Houston. (1919)

● New Moon　◗ First Quarter　○ Full Moon　◑ Last Quarter

Atmospheric and Astronomical data provided by NOAA, National Ocean Service and U.S. Naval Observatory.

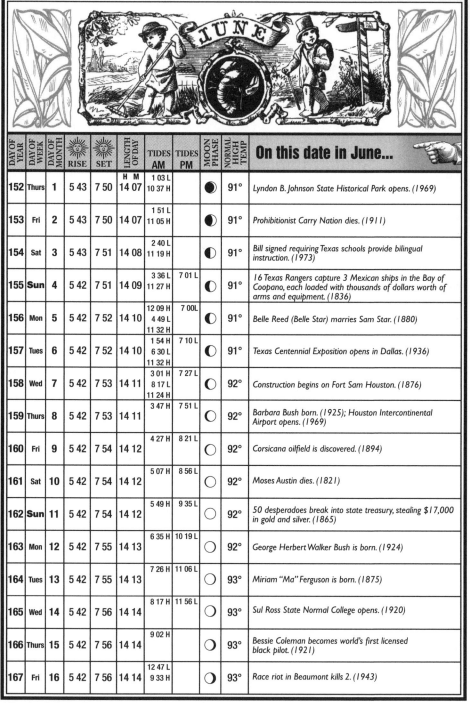

On this date in June...

DAY OF YEAR	DAY OF WEEK	DAY OF MONTH	RISE	SET	LENGTH OF DAY	TIDES AM	TIDES PM	MOON PHASE	NORMAL HIGH TEMP	On this date in June...
152	Thurs	1	5 43	7 50	H M 14 07	1 03 L 10 37 H		◖	91°	Lyndon B. Johnson State Historical Park opens. (1969)
153	Fri	2	5 43	7 50	14 07	1 51 L 11 05 H		◑	91°	Prohibitionist Carry Nation dies. (1911)
154	Sat	3	5 43	7 51	14 08	2 40 L 11 19 H		◑	91°	Bill signed requiring Texas schools provide bilingual instruction. (1973)
155	Sun	4	5 42	7 51	14 09	3 36 L 11 27 H	7 01 L	◑	91°	16 Texas Rangers capture 3 Mexican ships in the Bay of Coopano, each loaded with thousands of dollars worth of arms and equipment. (1836)
156	Mon	5	5 42	7 52	14 10	12 09 H 4 49 L 11 32 H	7 00 L	◑	91°	Belle Reed (Belle Star) marries Sam Star. (1880)
157	Tues	6	5 42	7 52	14 10	1 54 H 6 30 L 11 32 H	7 10 L	◑	91°	Texas Centennial Exposition opens in Dallas. (1936)
158	Wed	7	5 42	7 53	14 11	3 01 H 8 17 L 11 24 H	7 27 L	◑	92°	Construction begins on Fort Sam Houston. (1876)
159	Thurs	8	5 42	7 53	14 11	3 47 H	7 51 L	◑	92°	Barbara Bush born. (1925); Houston Intercontinental Airport opens. (1969)
160	Fri	9	5 42	7 54	14 12	4 27 H	8 21 L	◯	92°	Corsicana oilfield is discovered. (1894)
161	Sat	10	5 42	7 54	14 12	5 07 H	8 56 L	◯	92°	Moses Austin dies. (1821)
162	Sun	11	5 42	7 54	14 12	5 49 H	9 35 L	◯	92°	50 desperadoes break into state treasury, stealing $17,000 in gold and silver. (1865)
163	Mon	12	5 42	7 55	14 13	6 35 H	10 19 L	◯	92°	George Herbert Walker Bush is born. (1924)
164	Tues	13	5 42	7 55	14 13	7 26 H	11 06 L	◯	93°	Miriam "Ma" Ferguson is born. (1875)
165	Wed	14	5 42	7 56	14 14	8 17 H	11 56 L	◯	93°	Sul Ross State Normal College opens. (1920)
166	Thurs	15	5 42	7 56	14 14	9 02 H		◯	93°	Bessie Coleman becomes world's first licensed black pilot. (1921)
167	Fri	16	5 42	7 56	14 14	12 47 L 9 33 H		◯	93°	Race riot in Beaumont kills 2. (1943)

Add one hour for Daylight Saving Time, if and when in use.

June 2006

The month of June derives its name from the Roman goddess Juno, the wife of Jupiter.

June is the sixth month of the Gregorian calendar, and one of four months with 30 days. The summer solstice in the northern hemisphere and the winter solstice in the southern hemisphere occur during the month of June around the 21st.

No other month begins on the same day of the week as June.
June's flower is the rose.
June's birthstone is the pearl.
The signs of the zodiac during the month of June are Gemini and Cancer.

DAY OF YEAR	DAY OF WEEK	DAY OF MONTH	RISE	SET	LENGTH OF DAY	TIDES AM	TIDES PM	MOON PHASE	NORMAL HIGH TEMP	On this date in June...
					H M					
168	Sat	17	5 42	7 57	14 15	1 42 L 9 56 H	4 42 L 8 10 H	◗	93°	Rain begins falling in Brazos River area causing flooding. (1899)
169	Sun	18	5 42	7 57	14 15	2 42 L 10 12 H	5 10 L 11 04 H	◗	93°	Father's Day; Charles Goodnight and John Adair form A J Ranch. (1876)
170	Mon	19	5 42	7 57	14 15	4 00 L 10 24 H	5 47 L	◗	93°	Juneteenth. Union General Gordan Granger declares all slaves free in Texas. (1865)
171	Tues	20	5 43	7 57	14 14	1 13 H 5 56 L 10 33 H	6 26 L	◗	93°	German U-203 fails in its torpedo attack on the U. S. battleship Texas. (1941)
172	Wed	21	5 43	7 58	14 15	2 43 H 8 12 L 10 32 H	7 06 L	◗	93°	10 die in Baker Hotel fire in Dallas. (1946)
173	Thurs	22	5 43	7 58	14 15	3 46 H	7 47 L	◗	94°	Battle of Jones Creek fought between colonists and Karankawa Indians. (1824)
174	Fri	23	5 43	7 58	14 15	4 37 H	8 28 L	●	94°	Provisional Texas government declares independence from Spain. (1819)
175	Sat	24	5 44	7 58	14 14	5 22 H	9 09 L	●	94°	San Juan Bautista Mission is founded. (1699)
176	Sun	25	5 44	7 58	14 14	6 07 H	9 51 L	●	94°	Miriam "Ma" Ferguson dies. (1961)
177	Mon	26	5 44	7 58	14 14	6 51 H	10 31 L	●	94°	Battle of Velasco fought. (1832)
178	Tues	27	5 45	7 58	14 13	7 34 H	11 11 L	●	94°	Hurricane Audrey kills 526 people in Texas and Louisiana. (1957); Ross Perot is born. (1930)
179	Wed	28	5 45	7 58	14 13	8 14 H	11 48 L	●	94°	Texas Jack Omohundro dies. (1880)
180	Thurs	29	5 45	7 58	14 13	8 45 H		●	94°	Rain ends in Brazos River area. Floods kill 284 people and cause $10 million in damage. (1899)
181	Fri	30	5 46	7 58	14 12	12 23 L 9 07 H		◗	94°	Henry Flipper is dismissed from the Army. (1882)

● New Moon   ◗ First Quarter   ○ Full Moon   ◗ Last Quarter

Atmospheric and Astronomical data provided by NOAA, National Ocean Service and U.S. Naval Observatory.

DAY OF YEAR	DAY OF WEEK	DAY OF MONTH	☀ RISE	☀ SET	LENGTH OF DAY	TIDES AM	TIDES PM	MOON PHASE	NORMAL HIGH TEMP	On this date in July...
182	Sat	1	5 46	7 58	H M 14 12	12 55 L 9 23 H		◗	94°	Jake Atz is born. (1879)
183	Sun	2	5 46	7 58	14 12	1 25 L 9 35 H	5 30 L 10 15 H	◗	94°	Hood's Texas Brigade joins battle at Gettysburg. (1863)
184	Mon	3	5 47	7 58	14 11	1 53 L 9 41 H	5 32 L	◖	94°	City-County Hospital opens in Austin. (1884)
185	Tues	4	5 47	7 58	14 11	9 37 H	5 47 L	◖	94°	Independence Day; Texas Congress votes to annex to the United States. (1845)
186	Wed	5	5 48	7 58	14 10	2 50 H 6 55 L 8 43 H	6 10 L	◖	94°	Slats Rodgers, Texas' first licensed pilot dies. (1956)
187	Thurs	6	5 48	7 58	14 10	3 18 H	6 40 L	◖	94°	George W. Bush is born. (1946); Dr Pepper incorporates. (1923)
188	Fri	7	5 49	7 58	14 09	3 50 H	7 15 L	◖	94°	Port of Velasco opens on Brazos River. (1891)
189	Sat	8	5 49	7 58	14 09	4 25 H	7 55 L	○	94°	San Jacinto veteran Alfonso Steele dies. (1911); Phil Gramm born. (1942)
190	Sun	9	5 50	7 57	14 07	5 04 H	8 38 L	○	94°	Construction begins on Bonham Veterans Administration Hospital in Bonham. (1948)
191	Mon	10	5 50	7 57	14 07	5 46 H	9 24 L	○	94°	Ima Hogg is born. (1882); Jessica Simpson is born. (1980)
192	Tues	11	5 51	7 57	14 06	6 27 H 9 55 L	12 34 H 10 12 L	○	94°	Longview Race Riot. (1919)
193	Wed	12	5 51	7 57	14 06	7 04 H 10 29 L	1 51 H 11 00 L	○	94°	Baylor College of Medicine opens in former Sears, Roebuck store in Houston. (1943)
194	Thurs	13	5 52	7 56	14 04	7 33 H 11 29 L	3 12 H 11 48 L	○	94°	Juan Nepomuceno Cortina shoots Brownsville city marshall Robert Shears. (1859)
195	Fri	14	5 52	7 56	14 04	7 56 H	12 47 L 5 01 H	○	94°	Howard Hughes circles globe. (1938); First Cowboys training camp opens in Oregon. (1960)
196	Sat	15	5 53	7 55	14 02	12 36 L 8 15 H	2 07 L 7 19 H	◗	94°	Texas Bar Association is organized. (1882)
197	Sun	16	5 54	7 55	14 01	1 27 L 8 29 H	3 15 L 9 47 H	◗	94°	Cherokee War begins. (1839)

Add one hour for Daylight Saving Time, if and when in use.

July 2006 — July is named for the Roman Emperor Julius Caesar.

July is the seventh month of the Gregorian calendar, and one of seven months with 31 days. The month of July was originally *Quintilis* in Latin because it was the fifth month of the year in the Roman calendar. The name of the month was changed to July honoring the birth month of Julius Caesar. Because it was named for Julius Caesar, the month's name was pronounced "Julie" until the 18th century. July begins on the same day of the month as April during non-leap years and January during leap years.

DAY OF YEAR	DAY OF WEEK	DAY OF MONTH	RISE	SET	LENGTH OF DAY	TIDES AM	TIDES PM	MOON PHASE	NORMAL HIGH TEMP	On this date in July...
					H M					
198	Mon	17	5 54	7 55	14 01	2 26 L / 8 41 H	4 14 L	◑	94°	Clara Driscoll dies. (1945)
199	Tues	18	5 55	7 54	13 59	12 14 H / 4 13 L / 8 44 H	5 07 L	◑	95°	Thirty-sixth Infantry Division at Camp Bowie mobilized for WWI. (1917)
200	Wed	19	5 55	7 54	13 59	2 08 H	5 58 L	◑	95°	Sam Bass wounded during bank robbery in Round Rock. (1878)
201	Thurs	20	5 56	7 53	13 57	3 14 H	6 46 L	◐	95°	Jack Johnson recognized as heavyweight champion of the world. (1910)
202	Fri	21	5 57	7 53	13 56	4 04 H	7 34 L	◐	95°	Sam Bass is born. (1851); Sam Bass dies on 27th birthday from wound received in robbery. (1878)
203	Sat	22	5 57	7 52	13 55	4 49 H	8 20 L	◐	95°	Confederate General Barnard Bee, Jr. dies at Bull Run. (1861)
204	Sun	23	5 58	7 52	13 54	5 30 H	9 02 L	◐	95°	Actress Florence Arto is born. (1895)
205	Mon	24	5 59	7 51	13 52	6 07 H	9 42 L	◐	95°	Town of Kyle is founded. (1880)
206	Tues	25	5 59	7 50	13 51	6 35 H / 10 54 L	1 00 H / 10 17 L	●	95°	Buffalo soldiers from the 10th U.S. Cavalry and the 25th U.S. Infantry skirmish near Sulphur Springs. (1879)
207	Wed	26	6 00	7 50	13 50	6 55 H / 10 54 L	1 57 H / 10 49 L	●	95°	United States flag flies for first time over Texas at St. Joseph Island. (1845)
208	Thurs	27	6 00	7 49	13 49	7 09 H / 11 38 L	2 53 H / 11 17 L	●	94°	Randall County organized. (1888)
209	Fri	28	6 01	7 48	13 47	7 23 H / 11 44 L	12 40 L / 4 09 H	●	94°	"March for Justice" erupts into riot in Dallas. (1973)
210	Sat	29	6 02	7 48	13 46	7 35 H	1 41 L / 5 59 H	●	94°	President Dwight Eisenhower signs National Aeronautics & Space Act creating NASA. (1958)
211	Sun	30	6 02	7 47	13 45	12 09 L / 7 45 H	2 29 L / 8 12 H	●	94°	Elements of the 10th U.S. Cavalry (Buffalo Soldiers) and a band of Lipan Apache Indians clash across the Rio Grande in Mexico. (1876)
212	Mon	31	6 03	7 46	13 43	12 33 L / 7 48 H	3 09 L / 10 37 H	◑	94°	Frontier merchant Charles Rath dies. (1902)

● New Moon   ◑ First Quarter   ○ Full Moon   ◐ Last Quarter

Atmospheric and Astronomical data provided by NOAA, National Ocean Service and U.S. Naval Observatory.

The Great State of Texas Almanac 113

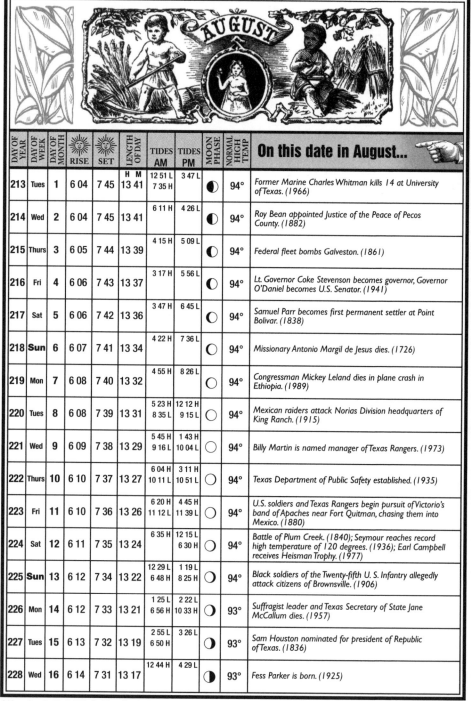

DAY OF YEAR	DAY OF WEEK	DAY OF MONTH	RISE	SET	LENGTH OF DAY	TIDES AM	TIDES PM	MOON PHASE	NORMAL HIGH TEMP	On this date in August...
213	Tues	1	6 04	7 45	H M 13 41	12 51 L 7 35 H	3 47 L	◗	94°	Former Marine Charles Whitman kills 14 at University of Texas. (1966)
214	Wed	2	6 04	7 45	13 41	6 11 H	4 26 L	◗	94°	Roy Bean appointed Justice of the Peace of Pecos County. (1882)
215	Thurs	3	6 05	7 44	13 39	4 15 H	5 09 L	◖	94°	Federal fleet bombs Galveston. (1861)
216	Fri	4	6 06	7 43	13 37	3 17 H	5 56 L	◖	94°	Lt. Governor Coke Stevenson becomes governor, Governor O'Daniel becomes U.S. Senator. (1941)
217	Sat	5	6 06	7 42	13 36	3 47 H	6 45 L	◯	94°	Samuel Parr becomes first permanent settler at Point Bolivar. (1838)
218	Sun	6	6 07	7 41	13 34	4 22 H	7 36 L	◯	94°	Missionary Antonio Margil de Jesus dies. (1726)
219	Mon	7	6 08	7 40	13 32	4 55 H	8 26 L	◯	94°	Congressman Mickey Leland dies in plane crash in Ethiopia. (1989)
220	Tues	8	6 08	7 39	13 31	5 23 H 8 35 L	12 12 H 9 15 L	◯	94°	Mexican raiders attack Norias Division headquarters of King Ranch. (1915)
221	Wed	9	6 09	7 38	13 29	5 45 H 9 16 L	1 43 H 10 04 L	◯	94°	Billy Martin is named manager of Texas Rangers. (1973)
222	Thurs	10	6 10	7 37	13 27	6 04 H 10 11 L	3 11 H 10 51 L	◯	94°	Texas Department of Public Safety established. (1935)
223	Fri	11	6 10	7 36	13 26	6 20 H 11 12 L	4 45 H 11 39 L	◯	94°	U.S. soldiers and Texas Rangers begin pursuit of Victorio's band of Apaches near Fort Quitman, chasing them into Mexico. (1880)
224	Sat	12	6 11	7 35	13 24	6 35 H	12 15 L 6 30 H	◯	94°	Battle of Plum Creek. (1840); Seymour reaches record high temperature of 120 degrees. (1936); Earl Campbell receives Heisman Trophy. (1977)
225	Sun	13	6 12	7 34	13 22	12 29 L 6 48 H	1 19 L 8 25 H	◯	94°	Black soldiers of the Twenty-fifth U. S. Infantry allegedly attack citizens of Brownsville. (1906)
226	Mon	14	6 12	7 33	13 21	1 25 L 6 56 H	2 22 L 10 33 H	◯	93°	Suffragist leader and Texas Secretary of State Jane McCallum dies. (1957)
227	Tues	15	6 13	7 32	13 19	2 55 L 6 50 H	3 26 L	◐	93°	Sam Houston nominated for president of Republic of Texas. (1836)
228	Wed	16	6 14	7 31	13 17	12 44 H	4 29 L	◗	93°	Fess Parker is born. (1925)

Add one hour for Daylight Saving Time, if and when in use.

August 2006
August is named for the Roman Emperor Augustus Caesar.

August is the eighth month of the year on the Gregorian calendar, and one of seven months with 31 days. The month of August was originally *Sextilis* in Latin because it was the sixth month of the Roman calendar. Renamed to honor Roman Emperor Augustus Caesar, August was placed where it is because it was the month of Cleopatra's death. Reputedly, August has 31 days because Augustus did not want it to have fewer days than Julius Caesar's July.
August's birthstone is the peridot.

DAY OF YEAR	DAY OF WEEK	DAY OF MONTH	RISE	SET	LENGTH OF DAY	TIDES AM	TIDES PM	MOON PHASE	NORMAL HIGH TEMP	On this date in August...
					H M					
229	Thurs	17	6 14	7 30	13 16	2 14 H	5 32 L	◑	93°	Davy Crockett is born. (1786)
230	Fri	18	6 15	7 29	13 14	3 13 H	6 32 L	◑	93°	Hurricane Alicia kills 17. (1983)
231	Sat	19	6 16	7 28	13 12	4 03 H	7 27 L	◑	93°	John Wesley Hardin dies in gunfight. (1895)
232	Sun	20	6 16	7 27	13 11	4 44 H	8 16 L	◑	93°	President Andrew Johnson officially ends Civil War issuing a proclamation of peace between U.S. and Texas. (1866)
233	Mon	21	6 17	7 26	13 09	5 15 H	8 57 L	◑	92°	Antisuffragist Pauline Wells dies. (1928)
234	Tues	22	6 17	7 25	13 08	5 29 H / 9 56 L	1 09 H / 9 30 L	◕	92°	Texas A&M University College of Medicine opens. (1977)
235	Wed	23	6 18	7 23	13 05	5 33 H / 9 58 L	2 10 H / 9 58 L	●	92°	12 killed in Houston race riot. (1917)
236	Thurs	24	6 19	7 22	13 03	5 37 H / 10 24 L	3 11 H / 10 23 L	●	92°	Town of Ben Ficklin is washed away by flooding. (1882)
237	Fri	25	6 19	7 21	13 02	5 44 H / 11 00 L	4 18 H / 10 47 L	●	92°	President Jackson offers to buy Texas from Mexico, the offer is rejected. (1829); Galveston hurricane kills 275 people, causes $50 million in damage. (1915)
238	Sat	26	6 20	7 20	13 00	5 52 H / 11 38 L	5 33 H / 11 12 L	●	91°	Alamo survivor and slave of William Travis, Joe, escapes to freedom. (1837)
239	Sun	27	6 21	7 19	12 58	5 58 H	12 16 L / 6 58 H / 11 40 L	●	91°	Stevie Ray Vaughn dies in helicopter crash. (1990)
240	Mon	28	6 21	7 17	12 56	5 58 H	12 54 L / 8 33 H	◐	91°	Sara Ann Horn, who later loses her husband and sons to Comanche Indians in Texas, moves to New York City. (1833)
241	Tues	29	6 22	7 16	12 54	12 09 L / 5 39 H	1 35 L	◐	91°	Alton Stricklin is born. (1908)
242	Wed	30	6 23	7 15	12 52	12 37 L / 4 47 H	2 21 L	◐	90°	Mob prevents enrollment of black students at Mansfield High School. (1956)
243	Thurs	31	6 23	7 14	12 51	4 04 H	3 15 L	◑	90°	James "Gentleman Jim" Ferguson born. (1871)

● New Moon   ◐ First Quarter   ○ Full Moon   ◑ Last Quarter

Atmospheric and Astronomical data provided by NOAA, National Ocean Service and U.S. Naval Observatory.

The Great State of Texas Almanac   115

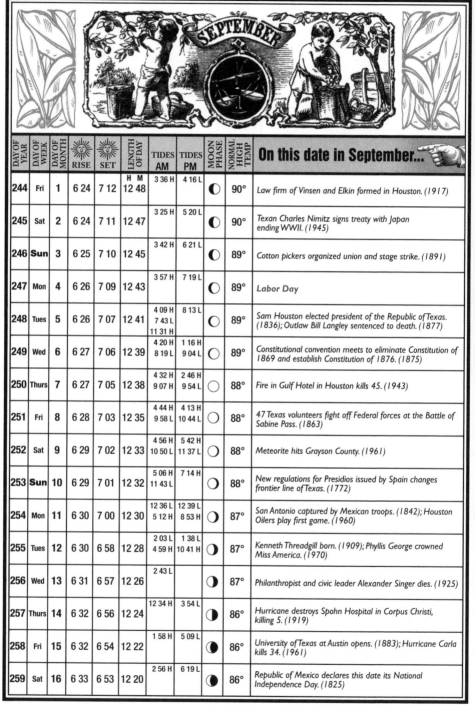

DAY OF YEAR	DAY OF WEEK	DAY OF MONTH	☼ RISE	☼ SET	LENGTH OF DAY	TIDES AM	TIDES PM	MOON PHASE	NORMAL HIGH TEMP	On this date in September...
244	Fri	1	6 24	7 12	H M 12 48	3 36 H	4 16 L	◖	90°	Law firm of Vinsen and Elkin formed in Houston. (1917)
245	Sat	2	6 24	7 11	12 47	3 25 H	5 20 L	◖	90°	Texan Charles Nimitz signs treaty with Japan ending WWII. (1945)
246	Sun	3	6 25	7 10	12 45	3 42 H	6 21 L	◖	89°	Cotton pickers organized union and stage strike. (1891)
247	Mon	4	6 26	7 09	12 43	3 57 H	7 19 L	◖	89°	Labor Day
248	Tues	5	6 26	7 07	12 41	4 09 H 7 43 L 11 31 H	8 13 L	◖	89°	Sam Houston elected president of the Republic of Texas. (1836); Outlaw Bill Langley sentenced to death. (1877)
249	Wed	6	6 27	7 06	12 39	4 20 H 8 19 L	1 16 H 9 04 L	◖	89°	Constitutional convention meets to eliminate Constitution of 1869 and establish Constitution of 1876. (1875)
250	Thurs	7	6 27	7 05	12 38	4 32 H 9 07 H	2 46 H 9 54 L	○	88°	Fire in Gulf Hotel in Houston kills 45. (1943)
251	Fri	8	6 28	7 03	12 35	4 44 H 9 58 L	4 13 H 10 44 L	○	88°	47 Texas volunteers fight off Federal forces at the Battle of Sabine Pass. (1863)
252	Sat	9	6 29	7 02	12 33	4 56 H 10 50 L	5 42 H 11 37 L	○	88°	Meteorite hits Grayson County. (1961)
253	Sun	10	6 29	7 01	12 32	5 06 H 11 43 L	7 14 H	○	88°	New regulations for Presidios issued by Spain changes frontier line of Texas. (1772)
254	Mon	11	6 30	7 00	12 30	12 36 L 5 12 H	12 39 L 8 53 H	○	87°	San Antonio captured by Mexican troops. (1842); Houston Oilers play first game. (1960)
255	Tues	12	6 30	6 58	12 28	2 03 L 4 59 H	1 38 L 10 41 H	◑	87°	Kenneth Threadgill born. (1909); Phyllis George crowned Miss America. (1970)
256	Wed	13	6 31	6 57	12 26	2 43 L		◑	87°	Philanthropist and civic leader Alexander Singer dies. (1925)
257	Thurs	14	6 32	6 56	12 24	12 34 H	3 54 L	◑	86°	Hurricane destroys Spohn Hospital in Corpus Christi, killing 5. (1919)
258	Fri	15	6 32	6 54	12 22	1 58 H	5 09 L	◑	86°	University of Texas at Austin opens. (1883); Hurricane Carla kills 34. (1961)
259	Sat	16	6 33	6 53	12 20	2 56 H	6 19 L	◑	86°	Republic of Mexico declares this date its National Independence Day. (1825)

Add one hour for Daylight Saving Time, if and when in use.

September 2006

The name September is derived from the Latin word septem, for "seven."

The name September is derived from the Latin word *septem,* for "seven" because September was the seventh month of the year in the Roman calendar.
September is the ninth month of the year in the Gregorian calendar, and one of four months with 30 days. The autumnal equinox in the northern hemisphere and the spring equinox in the southern hemisphere occur around the 21st of this month.
September's flower is the morning glory.
September's birthstone is the sapphire.

DAY OF YEAR	DAY OF WEEK	DAY OF MONTH	RISE	SET	LENGTH OF DAY	TIDES AM	TIDES PM	MOON PHASE	NORMAL HIGH TEMP	On this date in September...
					H M					
260	Sun	17	6 34	6 52	12 18	3 38 H	7 18 L	◐	86°	Lake Hawkins and Lake Winnsboro dams completed. (1962)
261	Mon	18	6 34	6 50	12 16	4 02 H 9 26 L 11 35 H	8 05 L	◑	85°	Lance Armstrong is born. (1971)
262	Tues	19	6 35	6 49	12 14	4 08 H 9 19 L	12 54 H 8 42 L	◑	85°	Texas units fight at Battle of Chickamauga. (1863)
263	Wed	20	6 35	6 48	12 13	4 06 H 9 22 L	2 00 H 9 11 L	◑	85°	Hurricane Beulah kills 38 people. (1967)
264	Thurs	21	6 36	6 46	12 10	4 06 H 9 36 L	3 03 H 9 36 L	◑	85°	American League approves move of Washington Senators to Arlington becoming the Texas Rangers. (1971); Dr Pepper truck hits school bus killing 21 children. (1989)
265	Fri	22	6 37	6 45	12 08	4 09 H 9 58 L	4 05 H 10 00 L	●	84°	Southern Methodist University holds first class. (1915)
266	Sat	23	6 37	6 44	12 07	4 13 H 10 23 L	5 07 H 10 26 L	●	84°	Rosh Hashana (Jewish)
267	Sun	24	6 38	6 42	12 04	4 16 H 10 52 L	6 10 H 10 57 L	●	84°	After release from a Mexican prison, members of the Mier Expedition begin journey home to Texas. (1844)
268	Mon	25	6 38	6 41	12 03	4 13 H 11 23 L	7 16 H 11 31 L	●	84°	Oliver Loving dies. (1867)
269	Tues	26	6 39	6 40	12 01	3 55 H 11 57 L	8 29 H	◐	83°	Western writer Andy Adams dies. (1935)
270	Wed	27	6 40	6 38	11 58	12 07 H 3 22 H 12 00 L	9 56 H	◐	83°	Mildred "Babe" Zaharias dies. (1956)
271	Thurs	28	6 40	6 37	11 57	12 39 H 3 02 H	1 25 L	◑	83°	WBAP-TV–Fort Worth begins broadcasting. (1948)
272	Fri	29	6 41	6 36	11 55	3 02 H	2 25 L	◑	83°	"Bum" Phillips is born. (1923)
273	Sat	30	6 42	6 35	11 53	3 17 H	3 34 L	◑	82°	Guadalupe Mountains National Park established. (1972)

● New Moon   ◑ First Quarter   ○ Full Moon   ◐ Last Quarter

Atmospheric and Astronomical data provided by NOAA, National Ocean Service and U.S. Naval Observatory.

The Great State of Texas Almanac **117**

DAY OF YEAR	DAY OF WEEK	DAY OF MONTH	RISE	SET	LENGTH OF DAY	TIDES AM	TIDES PM	MOON PHASE	NORMAL HIGH TEMP	On this date in October...
274	Sun	1	6 42	6 33	H M 11 51	3 09 H	4 48 L	◖	82°	General Land Office opens in Houston. (1837)
275	Mon	2	6 43	6 32	11 49	2 44 H	5 57 L	◖	82°	Yom Kippur (Jewish); Battle of Gonzales fought. (1835)
276	Tues	3	6 44	6 31	11 47	2 44 H 7 41 L 10 28 H	7 01 L	◖	82°	Stevie Ray Vaughan is born. (1954); The Daisy Bradford No. 3 strikes oil. (1930)
277	Wed	4	6 44	6 29	11 45	2 50 H 7 38 L	12 41 H 7 59 L	◯	81°	Agricultural and Mechanical College of Texas (Texas A&M) opens. (1876)
278	Thurs	5	6 45	6 28	11 43	2 58 H 8 13 L	2 15 H 8 54 L	◯	81°	Federal fleet occupies Galveston. (1863); Janis Joplin dies. (1970)
279	Fri	6	6 46	6 27	11 41	3 08 H 8 55 L	3 39 H 9 49 L	◯	81°	Reuben Ross wounds Ben McCullough in duel after years of feuding. (1839)
280	Sat	7	6 46	6 26	11 40	3 18 H 9 39 L	4 57 H 10 46 L	◯	80°	Alamo survivor Susanna Wilkerson Dickinson dies. (1883)
281	Sun	8	6 47	6 24	11 37	3 27 H 10 25 L	6 14 H 11 49 L	◯	80°	Witte Memorial Museum opens in San Antonio. (1926)
282	Mon	9	6 48	6 23	11 35	3 32 H 11 14 L	7 32 H	◯	80°	Columbus Day
283	Tues	10	6 48	6 22	11 34	1 13 L 3 17 H	12 05 L 8 55 H	◯	80°	First issue of **Telegraph and Texas Register** published in Houston. (1835)
284	Wed	11	6 49	6 21	11 32		1 01 L 10 29 H	◑	79°	Kiowa Chief Satanta commits suicide by jumping from prison window. (1878)
285	Thurs	12	6 50	6 20	11 30		2 05 L	◑	79°	Hurricane and tidal surges kill 250 in Indianola. (1886)
286	Fri	13	6 50	6 18	11 28	12 15 H	3 19 L	◑	79°	Last Day of Sukkot (Jewish)
287	Sat	14	6 51	6 17	11 26	1 34 H	4 40 L	◑	78°	Dwight Eisenhower is born. (1890)
288	Sun	15	6 52	6 16	11 24	2 17 H	5 54 L	◐	78°	First Sangerfest, or singer's festival, held in New Braunfels. (1853)
289	Mon	16	6 53	6 15	11 22	2 36 H	6 54 L	◑	78°	Texas School Board prohibits teaching of evolution. (1925)

Add one hour for Daylight Saving Time, if and when in use.

October 2006 — *October is derived from the Latin word* **octo**, *meaning "eight."*

The name October is derived from the Latin word *octo*, meaning "eight," because October was the eighth month of the year in the Roman calendar. October begins on the same day of the week as January in non-leap years.

October's flower is the marigold.
October's birthstone is the opal.
The signs of the zodiac during the month of October are Libra and Scorpio.

DAY OF YEAR	DAY OF WEEK	DAY OF MONTH	RISE	SET	LENGTH OF DAY	TIDES AM	TIDES PM	MOON PHASE	NORMAL HIGH TEMP	On this date in October...
290	Tues	17	6 53	6 14	11 21	2 39 H / 8 39 L	12 20 L / 7 41 L	●	77°	Texas President Lamar arrives in new capital city of Austin. (1839)
291	Wed	18	6 54	6 13	11 19	2 36 H / 8 42 L	1 39 H / 8 19 L	●	77°	Author Charles Siringo dies. (1928)
292	Thurs	19	6 55	6 11	11 16	2 35 H / 8 51 L	2 46 H / 8 50 L	●	77°	League of Women Voters organized in San Antonio. (1919)
293	Fri	20	6 56	6 10	11 14	2 36 H / 9 05 L	3 46 H / 9 20 L	●	76°	Aaron Burr found not guilty of treason. (1807)
294	Sat	21	6 56	6 09	11 13	2 38 H / 9 24 L	3 46 H / 9 20 L	●	76°	Texas' first bank, the Texas National Bank, established. (1822)
295	Sun	22	6 57	6 08	11 11	2 38 H / 9 47 L	5 32 H / 10 24 L	●	75°	Sam Houston inaugurated as first elected president of the Republic of Texas. (1836)
296	Mon	23	6 58	6 07	11 09	2 33 H / 10 14 L	6 23 H / 10 59 L	◑	75°	Abilene becomes county seat of Taylor County. (1883)
297	Tues	24	6 59	6 06	11 07	2 17 H / 10 44 L	7 17 H / 11 33 L	●	75°	Cowboys defeat Patriots 44-21 at the first game in Texas Stadium. (1971)
298	Wed	25	6 59	6 05	11 06	1 59 H / 11 20 L	8 21 H	●	74°	Texas State Fair opens in Dallas. (1886)
299	Thurs	26	7 00	6 04	11 04		12 03 L / 9 42 H	●	74°	SMU defeats Indiana in the first football game held at the Cotton Bowl. (1930)
300	Fri	27	7 01	6 03	11 02	12 12 L / 2 13 H	12 53 L	●	73°	Pan American Railway chartered to connect Texas and Brazil. The railway was never completed. (1891)
301	Sat	28	7 02	6 02	11 00	2 36 H	1 53 L	●	73°	Jim Bowie, James Fannin, and 90 Texans defeat 450 Mexicans at Battle of Concepcion. (1835)
302	Sun	29	7 03	6 01	10 58	2 35 H	3 01 L	◐	73°	Petition for a reservation for Alabama Indians presented to legislature. (1853)
303	Mon	30	7 03	6 00	10 57	1 09 H	4 15 L	○	72°	Furr Food Store founder, Crone Webster Furr, dies. (1946)
304	Tues	31	7 04	5 59	10 55	1 10 H	5 30 L	◐	72°	Halloween

● New Moon   ◐ First Quarter   ○ Full Moon   ◑ Last Quarter

Atmospheric and Astronomical data provided by NOAA, National Ocean Service and U.S. Naval Observatory.

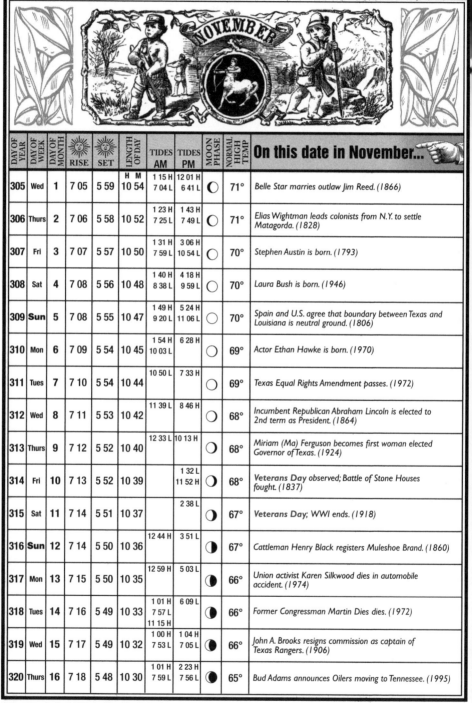

DAY OF YEAR	DAY OF WEEK	DAY OF MONTH	☀ RISE	☀ SET	LENGTH OF DAY	TIDES AM	TIDES PM	MOON PHASE	NORMAL HIGH TEMP	On this date in November...
305	Wed	1	7 05	5 59	H M 10 54	1 15 H 7 04 L	12 01 H 6 41 L	◐	71°	Belle Star marries outlaw Jim Reed. (1866)
306	Thurs	2	7 06	5 58	10 52	1 23 H 7 25 L	1 43 H 7 49 L	○	71°	Elias Wightman leads colonists from N.Y. to settle Matagorda. (1828)
307	Fri	3	7 07	5 57	10 50	1 31 H 7 59 L	3 06 H 10 54 L	○	70°	Stephen Austin is born. (1793)
308	Sat	4	7 08	5 56	10 48	1 40 H 8 38 L	4 18 H 9 59 L	○	70°	Laura Bush is born. (1946)
309	Sun	5	7 08	5 55	10 47	1 49 H 9 20 L	5 24 H 11 06 L	○	70°	Spain and U.S. agree that boundary between Texas and Louisiana is neutral ground. (1806)
310	Mon	6	7 09	5 54	10 45	1 54 H 10 03 L	6 28 H	○	69°	Actor Ethan Hawke is born. (1970)
311	Tues	7	7 10	5 54	10 44	10 50 L	7 33 H	○	69°	Texas Equal Rights Amendment passes. (1972)
312	Wed	8	7 11	5 53	10 42	11 39 L	8 46 H	○	68°	Incumbent Republican Abraham Lincoln is elected to 2nd term as President. (1864)
313	Thurs	9	7 12	5 52	10 40	12 33 L	10 13 H	◑	68°	Miriam (Ma) Ferguson becomes first woman elected Governor of Texas. (1924)
314	Fri	10	7 13	5 52	10 39		1 32 L 11 52 H	◑	68°	Veterans Day observed; Battle of Stone Houses fought. (1837)
315	Sat	11	7 14	5 51	10 37		2 38 L	◑	67°	Veterans Day; WWI ends. (1918)
316	Sun	12	7 14	5 50	10 36	12 44 H	3 51 L	◑	67°	Cattleman Henry Black registers Muleshoe Brand. (1860)
317	Mon	13	7 15	5 50	10 35	12 59 H	5 03 L	◑	66°	Union activist Karen Silkwood dies in automobile accident. (1974)
318	Tues	14	7 16	5 49	10 33	1 01 H 7 57 L 11 15 H	6 09 L	◐	66°	Former Congressman Martin Dies dies. (1972)
319	Wed	15	7 17	5 49	10 32	1 00 H 7 53 L	1 04 H 7 05 L	◐	66°	John A. Brooks resigns commission as captain of Texas Rangers. (1906)
320	Thurs	16	7 18	5 48	10 30	1 01 H 7 59 L	2 23 H 7 56 L	●	65°	Bud Adams announces Oilers moving to Tennessee. (1995)

Add one hour for Daylight Saving Time, if and when in use.

November 2006 — *November comes from the Latin word* novem, *for "nine."*

The name November comes from the Latin word *novem,* for "nine." November in the Roman calendar was the ninth month of the year. November begins on the same day of the week as March in non-leap years and February in leap years.

November's flower is the chrysanthemum. November's birthstone is the topaz. The signs of the zodiac during the month of November are Scorpio and Sagittarius.

DAY OF YEAR	DAY OF WEEK	DAY OF MONTH	RISE	SET	LENGTH OF DAY H M	TIDES AM	TIDES PM	MOON PHASE	NORMAL HIGH TEMP	On this date in November...
321	Fri	17	7 19	5 48	10 29	1 02 H 8 11 L	3 24 H 8 43 L	◐	65°	Delta Drilling Company founded in Longview. (1931)
322	Sat	18	7 20	5 47	10 27	1 02 H 8 27 L	4 13 H 9 28 L	◐	65°	Cavalry launches Canadian River Expedition against Indians in the Panhandle. (1868)
323	Sun	19	7 21	5 47	10 26	1 00 H 8 48 L	4 56 H 10 09 L	◐	64°	First group of Mormon settlers arrive in Texas near Fredericksburg. (1845)
324	Mon	20	7 22	5 46	10 24	12 51 H 9 14 L	5 38 H	●	64°	Black soldiers of Troop D of Ninth U. S. Cavalry allegedly fire on civilians at Rio Grande City. (1899)
325	Tues	21	7 22	5 46	10 24	9 45 L	6 23 H	◑	64°	Town of Thin Gravy changes name to Truman. (1945)
326	Wed	22	7 23	5 46	10 23	10 20 L	7 15 H	●	63°	President John F. Kennedy assassinated in Dallas. (1963)
327	Thurs	23	7 24	5 45	10 21	11 00 L	8 17 H 11 15 L	●	63°	Thanksgiving Day; Dr. Michael DeBakey performs first successful bypass surgery in Houston. (1964)
328	Fri	24	7 25	5 45	10 20	1 34 H 11 45 L	9 31 H 11 31 L	●	63°	Texas Rangers recognized by Texas State Government. (1835); Scott Joplin born. (1868)
329	Sat	25	7 26	5 45	10 19	2 05 H	12 35 L	●	63°	Texas Navy established. (1835); Barbara and Jenna Bush born. (1981)
330	Sun	26	7 27	5 45	10 18	2 22 H	1 30 L 11 09 H	◑	62°	H.L. Hunt acquires the Daisy Bradford oil well from "Dad" Joiner. (1930)
331	Mon	27	7 28	5 44	10 16		2 31 L 11 23 H	◑	62°	Former Texas Ranger Frank Hamer completes his first month as city marshal of Navasota. (1908)
332	Tues	28	7 29	5 44	10 15		3 41 L 11 33 H	◑	62°	Texas Confederate Home for Veterans chartered. (1884)
333	Wed	29	7 29	5 44	10 15	6 11 L 11 12 H	5 03 L 11 42 H	◑	62°	Jesse Hord, founder of Methodism in Texas, enters state. (1838)
334	Thurs	30	7 30	5 44	10 14	6 29 L	1 11 H 6 34 L 11 51 H	◑	62°	Confederate troops vacate Fort Esperanza. (1863)

● New Moon   ◑ First Quarter   ○ Full Moon   ◐ Last Quarter

Atmospheric and Astronomical data provided by NOAA, National Ocean Service and U.S. Naval Observatory.

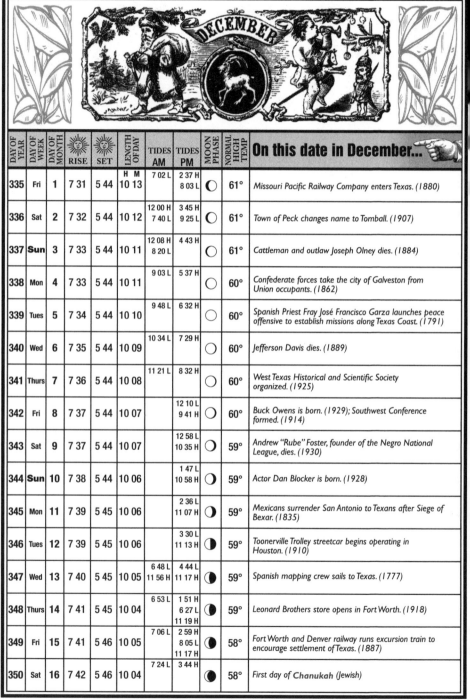

On this date in December...

DAY OF YEAR	DAY OF WEEK	DAY OF MONTH	RISE	SET	LENGTH OF DAY	TIDES AM	TIDES PM	MOON PHASE	NORMAL HIGH TEMP	On this date in December...
335	Fri	1	7 31	5 44	H M 10 13	7 02 L	2 37 H 8 03 L	◖	61°	Missouri Pacific Railway Company enters Texas. (1880)
336	Sat	2	7 32	5 44	10 12	12 00 H 7 40 L	3 45 H 9 25 L	○	61°	Town of Peck changes name to Tomball. (1907)
337	Sun	3	7 33	5 44	10 11	12 08 H 8 20 L	4 43 H	○	61°	Cattleman and outlaw Joseph Olney dies. (1884)
338	Mon	4	7 33	5 44	10 11	9 03 L	5 37 H	○	60°	Confederate forces take the city of Galveston from Union occupants. (1862)
339	Tues	5	7 34	5 44	10 10	9 48 L	6 32 H	○	60°	Spanish Priest Fray José Francisco Garza launches peace offensive to establish missions along Texas Coast. (1791)
340	Wed	6	7 35	5 44	10 09	10 34 L	7 29 H	○	60°	Jefferson Davis dies. (1889)
341	Thurs	7	7 36	5 44	10 08	11 21 L	8 32 H	○	60°	West Texas Historical and Scientific Society organized. (1925)
342	Fri	8	7 37	5 44	10 07		12 10 L 9 41 H	○	60°	Buck Owens is born. (1929); Southwest Conference formed. (1914)
343	Sat	9	7 37	5 44	10 07		12 58 L 10 35 H	◗	59°	Andrew "Rube" Foster, founder of the Negro National League, dies. (1930)
344	Sun	10	7 38	5 44	10 06		1 47 L 10 58 H	◗	59°	Actor Dan Blocker is born. (1928)
345	Mon	11	7 39	5 45	10 06		2 36 L 11 07 H	◗	59°	Mexicans surrender San Antonio to Texans after Siege of Bexar. (1835)
346	Tues	12	7 39	5 45	10 06		3 30 L 11 13 H	◗	59°	Toonerville Trolley streetcar begins operating in Houston. (1910)
347	Wed	13	7 40	5 45	10 05	6 48 L 11 56 H	4 44 L 11 17 H	◗	59°	Spanish mapping crew sails to Texas. (1777)
348	Thurs	14	7 41	5 45	10 04	6 53 L	1 51 H 6 27 L 11 19 H	◗	59°	Leonard Brothers store opens in Fort Worth. (1918)
349	Fri	15	7 41	5 46	10 05	7 06 L	2 59 H 8 05 L 11 17 H	◖	58°	Fort Worth and Denver railway runs excursion train to encourage settlement of Texas. (1887)
350	Sat	16	7 42	5 46	10 04	7 24 L	3 44 H	●	58°	First day of Chanukah (Jewish)

Add one hour for Daylight Saving Time, if and when in use.

December 2006

December, the tenth month in the Roman calendar, derives its name from the Latin word decem, for "ten."

December is the twelfth month of the year in the Gregorian calendar and one of seven months of the year with 31 days. The winter solstice in the northern hemisphere and the summer solstice in the southern hemisphere occur during the month of December around the 21st. December begins on the same day of the week as September. December's flower is the holly. December's birthstone is turquoise. The signs of the zodiac during the month of December are Sagittarius and Capricorn.

DAY OF YEAR	DAY OF WEEK	DAY OF MONTH	RISE	SET	LENGTH OF DAY H M	TIDES AM	TIDES PM	MOON PHASE	NORMAL HIGH TEMP	On this date in December...
351	Sun	17	7 43	5 46	10 03	7 48 L	4 21 H	●	58°	"John Henry Faulk Show" debuts on WCBS. (1951)
352	Mon	18	7 43	5 47	10 04	8 16 L	4 57 H	●	58°	Texas Rangers attack Commanche hunting camp rescuing Cynthia Ann Parker. (1860)
353	Tues	19	7 44	5 47	10 03	8 49 L	5 37 H	●	58°	Towns of Lubbock and Monterey consolidate. (1890)
354	Wed	20	7 44	5 48	10 04	9 26 L	6 22 H / 10 05 L	●	58°	Garrison at Goliad declares independence from Mexico. (1835); Driskill Hotel opens in Austin. (1886)
355	Thurs	21	7 45	5 48	10 03	12 20 H / 10 07 L	7 11 H / 10 10 L	●	57°	Legislature establishes Frontier Regiment. (1861)
356	Fri	22	7 45	5 49	10 04	1 10 H / 10 50 L	8 01 H / 10 37 L	●	57°	Oilers play last game in Houston. (1996)
357	Sat	23	7 46	5 49	10 03	1 56 H / 11 35 L	8 43 H / 11 34 L	●	57°	Last day of Chanukah (Jewish)
358	Sun	24	7 46	5 50	10 04	2 41 H	12 22 L / 9 11 H	●	57°	First railroad locomotive comes to Texas. (1852)
359	Mon	25	7 47	5 50	10 03	1 16 L / 3 35 H	1 11 L / 9 30 H	◐	57°	Christmas Day
360	Tues	26	7 47	5 51	10 04	3 25 L / 6 48 H	2 05 L / 9 44 H	◐	57°	First commercial buffalo hunt held in Fort Griffin. (1874)
361	Wed	27	7 48	5 52	10 04	4 23 L / 10 05 H	3 12 L / 9 55 H	◑	57°	Stephen F. Austin dies. (1836)
362	Thurs	28	7 48	5 52	10 04	5 09 L	12 28 H / 4 57 L / 10 03 H	○	57°	Bluesman Freddie King dies. (1976)
363	Fri	29	7 48	5 53	10 05	5 53 L	2 08 H / 7 26 L / 10 05 H	◑	57°	Texas admitted as 28th state. (1845)
364	Sat	30	7 48	5 54	10 06	6 37 L	3 16 H	○	56°	San Antonio Mayor Charles Quin indicted for misapplication of funds. (1938)
365	Sun	31	7 49	5 54	10 05	7 22 L	4 09 H	○	56°	Aransas National Wildlife Refuge established. (1937)

● New Moon   ◐ First Quarter   ○ Full Moon   ◑ Last Quarter

Atmospheric and Astronomical data provided by NOAA, National Ocean Service and U.S. Naval Observatory.

TEXAS

WEATHER RECORDS

Event	Record	Location	Date
Temperature (F)			
Coldest	-23	Tulia	February 12, 1899
		Seminole	February 8, 1933
Hottest	120	Seymour	August 12, 1936
		Monahans	July 27, 1994
Highest monthly average	102.4	Presidio	June 1962
Lowest monthly average	19.4	Dalhart	January 1959
Highest annual average	74.1	McAllen	1988
Lowest annual average	56.1	Dalhart	1959
Rainfall (inches)			
Greatest in a 24-hour period	29.05	Albany	August 4 1978
Greatest in one month	35.7	Alvin	July 1979
Greatest in one year	109.38	Clarksville	1873
Least in one year	1.64	Presidio	1956
Snowfall (inches)			
Greatest in a 24-hour period	24.0	Plainview	February 3 to 5, 1956
Greatest maximum depth	33.0	Hale Center	February 4, 1956
		Vega	February 4, 1956
Greatest in a single storm	61.0	Vega	February 1 to 8, 1956
Greatest in one month	61.0	Vega	February 1956
Greatest in one season	65.0	Romero	1923 to 1924
Wind (mph)			
Highest sustained speed	145	Matagorda (Hurricane Carla)	September 11, 1961
	145	Port Lavaca (Hurricane Carla)	September 11, 1961
Highest peak gust	180	Aransas Pass (Hurricane Celia)	August 3, 1970
Hazardous Weather			
Longest and worst drought			1950 to 1956
Worst heat wave			1980
Most damage from 1 tornado	$442 million	Wichita Falls	April 10, 1979
Most tornadoes in one year	232		1905
Most tornadoes in one month	124		September 1967
Deadliest hurricane	6,000 to 8,000	Galveston	September 8, 1900
Most damaging hurricane	$3 billion	Hurricane Alicia	August 18, 1983

Pro Football Hall of Fame ★ ★ ★

Players, coaches, and others who have been inducted into the Pro Football Hall of Fame from Texas teams are listed below, followed by the year of induction and the year(s) of association with their team.

The following compilation lists the current members of the Pro Football Hall of Fame who were born in Texas, followed by their birthplace and the year of induction into the Hall.

Dallas Cowboys

Herb Adderley	1980	1970-1972
Lance Alworth	1978	1971-1972
Mike Ditka	1988	1969-1972
Tony Dorsett	1994	1977-1987
Forrest Gregg	1977	1971
Tom Landry	1990	1960-1988
Bob Lilly	1980	1961-1974
Tommy McDonald	1998	1964
Mel Renfro	1996	1964-1977
Tex Schramm	1991	1960-1989
Jackie Smith	1994	1978
Roger Staubach	1985	1969-1979
Randy White	1994	1975-1988

Houston Oilers

Elvin Bethea	2003	1968-1983
George Blanda	1981	1960-1966
Earl Campbell	1991	1978-1984
Dave Casper	2002	1980-1983
Sid Gillman	1983	1973-1974
Ken Houston	1986	1967-1972
John Henry Johnson	1987	1966
Charlie Joiner	1996	1969-1972
Mike Munchak	2001	1982-1993

Dallas Texans

Lamar Hunt	1972	1959-1962
Hank Stram	2003	1960-1962

Lance Alworth	Houston	1978
Sammy Baugh	Temple	1963
Raymond Berry	Corpus Christi	1973
Earl Campbell	Tyler	1991
Eric Dickerson	Sealy	1999
Joe Greene	Temple	1987
Forrest Gregg	Birthright	1977
Mike Haynes	Denison	1997
Ken Houston	Lufkin	1986
Jimmy Johnson	Dallas	1994
Tom Landry	Mission	1990
Dick (Night Train) Lane	Austin	1974
Yale Lary	Fort Worth	1979
Bobby Layne	Santa Anna	1967
Bob Lilly	Olney	1980
Ollie Matson	Trinity	1972
Don Maynard	Crosbyton	1987
Mel Renfro	Houston	1996
Mike Singletary	Houston	1988
Charley Taylor	Grand Prairie	1984
Y. A. Tittle	Marshall	1971
Clyde (Bulldog) Turner	Plains	1966
Gene Upshaw	Robstown	1987
Doak Walker	Dallas	1986

Source: Pro Football Hall of Fame Website – www.profootballhof.com

Tom Landry on the Basics of Coaching...

"When you want to win a game, you have to teach. When you lose a game, you have to learn."

"Leadership is getting someone to do what they don't want to do in order to achieve what they want to achieve."

Tom Landry,
Former Head Coach of the Dallas Cowboys.

Earl Campbell
THE TYLER ROSE

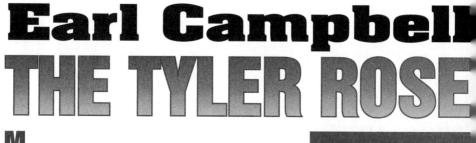

Many football aficionados claim that Earl Campbell was the best running back ever to play in the NFL. And many others, particularly Texans, vow that he was the finest football player to hail from the Lone Star State.

Born on March 29, 1955, the sixth of eleven children, Campbell worked as a youth with his father in the vast rose fields that surrounded his birthplace of Tyler. By the time he had reached the fifth grade in school, football had grabbed the boy's attention and, befriended and guided by his coach, he played quite well. In 1973, as a senior at John Tyler High School, young Campbell led his squad to the state championship, winning the final game at his future home, the Houston Astrodome, by a score of 21-14. He rushed for 200 yards during the game.

During his last season at John Tyler High School, Campbell had caught the attention of scouts for the University of Texas Longhorns. One of the excited scouts persuaded the legendary Darrell Royal to come to Tyler to observe the fast-running Campbell in person. Royal liked what he saw and thus began a long campaign to entice Earl to come to Austin and play for the Longhorns.

Many other teams were eyeing Campbell at the same time, but the one that Earl was seriously considering, other than UT, was the University of Oklahoma. When the night before the day for him to make his decision approached and he had still not chosen a team, the deeply religious Campbell prayed that God would give him a sign: if he was awakened during the night with the urge to urinate, he would select Texas. Otherwise, Oklahoma would be his next home.

As the old saying goes, the rest is history. Earl stumbled to the bathroom during the night and decided that God wanted him to be a Longhorn. Years later when Oklahoma's long-time coach Barry Switzer heard of Earl's pact with God, he exclaimed that had he known such a deal was in the works, he would have "flown to Tyler and laid underneath his bed all night."

★

Total Number of Yards at the University of Texas

4,443

EARL CAMPBELL BY THE NUMBERS

Earl's Jersey Number at the University of Texas	20
Earl's Jersey Number at the Houston Oilers	34
Career Total Yards (Professional)	10,213
Career Touchdowns (Professional)	74
Career Total Yards Rushing (Professional)	9,407
Career Total Yards Receiving (Professional)	806
Rank in the NFL for Total Rushing	10
Number of Times Earl Appeared on Cover of *Sports Illustrated*	6
The Year Earl Won the Heisman Trophy	1977
Total Number of Touchdowns at the University of Texas	41
The Year Earl Was Inducted into the NFL Hall of Fame	1991

Earl graduated from UT in 1977, following an illustrious career on the football field. When his days as a Longhorn were over, he had rushed for nearly 4,500 yards, scored 41 touchdowns, and won the coveted Heisman Trophy.

While at Texas, Campbell had been watched by the discerning eyes of Houston Oilers owner, Bud Adams, and the team's coach, Bum Phillips, who snapped up the "Tyler Rose" as their first draft choice. It was a good decision; during his first year as an Oiler, Earl was named both "Rookie of the Year" and the NFL's "Most Valuable Player." Campbell's years at Houston were good ones; he not only excelled on the field, but was admired by sports fans everywhere. In 1981, the Texas Legislature passed an act declaring Earl a "state hero of Texas," alongside three other legends: Davy Crockett, Sam Houston, and Stephen Austin.

Campbell was eventually traded to the New Orleans Saints and there he rejoined his old coach and good friend, Bum Phillips, who had been released from the Oilers several years earlier. By now Earl was growing tired and following a short-lived and uneventful career with the Saints, he retired from football in August, 1986. Five years later, he was inducted into the NFL Hall of Fame and was introduced at the occasion by Bum Phillips.

Today, Earl Campbell is a successful Austin businessman and sits as president of Earl Campbell Meat Products, Inc. ★

DUTCH MEYER

Leo "Dutch" Meyer's tenure at Texas Christian University from 1934-1952 was very successful, but it was his innovative use of the "spread" formation that brought him the most attention. He was really way ahead of his time. He implemented a formation using a double wing with two split ends and two or three wingbacks. This new look improved the college passing game, and Meyer's 1938 team won the National Championship after going 11-0 and defeating Carnegie Tech 15-7 in the 1939 Sugar Bowl. The fact is that the offense Meyer developed is not much different than the "West Coast" offenses that are being used today.

BASKETBALL HALL of FAME

Players, coaches, and others who have been inducted into the Basketball Hall of Fame from Texas teams are listed below, followed by the year of induction, and the year(s) of association with their team.

Dallas Diamonds (WBL)
Nancy Leiberman	1996	1980

Dallas Fury
Nancy Lieberman	1996	2004 - present – Coach

Dallas Mavericks
Alex English	1997	1990-1991

Houston Rockets
Rick Barry	1987	1978-1979
Clyde Drexler	2004	1995-1998
Elvin Hayes	1990	1971-1972, 1981-1984
Calvin Murphy	1993	1971-1983
Moses Malone	2001	1976-1977, 1981-1982

San Antonio Spurs
George Gervin	1996	1974-1985
Clifford Hagan	1978	1967-1970 – Player/coach
		(Dallas Chaparrals)
Moses Malone	2001	1994-1995
Larry Brown	2002	1989-1992 – Coach

The following compilation lists the current members of the Basketball Hall of Fame who were born in Texas, followed by their birthplace, and year of induction into the Hall.

Jody Conradt	Goldthwaite	1998 - Coach
Bruce Drake	Gentry	1973 - Coach
K.C. Jones	Taylor	1989 - Player
Slater "Dugie" Martin	Elmira	1982 - Player
Bill Sharman	Abilene	1976 - Player/coach-2004

Source: Basketball Hall of Fame – www.hoophall.com

Moses Malone Professional Stats

Lifetime Goals	1,329
Field Goal Percent	49.1 %
Three-point Field Goal Percent	10.0 %
Free Throw Percent	76.9 %
Rebounds	16,212
Assists	1,796
Total Points	27,409
Average Points per Game	20.6

★

Moses Malone

In 1974, just prior to graduating from Petersburg (Virginia) High School, nineteen-year-old Moses Malone was, without doubt, one of the hottest basketball players in the United States. Even before he had time to plan for college, the six-foot, ten-inch center was drafted by the Utah Stars in the American Basketball Association's third round. By the fall of 1976, he had been traded to the Houston Rockets where he played for the next six years and was named the NBA's most valuable player in 1979. Malone's professional career lasted twenty-one seasons, ending with a stint with the San Antonio Spurs, beginning in 1994. Two years later, he was named one of the fifty greatest players in NBA history. Malone is the third-leading rebounder and the sixth-leading scorer in the combined history of the ABA and NBA.

★

★ NATIONAL ★
BASEBALL
HALL OF FAME

Players, managers, and others who have been inducted into the Baseball Hall of Fame from Texas teams are listed below, followed by the year of induction and the year(s) of association with their team.

Houston Astros

Leo Durocher	1994	1972-1973
Nellie Fox	1997	1964-1965
Eddie Mathews	1978	1967
Joe Morgan	1990	1963-1971, 1980
Robin Roberts	1976	1965-1966
Nolan Ryan	1999	1980-1988
Don Sutton	1998	1981-1982

Texas Rangers

Ferguson Jenkins	1991	1974-1975, 1978-1981
Gaylord Perry	1991	1975-1977, 1980
Nolan Ryan	1999	1989-1993
Ted Williams	1966	1972

The following compilation lists the current members of the Baseball Hall of Fame who were born in Texas, followed by their birthplace and year of induction into the Hall.

Ernie Banks	Dallas	1977
Bill Foster	Calvert	1996
Rube Foster	Calvert	1981
Rogers Hornsby	Winters	1942
Eddie Mathews	Texarkana	1978
Joe Morgan	Bonham	1990
Frank Robinson	Beaumont	1982
Nolan Ryan	Refugio	1999
Hilton Smith	Giddings	2001
Tris Speaker	Hubbard	1937
Willie Wells	Austin	1997
Joe Williams	Seguin	1999
Ross Youngs	Shiner	1972

Source: National Baseball Hall of Fame and Museum, Inc. Website – www.baseballhalloffame.org

The summer of **1989** was a hot one for most Texans, including the recently signed pitcher for the Texas Rangers, **Nolan Ryan.** Most fans were skeptical. Ryan was forty-plus years old with chronic back trouble and a pulled hamstring to boot. But Nolan Ryan proved to be hotter than than a west Texas wind. Instead of becoming the "Ole Man" of the team, he pitched like a machine. His fastball was clocked at over 96 miles per hour and he had good stuff on everything else. When the dust settled at the end of the season, Ryan had won **16 games**, and led the American League with an blistering **301 strikeouts**. Ryan became the oldest pitcher

On June 11, 1990, at the age of forty-three and one half years old, Nolan Ryan pitched the sixth no-hitter of his baseball career.

ever to strike out more than 300 batters in a single season. 'Nuff said.

Did You Know?....

Nolan Ryan has the distinction of being the only pitcher ever to strike out the side on nine pitched balls in both the National League (pitching April 19, 1968) and the American League (pitching July 9, 1972).

Nolan Ryan *A man for all seasons!*

For Nolan Ryan's seventh birthday in 1954, he received a brand new baseball glove from his father and, from that point on, the youth knew where his future lay. Two years later, he was playing in the Little League and, since he was accurate at hurling a baseball, he was persuaded to try his hand at pitching. Ryan grew up in the small town of Alvin, Texas, located a few miles south of Houston, and he attended as many games as he could when the Houston Colt .45s played. A few years later, when the team became the Houston Astros and began playing indoors in the newly-completed Astrodome, young Ryan continued his loyalty.

Legendary baseball scout Red Murff "discovered" Ryan in 1963 when Nolan

the next two years, always encouraging the team's coaching staff to continue working with Ryan. Ryan was described by the scout as having "one of the ten best arms in the world" and was encouraged to improve his pitching skills.

During Nolan's senior year in high school, he carried the Yellowjackets to second place in the state. In the meantime, he had been selected by Murff's team, the New York Mets, in the 1965 amateur draft. On June 28, Ryan and the Mets inked a contract worth $20,000. The hurler was soon off to the Mets' farm team in Marion, Virginia, where he experienced a horrible rookie year, winning only three games and losing six. His second year in professional baseball carried him to the Class A team at Greenville, North Carolina, and he finished

Nolan Ryan *By The Numbers*

Number of Years in Professional Baseball	27
Number of No-hitters Pitched	7
Number of One-hitters Pitched	12
Number of Strikeouts	5,714
Most Strikeouts in a Single Season	383
Number of Strikeout "Victims"	1,176
Number of Times Ryan Struck Out Pete Rose	13
Number of Times Ryan Struck Out Mark McGwire	6
Number of Times Ryan Struck Out Roger Maris	2
Number of Times Ryan Struck Out Carlton Fisk	24
Number of Times Ryan Struck Out Reggie Jackson	22
Number of Shutout Games	61

pitched for his high school team, the Yellowjackets. Impressed by the youngster's speed, Murff estimated that the pitches he observed were in excess of 100 miles per hour, faster than two well-respected "ninety-five-mile-per-hour" major league pitchers, Jim Maloney and Turk Farrell. Murff made several visits to Alvin over

the season with seventeen games won and two lost. In a single game, he struck out nineteen batters in only seven innings. He so impressed the New York front office that the Mets called him up at the end of the minor league season.

Following a stint with the Mets' AAA Jacksonville, Florida, affiliate, Ryan finally graduated to the majors where he spent most of his time in the bullpen, although he did assist his team in winning the 1969 World Series against the Baltimore Orioles. Ryan spent two more rather gloomy years with the Mets before, at his own request, he was traded to the California Angels. Whitey Hertzog of the Mets later lamented that the trade "might be the worst deal in history."

Ryan's career with the Angels was mixed. On the positive side, during one season, he tied Sandy Koufax's record by pitching four no-hitters and broke Bob Feller's legendary fastball speed record with several pitches thrown in excess of 100 miles per hour. But, on the downside, he also faced several health issues that, fortunately, were overcome with surgery and rest. By 1979, he had grown weary of California and wanted to go home to Texas. The New York Yankees offered him a one million dollar per year contract, a huge amount of money in those days and the highest salary ever extended to a major league baseball player to date. When the Houston Astros matched the deal, a happy Ryan packed up his family and headed home for Alvin.

Ryan's years at Houston were good ones. While with the Astros, he broke Walter Johnson's strikeout record and became the first pitcher in history to fan 4,000 hitters. At the end of the 1988 season, however, when team management asked him to take a pay cut, he signed on with the Texas Rangers at twice his previous salary.

While with the Rangers, Ryan threw his 5,000th strikeout on August 22, 1989. He also racked up his 300th win at Texas, only the twentieth player in history to do so. By the end of the 1993 season, however, after twenty-seven years in baseball during which time he set fifty-three all time records, Ryan's body was in constant pain and he decided to retire from the sport he loved so well. In 1999, he was inducted into the Baseball Hall of Fame at Cooperstown, New York, where he joined his boyhood idol, Sandy Koufax, and so many of his other heroes. ★

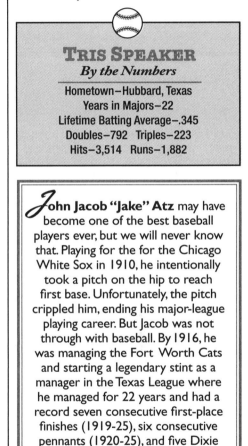

TRIS SPEAKER
By the Numbers

Hometown–Hubbard, Texas
Years in Majors–22
Lifetime Batting Average–.345
Doubles–792   Triples–223
Hits–3,514   Runs–1,882

*J*ohn Jacob "Jake" Atz may have become one of the best baseball players ever, but we will never know that. Playing for the for the Chicago White Sox in 1910, he intentionally took a pitch on the hip to reach first base. Unfortunately, the pitch crippled him, ending his major-league playing career. But Jacob was not through with baseball. By 1916, he was managing the Fort Worth Cats and starting a legendary stint as a manager in the Texas League where he managed for 22 years and had a record seven consecutive first-place finishes (1919-25), six consecutive pennants (1920-25), and five Dixie Series titles (1920, 1921, 1923-25).

TEXAS BASEBALL
Did You Know?

Simply Perfect! *Did you know that Football Hall of Fame quarterback* **Bobby Layne** *still holds the record for the* **University of Texas baseball team** *against conference opponents? His record was a perfect 28-0.*

THE SOUTHWEST CONFERENCE

1 ★ 9 ★ 1 ★ 4

On December 8, 1914, representatives of the Universities of Texas and Arkansas, along with those of Texas A&M, Baylor, Oklahoma, Oklahoma A&M, Rice, and Southwestern Universities signed an agreement that created the Southwest Intercollegiate Athletic Conference. The idea for the consortium came from the fertile brain of Theodore (Theo) Bellmont, the athletic director and a professor at the University of Texas. Bellmont, a graduate of the University of Tennessee, had already served as secretary of the Houston YMCA for a number of years before joining UT in its athletic department in 1913.

Vitally interested in furthering the athletic reputations as well as the ethical principles and academic standards of the larger universities in the region, Bellmont soon invited Louisiana State University and the University of Mississippi to join the conference, but both schools declined. Undaunted, the tireless leader was encouraged when Southern Methodist University joined the group in 1918 and Texas Christian came on board five years later. In the meantime, however, Southwestern, Oklahoma, and Oklahoma A&M had dropped their memberships in the now renamed Southwest Conference (SWC), leaving only seven active schools.

Texas Tech joined in 1958, followed by the University of Houston in 1972. When multiple NCAA sanctions were placed against several SWC teams during the 1980s, the conference's reputation suffered a severe blow and its members' athletic recruiting programs

suffered tremendously. In 1990, the University of Arkansas parted ways with the SWC and affiliated itself with the Southeastern Conference (SEC). The eight remaining university programs were further reduced during 1993-1994, when UT, Texas A&M, Baylor, and Texas Tech left the fold to join the Big Eight Conference, which then became the Big Twelve. Rice, Texas Christian, and Southern Methodist then affiliated with the Western Athletic Conference (WAC), while the University of Houston helped organize, along with other schools in the region, a brand new league called Conference USA. In 1996, the Southwest Conference ceased to exist.

The trademark of the Southwest Conference was the Cotton Bowl, first played in 1937 between Texas Christian and Marquette (TCU won 16-6). Between 1940 and 1995, the classic football game pitted the SWC champion against a leading team from another conference.

During its eighty-two year existence, the SWC produced some of the most successful sports programs in the country. In football alone, conference teams have won eight national championships, and five of its players have been awarded the coveted Heisman Trophy: Robert David (Davey) O'Brien, TCU, 1938; Doak Walker, SMU, 1948; John David Crow, Texas A&M, 1957; Earl Campbell, UT, 1977; and Andre Ware, Houston, 1989. Overall, SWC athletic teams have garnered sixty-two national championships representing fifteen sports. ★

Southwest Conference Champions

1915 -1995

1915 – Oklahoma	1937 – Rice	1958 – TCU	1977 – Texas
1916 – None	1938 – TCU	1959 – Texas,	1978 – Houston
1917 – Texas A&M	1939 – Texas A&M	Arkansas, and TCU	1979 – Arkansas and
1918 – None	1940 – Texas A&M	1960 – Arkansas	Houston
1919 – Texas A&M	1941 – Texas A&M	1961 – Arkansas	1980 – Baylor
1920 – Texas	1942 – Texas	and Texas	1981 – SMU
1921 – Texas A&M	1943 – Texas	1962 – Texas	1982 – SMU
1922 – Baylor	1944 – TCU	1963 – Texas	1983 – Texas
1923 – None	1945 – Texas	1964 – Arkansas	1984 – Houston
1924 – Baylor	1946 – Rice	1965 – Arkansas	1985 – Texas A&M
1925 – Texas A&M	1947 – SMU	1966 – SMU	1986 – Texas A&M
1926 – SMU	1948 – SMU	1967 – Texas A&M	1987 – Texas A&M
1927 – Texas A&M	1949 – Rice	1968 – Texas and	1988 – Arkansas
1928 – Texas	1950 – Texas	Arkansas	1989 – Arkansas
1929 – TCU	1951 – TCU	1969 – Texas	1990 – Texas
1930 – Texas	1952 – Texas	1970 – Texas	1991 – Texas A&M
1931 – SMU	1953 – Rice and	1971 – Texas	1992 – Texas A&M
1932 – TCU	Texas	1972 – Texas	1993 – Texas A&M
1933 – None	1954 – Arkansas	1973 – Texas	1994 – Texas, TCU, Rice,
1934 – Rice	1955 – TCU	1974 – Baylor	Baylor, Texas Tech
1935 – SMU	1956 – Texas A&M	1975 – Arkansas	(5-way tie)
1936 – Arkansas	1957 – Rice	1976 – Houston	1995 – Texas

Source: www.texasalmanac.com/history/highlights/swc

Sooner Logic

New students from various states were attending their first psychiatry class at UT.

"Just to establish some parameters and to get us on our way, I would like to ask you a few questions," said the professor.

To the student from Houston, "What is the opposite of joy?," asked the professor. *"Sadness,"* said the student.

"And the opposite of depression?" he asked of the young lady from the Austin. *"Elation,"* she said.

"And you sir," he said to the young man from Tulsa, "how about the opposite of woe?" The student thought a minute and then said, *"I believe that would be giddy-up."*

"How can you be in this class?," replied the professor, "It's obvious that you have already been through the University of Oklahoma!"

A TEXAS FOOTBALL LEGEND

When O. A. "Bum" Phillips accepted his diploma from Nederland High School in the spring of 1941, he could hardly wait until the new school season opened. He intended to follow his high school passion of playing football, only now at Lamar Junior College in nearby Beaumont. When fall arrived, Bum enrolled at Lamar and, based on his high school athletic record, was immediately accepted on the football team. The season had barely opened when the Japanese bombed Pearl Harbor on December 7, and President Franklin D. Roosevelt declared war.

Phillips served in the South Pacific, where he was wounded. Leaving the military after the war, he enrolled in Stephen F. Austin State College in Nacogdoches and again received a place on the school's football team. He played first string during the 1948 and 1949 seasons and graduated with an education degree.

For his career, he selected high school teaching and, over the next few years, he taught and coached football at Jacksonville, Amarillo, and Nederland. As head coach of the Nederland Bulldogs, he took his team to the state playoffs in 1955.

Bum left high school coaching when he was hired as an assistant coach at Texas A&M under the tutelage of the legendary Paul "Bear" Bryant, who had come on board with the Aggies in 1954. Many of his tricks of the trade he learned under the elusive "Bear." Leaving the

Aggies, Bum migrated to the University of Houston, under Coach Bill Yeoman, and then returned to high school sports. Returning to college football, he spent time as an assistant at SMU, Texas-El Paso, and Oklahoma State, before eventually signing on in the NFL as a defensive assistant coach in San Diego. When San Diego head coach Sid Gillman eventually took over the Houston Oilers, he hired Bum as his defensive coordinator. Gillman gave up active coaching for the front office in 1975, and Phillips became head coach of the Oilers.

The Oilers team that Bum inherited had seen hard times lately. Since its founding in 1960, when it was the AFL's dream team, winning the league's championship with the assistance of such stalwarts as George Blanda and Billy Cannon, it had fallen significantly in the ratings and had gone through nine coaches. Now, it was Bum's job to bring the team out of the doldrums and make them a nationally recognized contender.

During the 1975 season, Phillips took the Oilers to their first winning season in seven years, winning ten games and losing only four. The next year saw the team end up with a disappointing five wins and nine losses. Player injuries plagued the Oilers during the 1977 season, but they finished with a respectable 8-6 record.

With running back Earl Campbell racking up 1,450 yards in 1978, the Oilers finished the regular season with a 10-6 record. They went on to beat the Miami

Dolphins in the Wild Card playoff, then surpassed the New England Patriots, thereby earning a spot to play Pittsburgh in the playoffs. The Steelers won the game 34-5, and the Oilers sadly returned to Houston.

"Wait'll next year," was the Houston war chant as the 1979 season, with Earl Campbell again giving a stellar performance, progressed. The Oilers completed the year with an 11-5 record, won the Wild Card game against Denver, and beat the Chargers in the Divisional Playoffs, before being shut down in the AFC championship game, again by Pittsburgh,

27-13. The 1980 season ended with an 11-5 record and, after losing to Oakland in the Wild Card game, Bum Phillips was released from the Oilers by owner Bud Adams, to be replaced by Ed Biles. Bum's overall record with the Oilers was 55-35.

The New Orleans Saints hired Phillips and he served there from 1981-85, ending his overall professional career with an 88-77 record. After working as an analyst with local radio and television stations across Texas, Bum retired to his ranch in South Texas, where, with his wife, he breeds cutting horses. ★

BUM PHILLIPS on the Record.

On the business of coaching...

"There are two kinds of coaches. Them that have been fired and them that are going to be fired."

On losing a game...

"The behinder we got, the worse it got."

Grant Teaff has had as much success in leading the Baylor Bears to football success as anyone who ever coached at the Waco school. When he was hired years ago, the coach was given a plaque to commemorate the occasion at the traditionally religious school. That plaque read *"God, grant Teaff the serenity to accept the things that he cannot change and the courage to change the things he can...and the wisdom to have us in the Cotton Bowl in a couple of years."*

The Bear and the Aggies

Bum Phillips's mentor at Texas A&M was the legendary Paul "Bear" Bryant. Bryant, arguably the most recognized name in college football, had come to the Aggies from Kentucky in 1954, ending up his first year in Texas with a miserable 1-9 record. The following year, the Bear racked up a 7-2-1 record; then, in 1956, he carried his team through the season unbeaten, with one tie. During his last year at A&M, Bryant's team won eight games and lost three, before he was lured away to his destiny at the University of Alabama where he coached until his retirement in 1982. Bear's lifetime record was 323-85-17. When he was carried off the field at the Liberty Bowl in Memphis, Tennessee, at the end of his last game—Alabama 21, Illinois 15— the lights on the scoreboard spelled out, *"Good-bye, Bear, We'll Miss You."*

University Interscholastic League State
FOOTBALL CHAMPIONSHIPS 1920 2004

Year	League	Opponents/Score	Year	League	Opponents/Score
1920	—	Houston Heights 0, Cleburne 0	1954	4A	Abilene 14, Houston Austin 7
1921	—	Bryan 35, Dallas Oak Cliff 13		3A	Breckenridge 20, Port Neches 7
1922	—	Waco 13, Abilene 10		2A	Phillips 21, Killeen 13
1923	—	Abilene 3, Waco 0		1A	Deer Park 26, Albany 6
1924	—	Dallas Oak Cliff 31, Waco 0	1955	4A	Abilene 33, Tyler 13
1925	—	Waco 20, Dallas Forest 7		3A	Port Neches 20, Garland 14
1926	—	Waco 20, Dallas Oak Cliff 7		2A	Stamford 34, Hillsboro 7
1927	—	Waco 21, Abilene 14		1A	Deer Park 7, Stinnett 0
1928	—	Abilene 38, Port Arthur 0	1956	4A	Abilene 14, Corpus Christi Ray 0
1929	—	Port Arthur 0, Breckenridge 0 (tie)		3A	Garland 3, Nederland 0
1930	—	Tyler 25, Amarillo 13		2A	Stamford 26, Brady 13
1931	—	Abilene 13, Beaumont 0		1A	Stinnett 35, Hondo 13
1932	—	Corsicana 0, Fort Worth Masonic Home 0	1957	4A	Highland Park 21, Port Arthur 9
		(Corsicana won on penetrations, 3-0)		3A	Nederland 20, Sweetwater 7
1933	—	Greenville 21, Dallas Tech 0		2A	Terrell 41, Brady 6
1934	—	Amarillo 48, Corpus Christi 0		1A	Mart 7, White Oak 7
1935	—	Amarillo 13, Greenville 7	1958	4A	Wichita Falls 48, Pasadena 6
1936	—	Amarillo 19, Kerrville 6		3A	Breckenridge 42, Kingsville 14
1937	—	Longview 19, Wichita Falls 12		2A	Stamford 23, Angelton 0
1938	—	Corpus Christi 20, Lubbock 6		1A	White Deer 44, Elgin 22
1939	—	Lubbock 20, Waco 14	1959	4A	Corpus Christi Ray 20, Wichita Falls 6
1940	—	Amarillo 20, Temple 7		3A	Breckenridge 20, Cleburne 20
1941	—	Wichita Falls 13, Temple 0		2A	Stamford 19, Brady 14
1942	—	Austin 20, Dallas Sunset 7		1A	Katy 16, Sundown 6
1943	—	San Angelo 26, Lufkin 13	1960	4A	Corpus Christi Miller 13, Wichita Falls 6
1944	—	Port Arthur 20, Dallas Highland Park 7		3A	Brownwood 26, Port Lavaca 6
1945	—	Dallas Highland Park 7, Waco 7 (tie)		2A	Denver City 26, Bellville 21
1946	—	Odessa 21, San Antonio Jefferson 14		1A	Albany 20, Crosby 0
1947	—	San Antonio Brackenridge 23,	1961	4A	Wichita Falls 21, Galena Park 14
		Dallas Highland Park 13		3A	Dumas 6, Nederland 0
1948	City	Fort Worth Arlington Heights 20,		2A	Donna 28, Quanah 21
		Houston Lamar 0		1A	Albany 18, Hull-Daisetta 12
	2A	Waco 21, Amarillo 0	1962	4A	San Antonio Breckenridge 30, Borger 26
	1A	Monahans 14, New Braunfels 0		3A	Dumas 14, Pharr 3
1949	City	San Antonio Jefferson 31, Dallas Sunset 13		2A	Jacksboro 52, Rockdale 0
	2A	Wichita Falls 14, Austin 13		1A	Rotan 39, Ingleside 6
	1A	Littlefield 13, Mexia 0	1963	4A	Garland 17, Corpus Christi Miller 0
1950	City	Dallas Sunset 14, Houston Reagan 6		3A	Corsicana 7, Pharr 0
	2A	Wichita 34, Austin 13		2A	Rockwall 7, Houston Dulles 6
	1A	Wharton 13, Kermit 9		1A	Petersburg 20, George West 12
1951	4A	Lubbock 14, Baytown 12	1964	4A	Garland 26, Galena Park 21
	3A	Breckenridge 20, Temple 14		3A	Palestine 24, San Marcos 15
	2A	Arlington 7, Waco LeVega 0		2A	Palacios 12, Marlin 0
	1A	Giddings 25, Newcastle 14		1A	Archer City 13, Ingleside 6
1952	4A	Lubbock 12, Baytown 7	1965	4A	Odessa Permian 11, San Antonio Lee 6
	3A	Breckenridge 28, Temple 20		3A	Brownwood 14, Bridge City 0
	2A	Terrell 61, Yoakum 13		2A	Plano 20, Edna 17
	1A	Wink 26, Deer Park 20		1A	Wills Point 14, White Deer 0
1953	4A	Houston Lamar 33, Odessa 7	1966	4A	San Angelo 21, Houston Spring Branch 14
	3A	Port Neches 24, Big Spring 13		3A	Bridge City 30, McKinney 6
	2A	Huntsville 40, Ballinger 6		2A	Sweeny 29, Granbury 7
	1A	Ranger 34, Luling 21		1A	Sonora 40, Schulenburg 14

Year	League	Opponents/Score
1967	4A	Austin Reagan 20, Abilene Cooper 19
	3A	Brownwood 36, El Campo 12
	2A	Plano 27, Universal City Randolph 8
	1A	Tidehaven 7, Clifton 6
1968	4A	Austin Reagan 17, Odessa Permian 11
	3A	Lubbock Estacado 14, Refugio 0
	2A	Daingerfield 7, Lufkin Dunbar 6
	1A	Sonora 9, Poth 0
1969	4A	Wichita Falls 28, San Antonio Lee 20
	3A	Brownwood 34, West Columbia 16
	2A	Iowa Park 31, Klein 14
	1A	Mart 28, Sonora 0
1970	4A	Austin Reagan 21, Odessa Permian 14
	3A	Brownwood 14, Cuero 0
	2A	Refugio 7, Iowa Park 7 (tie)
	1A	Sonora 45, Pflugerville 6
1971	4A	San Antonio Lee 28, Wichita Falls 27
	3A	Plano 21, Gregory-Portland 20
	2A	Jacksboro 20, Rosebud-Lott 14
	1A	Mont Belvieu Barbers Hill 3, Sonora 3
1972	4A	Odessa Permian 37, Baytown Sterling 7
	3A	Uvalde 33, Lewisville 27
	2A	Boling 20, Rockwell 0
	1A	Schulenburg 14, Clarendon 10
	B	Chilton 6, Windthorst 0
	Eight-Man	Goree 28, Harold 24
	Six-Man	O'Brien 60, Jarrell 14
1973	4A	Tyler John Tyler 21, Austin Reagan 14
	3A	Cuero 21, Mount Pleasant 7
	2A	Friendswood 38, Hooks 15
	1A	Troup 28, Vega 7
	B	Big Sandy 25, Rule 0
	Eight-Man	Goree 52, La Pryor 12
	Six-Man	Cherokee 43, Marathon 12
1974	4A	Brazoswood 22, Mesquite 12
	3A	Cuero 19, Gainesville 7
	2A	Newton 56, Spearman 26
	1A	Grapeland 19, Aledo 18
	B	Big Sandy 0, Celina 0
	Eight-Man	Follett 28, La Pryor 22
	Six-Man	Marathon 60, Cherokee 58
1975	4A	Port Neches-Groves 20, Odessa Permian 10
	3A	Ennis 13, Cuero 0
	2A	LaGrange 27, Childress 6
	1A	DeLeon 28, Schulenburg 15
	B	Big Sandy 28, Groom 2
	Eight-Man	Leakey 32, Follett 14
	Six-Man	Cherokee 40, Marathon 26

Year	League	Opponents/Score
1976	4A	San Antonio Churchill 10, Temple 0
	3A	Beaumont Hebert 35, Gainesville 7
	2A	Rockdale 23, Childress 6
	1A	Mont Belvieu Barbers Hill 17, DeLeon 8
	B	Gorman 18, Ben Bolt 6
	Six-Man	Marathon 62, May 16
1977	4A	Plano 13, Port Neches-Groves 10
	3A	Dickinson 40, Brownwood 28
	2A	Wylie 22, Bellville 14
	1A	East Bernard 27, Seagraves 10
	B	Wheeler 35, Lone Oak 13
	Six-Man	May 42, Marathon 35
1978	4A	Houston Stratford 29, Plano 13
	3A	Brownwood 21, Gainesville 12
	2A	Sealy 42, Wylie 20
	1A	China Spring 42, Lexington 3
	B	Union Hill 14, Wheeler 7
	Six-Man	Cherokee 29, Cotton Center 27
1979	4A	Temple 28, Houston Memorial 6
	3A	McKinney 20, Bay City 7
	2A	Van 25, McGregor 0
	1A	Hull-Daisetta 28, China Spring 18
	B	Wheeler 33, High Island 21
	Six-Man	Milford 53, Cotton Center 34
1980	5A	Odessa Permian 28, Port Arthur Jefferson 19
	4A	Hunstville 19, Paris 0
	3A	Pittsburg 13, Van Vleck 2
	2A	Pilot Point 0, Tidehaven 0
	1A	Valley View 7, Rankin 6
	Six-Man	Milford 9, Highland 16
1981	5A	Richardson Lake Highlands 19, Houston Yates 6
	4A	Brownwood 14, Fort Bend Willowridge 9
	3A	Cameron 26, Gilmer 3
	2A	Pilot Point 32, Garrison 0
	1A	Bremond 12, Wink 9
	Six-Man	Whitharral 56, Mullin 36
1982	5A	Beaumont West Brook 21, Hurst Bell 10
	4A	Fort Bend Willowridge 22, Coriscana 17
	3A	Refugio 22, Littlefield 21
	2A	Eastland 28, East Bernard 6
	1A	Union Hill 13, Roscoe 0
	Six-Man	Highland 60, Mullin 13
1983	5A	Converse Judson 25, Midland Lee 21
	4A	Bay City 30, Lubbock Estacado 0
	3A	Daingerfield 42, Sweeny 0
	2A	Boyd 16, Groveton 8
	1A	Knox City 27, Bremond 20
	Six-Man	Highland 67, Mozelle 50
1984	5A	Odessa Permian 21, Beaumont French 21
	4A	Denison 27, Tomball 13
	3A	Medina Valley 21, Daingerfield 13
	2A	Groveton 38, Panhandle 7
	1A	Munday 13, Union Hill 0
	Six-Man	Jayton 44, May 28

BIG TEX

at the Texas State Fair is really a **big boy**! *His Lee jeans are size 276 with a 23-foot waist, and his boots are size 70. Whewee!.... and he has never been recruited?*

FOOTBALL CHAMPIONSHIPS continued...

Year	League	Opponents/Score
1985	5A	Houston Yates 37, Odessa Permian 0
	4A	Sweetwater 17, Tomball 7
	3A	Daingerfield 47, Cuero 22
	2A	Electra 29, Groveton 13
	1A	Goldthwaite 27, Runge 7
	Six-Man	Jayton 64, Christoval 14
1986	5A	Plano 24, LaMarque 7
	4A	West Orange-Stark 21, McKinney 9
	3A	Jefferon 24, Cuero 0
	2A	Shiner 18, Mart 0
	1A	Burkeville 33, Throckmorton 7
	Six-Man	Fort Hancock 50, Christoval 36
1987	5A	Plano 28, Houston Stratford 21
	4A	West Orange-Stark 17, Rockwall 7
	3A	Cuero 14, McGregor 6
	2A	Lorena 8, Refugio 7
	1A	Wheeler 23, Bremond 21
	Six-Man	Lohn 58, Wellman 30
1988	5A	Converse Judson 1, Dallas Carter 0
		(Dallas Carter stripped of title)
	4A	Paris 31, West Orange-Stark 13
	3A	Southlake Carroll 42, Navasota 8
	2A	Corrigan-Camden 35, Quanah 14
	1A	White Deer 14, Flatonia 13
	Six-Man	Fort Hancock 76, Zephyr 30
1989	5A	Odessa Permian 28, Aldine 14
	4A	Tyler Chapel Hill 14, A&M Consolidated 0
	3A	Mexia 22, Vernon 21
	2A	Groveton 20, Lorena 13
	1A	Thorndale 42, Sudan 24
	Six-Man	Fort Hancock 48, Jayton 24
1990	5A Div I	Marshall 21, Converse Judson 19
	5A Div II	Aldine 27, Arlington Lamar 10
	4A	Wilmer-Hutchins 19, Austin Westlake 7
	3A	Vernon 41, Crockett 20
	2A	Groveton 25, DeLeon 19
	1A	Barlett 36, Munday 28
	Six-Man	Fort Hancock 66, Christoval 17
1991	5A Div I	Killeen 14, Fort Bend Dulles 10
	5A Div II	Odessa Permian 27, San Antonio Marshall 14
	4A	A&M Consolidated 35, Carthage 16
	3A	Groesbeck 7, Burnet 0
	2A	Schulenburg 21, Albany 0
	1A	Memphis 21, Oakwood 14
	Six-Man	Fort Hancock 64, Christoval 14
1992	5A Div I	Converse Judson 52, Euless Trinity 0
	5A Div II	Temple 38, Houston Yates 20
	4A	Waxahachie 28, A&M Consolidated 24
	3A	Southlake Carroll 48, Coldspring 0
	2A	Schulenburg 35, Goldthwaite 20
	1A	Barlett 33, Sudan 26
	Six-Man	Panther Creek 54, Fort Hancock 26

Year	League	Opponents/Score
1993	5A Div I	Converse Judson 36, Plano 13
	5A Div II	Lewisville 43, Aldine MacArthur 37
	4A	Stephenville 26, LaMarque 13
	3A	Southlake Carroll 14, Cuero 6
	2A	Goldthwaite 21, Omaha Pewitt 8
	1A	Sudan 54, Bremond 0
	Six-Man	Panther Creek 56, Dell City 28
1994	5A Div I	Plano 28, Katy 7
	5A Div II	Tyler John Tyler 35, Austin Westlake 24
	4A	Stephenville 32, LaMarque 17
	3A	Sealy 36, Atlanta 15
	2A	Goldthwaite 20, Schulenburg 16
	1A	Thorndale 36, Crawford 13
	Six-Man	Amherst 30, Milford 30
1995	5A Div I	Converse Judson 31, Odessa Permian 28
	5A Div II	San Antonio Roosevelt 17,
		Flower Mound Marcus 10
	4A	La Marque 31, Denison 8
	3A	Sealy 21, Commerce 20
	2A	Celina 32, Alto 28
	1A	Thorndale 14, Roscoe 7
	Six-Man	Amherst 72, Milford 48
1996	5A Div I	Lewisville 58, Converse Judson 34
	5A Div II	Austin Westlake 55, Abilene Cooper 15
	4A Div I	Grapevine 34, Hays Consolidated 19
	4A Div II	LaMarque 34, Denison 3
	3A	Sealy 36, Tatum 27
	2A	Iraan 14, Groveton 7
	1A	Windthorst 41, Bedford 12
	Six-Man	Gordon 51, Whitharral 50
1997	5A Div I	Katy 24, Longview 3
	5A Div II	Lewisville Marcus 59, Alief Hastings 20
	4A Div I	Texas City 37, Corsicana 34
	4A Div II	La Marque 17, Denison 0
	3A	Sealy 28, Commerce 21
	2A	Stanton 33, Rogers 7
	1A	Granger 40, Wheeler 0
	Six-Man	Gail Borden County 48,
		Valera Panther Creek 16
1998	5A Div I	Duncanville 24, Converse Judson 21
	5A Div II	Midland Lee 54, San Antonio MacArthur 0
	4A Div I	Grapevine 22, Bay City 0
	4A Div II	Stephenville 34, La Marque 7
	3A Div I	Aledo 14, Cuero 7
	3A Div II	Newton 21, Daingerfield 0
	2A Div I	Omaha Pewitt 28, Brookshire Royal 26
	2A Div II	Celina 21, Elysian Fields 0
	1A - 11-Man	Teneha 20, Wheeler 13
	1A - Six-Man	Trinidad 62, Gail Borden 16

> *"Football is an incredible game. Sometimes it's so incredible, it's unbelievable."*
>
> Tom Landry,
> *Former Head Coach of the Dallas Cowboys*

Year	League	Opponents/Score
1999	5A Div I	Midland Lee 42, Houston Eisenhower 21
	5A Div II	Garland 37, Katy 25
	4A Div I	Texas City 27, Hereford 14
	4A Div II	Stephenville 28, Port Neches-Groves 18
	3A Div I	Texarkana Liberty-Eylau 49, Mathis 6
	3A Div II	Commerce 17, Sealy 10
	2A Div I	Mart 40, Boyd 7
	2A Div II	Celina 38, Elysian Fields 7
	1A - 11-Man	Bartlett 35, Aspermont 6
	1A - Six-Man	Gordon 54, Groom 34
2000	5A Div I	Midland Lee 33, Austin Westlake 21
	5A Div II	Katy 35, Tyler 20
	4A Div I	Bay City 24, Denton Ryan 2
	4A Div II	Ennis 38, West Orange Stark 24
	3A Div I	Gatesville 14, Abilene Wylie 10
	3A Div II	La Grange 20, Forney 17
	2A Div I	Sonora 27, Blanco 24
	2A Div II	Celina 21, Mart 17
	1A - 11-Man	Stratford 49, Burkeville 14
	1A - Six-Man	Valera Panther Creek 42, Roscoe Highland 36
2001	5A Div I	Mesquite 14, San Antonio Taft 13
	5A Div II	Lufkin 38, Austin Westlake 24
	4A Div I	Denton Ryan 42, Smithson Valley 35 OT
	4A Div II	Ennis 22, Bay City 0
	3A Div I	Everman 25, Sinton 14
	3A Div II	Commerce 14, La Grange 11
	2A Div I	Blanco 16, Van Alstyne 0
	2A Div II	Celina 41, Garrison 35
	1A - 11-Man	Burkeville 27 Celeste 8
	1A - Six-Man	Whitharral 27, Richland Springs 21
2002	5A Div I	Converse Judson 33, Midland 32
	5A Div II	Southlake Carroll 45, Smithson Valley 14
	4A Div I	Texarkana Texas 42, New Braunfels 11
	4A Div II	Denton Ryan 38, Brenham 8
	3A Div I	Everman 35, Burnet 14
	3ADiv II	Bandera 27, Greenwood 24 (2OT)
	2A Div I	Corrigan-Camden 33, Bangs 14
	2A Div II	Rosebud-Lott 34, Cisco 0
	1A - 11-Man	Petrolia 39, Celeste 18
	1A - Six-Man	Calvert 51, Sanderson 46
2003	5A Div I	Galena Park North Shore 23, Conroe The Woodlands 7
	5A Div II	Katy 16, Southlake Carroll 15
	4A Div I	North Crowley 20, Bay City 6
	4A Div II	La Marque 43, Denton Ryan 35 (3 OT)
	3A Div I	Gainesville 35, Burnet 24
	3A Div II	Atlanta 34, Marlin 0
	2A Div I	San Augustine 28, Tuscola Jim Ned 7
	2A Div II	Garrison 27, Bangs 0
	1A - 11-Man	Windthorst 28, Shiner 27
	1A - Six-Man	Strawn 67, Ft. Davis 62

Year	League	Opponents/Score
2004	5A Div I	Tyler Lee 28, Westfield 21
	5A Div II	Southlake Carroll 27, Smithson Valley 24
	4A Div I	Ennis 23, Marshall 21
	4A Div II	Kilgore 33, Lincoln 27
	3A Div I	Abilene Wylie 17, Cuero 14
	3A Div II	Gilmer 49, Jasper 47
	2A Div I	Boyd 17, Newton 14
	2A Div II	Crawford 28, Troup 14
	1A - 11-Man	Shiner 33, Stratford 19
	1A - Six-Man	Richland Springs 58, Turkey Valley 38

Source: University Interscholastic League Website

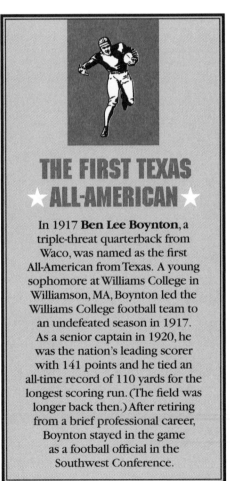

THE FIRST TEXAS
★ ALL-AMERICAN ★

In 1917 **Ben Lee Boynton**, a triple-threat quarterback from Waco, was named as the first All-American from Texas. A young sophomore at Williams College in Williamson, MA, Boynton led the Williams College football team to an undefeated season in 1917. As a senior captain in 1920, he was the nation's leading scorer with 141 points and he tied an all-time record of 110 yards for the longest scoring run. (The field was longer back then.) After retiring from a brief professional career, Boynton stayed in the game as a football official in the Southwest Conference.

Interesting and Unique High School Mascots

City or Town	Mascot
Aubrey	Chaparrals
Austin - Living Water Academy	Doves
Baytown - Lee	Ganders
Big Spring	Steers
Booker	Kiowas
Boys Ranch	Roughriders
Cameron - Yoe	Yoemen
Comanche	Indians
Crane	Cranes
Dallas - The Hockaday School	Daisies
East Bernard	Brahmas
El Campo	Ricebirds
Farmersville	Fightin' Farmers
Floydada	Whirlwinds
Fredericksburg	Battlin' Billies
Freeport - Brazosport	Exporters
Galveston - Ball	Tors
Grapeland	Sandies
Groesbeck	Goats
Houston - Morris Academy	Praying Hands
Hutto	Hippos
Itasca	Wampus Cats
Knippa	Rockcrushers
Lewisville	Farmers
Mason	Punchers
Mesquite	Skeeters
Munday	Moguls
Nazareth	Swifts
Pampa	Harvesters
Port Lavaca - Calhoun	Sandcrabs
Robstown	Cotton Pickers
Rockspring	Angores
Roscoe	Plowboys
Rotan	Yellow Hammers
St. Joseph Academy	Bloodhounds
San Antonio - Central Catholic	Buttons
Somerville	Yeguas
Springtown	Porcupines
Texas City	Stingarees
Van	Vandals
White Deer	Bucks

TEXAS SPORTS
Did You Know?

W. M. "Matty" Bell

is the only person to enjoy coaching success with three Southwest Conference football teams? Bell first coached Texas Christian University in 1923, where Bell's Horned Frogs went 33-17-5. In 1929, Bell left to replace Dana Bible at Texas A&M and went 24-21-3. In 1935, Bell changed schools again to become head coach at Southern Methodist University. It was a pretty good move for Bell because the Mustangs went 12-0 and won the national championship!

How many sweaters do you need?

By the time that 6'5" 210 pound **Bill "Jitterbug" Henderson** graduated from Texas A&M, he had earned more letters than any other athlete in Southwest Conference history. In a varsity career that spanned from 1940-1942, Henderson won three letters in football, basketball, and track, and one in swimming and baseball. He was the first Aggie to earn four letters in one scholastic year (1940-41) when he lettered **in football, basketball, baseball, and track.**

Hand Signs-A Texas College Tradition

The first day of orientation at all Texas colleges begins the same way—learning their school's hand sign. From "hook 'em horns" to "pony ears," hand signs are deeply ingrained in the hearts of all Texas collegians. Probably no other tradition is as practiced in Texas colleges as that of the hand sign. During the reign of the Southwest Conference, all Texas colleges were identified by a hand held high representing their mascot.

It's hard to remember a time when hand signs were not part of every Texas college football game. Hand signs, like other college traditions, have evolved over time. This uniquely Texas tradition reportedly started with an Aggie named Pinky Downs. Downs graduated from Texas A&M in 1906 and was an avid supporter of his alma mater. Always attending games and pep rallies, Downs was at the 1930 match up between his beloved Aggies and the TCU Horned Frogs. During a yell practice before the game, Downs exclaimed, "What are we going to do to those Horned Frogs." "Gig'em, Aggies," he responded. Downs made a fist with his thumb extended straight up and the first hand sign of the Southwest Conference was born.

Other colleges, feeling left out of the craze, decided to try their hand at a sign. In 1955, a University of Texas cheerleader named Harley Clark created a sign to rival that of the Aggies. Inspired by their mascot, Clark held up his right hand pointing his index and little finger up while his thumb and other fingers were tucked away. Quickly the Longhorn hand sign swept the stadium and fans of all ages were rallying the team. In the late 1950s, the SMU Mustangs adopted the "pony ears" as their official hand sign. The cheering crowds raised their index and middle fingers, slightly curved, representing the ears of their mighty Mustangs. Eventually Baylor followed suit in 1960 when cheerleader Bobby Schrade developed the "bear claw," five fingers curved as if to pounce on the opponent. The University of Houston Cougars developed the "cougar claw," a sign resembling that of the UT Longhorn but with the middle finger added to represent a claw. The Red Raiders of Texas Tech chose thumb and index finger pistols to rally their team. The Horned Frogs of TCU had a bit of a challenge coming up with something to symbolize their beloved mascot. After several tries, TCU cheerleaders decided that a bent index and middle finger along with a bent thumb would represent the menacing horned frog.

Through the years, many traditions have come and gone, the Southwest Conference has been dissolved, and the schools of Texas are divided into other divisions. But the rivalry among Texas colleges remains strong as do the unique hand signs which represent school spirit and pride.

THE EIGHTH WONDER OF THE WORLD

When it opened to the public on April 12, 1965, Houston's Astrodome, the first completely covered stadium in history, was hailed as the **"Eighth Wonder of the World."** The brainchild of the controversial former Houston mayor Roy Mark Hofheinz, the idea for the indoor stadium evolved after the city received the promise of a major league sports franchise if it would provide a suitable playing field and public facilities. Hofheinz formedthe Houston Sports Association and, by successfully floating several local bond issues, was able to raise the $35 million dollar construction tab.

Upon completion, the Astrodome occupied nearly 10 acres, measured 710 feet in diameter, and could seat 42,217 spectators. The ceiling soared nearly 210 feet in the air, enough height to accommodate an 18-story building. The playing field was placed 25 feet below street level and the foul lines measured 340 feet. Center field had a depth of 406 feet. The central air conditioning system circulated 2.5 million cubic feet of air per minute and the electricity required to light the field was equal to that used by a town of 9,000 people. The scoreboard alone cost two million dollars. Five restaurants offered fare to throngs of sports fans.

The Colt .45s, Houston's major league baseball team, after playing three years at a neighboring facility, changed its name to the Houston Astros when the move to the Astrodome was made. The first baseball game at the Dome was played on April 9, 1965, between the Astros and the New York Yankees where Mickey Mantle hit the first homerun at the stadium. Three weeks later, legendary sports announcer Lindsey Nelson broadcast an Astros-Mets game from a gondola suspended 208 feet above second base.

The Houston Oilers and the University of Houston both moved into the Astrodome in 1965 and, although modifications were required to configure the playing field for football, both football and baseball shared the facility for the next several years. The Astrodome was further modified at the end of the first season when the sunlight streaming through the dome's roof had to be minimized because of complaints from the players about the glare. Although the diminished sunlight was ideal for the players, the grass in the Astrodome failed to grow. The natural grass covering the playing field was replaced by artificial grass, appropriately named "Astroturf."

The Guide to Texas Golf

Texas has produced some of the greatest golfers of all time. This list, led by Ben Hogan, includes the likes of Lee Trevino, Ben Crenshaw, and Byron Nelson, but most Texas golfers do not have the swing of Hogan or possess the witty personality of Trevino. For the rest of us, there is a brand new book that is about to be published. We thought you might like a preview…

Chapter 1 - How to Properly Line Up Your Fourth Putt

Chapter 2 - How to Hit a Nike Out of the Rough When You Hit a Titleist from the Tee

Chapter 3 - How to Avoid the Water When You Lie 6 in a Bunker

Chapter 4 - How to Get More Distance Off a Shank

Chapter 5 - When to Give Your Opponent the Finger (Without Him Knowing It)

Chapter 6 - Using Your Shadow on the Greens to Maximize Earnings

Chapter 7 - Crying, Cussing, and Complaining: The 3 Cs and How They Can Get More Strokes at the Turn

Chapter 8 - Proper Excuses for Drinking Beers Before 10 a.m.

Chapter 9 - How to Rationalize a 6 Hour Round

Chapter 10 - How to Find The Ball That Everyone Else Saw Go in the Water

Chapter 11 - Yippee for the Yips!

Chapter 12 - How to Properly Let a Foursome Play Through Your Twosome

Chapter 13 - How to Relax When You Are Hitting Three Off the Tee

Chapter 14 - When to Suggest Major Swing Corrections to Your Opponent

Chapter 15 - God and the Meaning of the Birdie-to-Bogey Three Putt

Chapter 16 - The Foot Wedge: Ten Proven Methods to Shave Strokes and Not Get Caught

Several notable events occurred at the Astrodome during its lifetime. Willie Mayes hit his 500th homerun there on September 13, 1965, the facility hosted two All-Star games, in 1968 and 1986, and favorite son Nolan Ryan pitched his fifth no-hitter there on September 26, 1981.

In 1989, the Astrodome underwent major renovations, bringing it closely to its present-day configuration. During the mid-1990s, both the Oilers and the Astros petitioned for new facilities, and after the 1996 football season, when negotiations with the Oilers failed, the team moved to Nashville and changed its name to the Tennessee Titans. A new stadium, Minute Maid Park, was built in downtown Houston for the Astros, who played their last game in the Astrodome on October 9, 1999.★

The world's littlest skyscraper is found at 701 LaSalle in Wichita Falls. Planned in the early 20th century to be 120 feet tall, it was built in inches—not feet—only 4 stories tall and 1 room wide. The scheme bilked investors out of hundreds of thousands of dollars.

BY THE NUMBERS

SAMMY BAUGH *The Great Texas Quarterback*

While his numbers might not awe a coach today, the passing numbers that Sammy Baugh put up in the '30s and '40s were staggering. Baugh played during a time when most teams would run three or four times for everytime they passed. *Baugh changed all that!*

Year	Team	Games	Completions	Attempts	Comp.%	Yards	TDs	Int.
1937	Washington	11	81	171	47.4%	1,127	8	14
1938	Washington	9	63	128	49.2%	853	5	11
1939	Washington	9	53	96	55.2%	518	6	9
1940	Washington	11	11	177	6.2%	1,367	12	10
1941	Washington	11	106	193	54.9%	1,236	10	19
1942	Washington	11	132	225	58.7%	1,524	16	11
1943	Washington	10	133	239	55.6%	1,754	23	19
1944	Washington	8	82	146	56.2%	849	4	8
1945	Washington	8	128	182	70.3%	1,669	11	4
1946	Washington	11	87	161	54.0%	1,163	8	17
1947	Washington	12	210	354	59.3%	2,938	25	15
1948	Washington	12	185	315	58.7%	2,599	22	23
1949	Washington	12	145	255	56.9%	1,903	18	14
1950	Washington	11	90	166	54.2%	1,130	10	11
1951	Washington	12	67	154	43.5%	1,104	7	17
1952	Washington	7	20	33	60.6%	152	2	1
Totals		**165**	**1,593**	**2,995**	**53.2%**	**21,886**	**187**	**203**

HEISMAN TROPHY WINNERS

Since 1935, the coveted Heisman Trophy has been awarded to the most outstanding college football player in the country. In the Trophy's seventy-one year history, six athletes hailing from Texas colleges have been immortalized with the most prestigious award in college football.

Year	Name	School	Position
1938	Davey O'Brien	TCU	QB
1948	Doak Walker	SMU	RB
1957	John David Crow	Texas A&M	RB
1977	Earl Campbell	Texas	RB
1989	Andre Ware	Houston	QB
1998	Ricky Williams	Texas	RB

Source: www.heisman.com

The Fajita Phenomenon

It is hard to remember a time when a sizzling plate of fajitas served from a cast iron skillet was not commonplace in restaurants across America.

Contrary to the popular belief of anyone under twenty, fajitas have not always been on the menu. Fajitas, like most Tex-Mex food, can be traced back to West Texas of the early 1900s. Then, Hispanic ranch hands were often given the unwanted cuts of beef as part of their pay. The innovative workers would pound the tough meat to tenderize it, marinate it in lemon juice, and grill it. After grilling, they would combine the flavorful meat with salsa and condiments on flour tortillas. So, we have a few of the frugal ranchers of the dusty plains of West Texas to thank for our passion for fajitas.

Fajitas were a staple in most Mexican-American homes throughout the early 1900s, but they did not hit mainstream America until the late 1960s. In 1969, at an outdoor festival in Kyle, Texas, the first commercial sale of a fajita was made by Sonny Falcon, also known as the Fajita King. Falcon grilled a tender cut of meat, chopped it, and served it in flour tortillas. Shortly after this, the Round-Up Restaurant in Phar, Texas, became the first restaurant to serve fajitas, originating the concept of the sizzling platter of meat and condiments. Around the same time, Ninfa's, on Navigation in Houston, coined the name "fajita" becoming the first restaurant to refer to the new Tex-Mex wonder. Even though the word "fajita" did not appear in print until 1975, it was a term used by butchers in the 1940s, referring to the diaphragm muscle of a steer, which resembles a belt, or *faja* in Spanish.

The fajita phenomenon spread quickly across the country, and by the early 1980s, fajitas were the Tex-Mex rage. In 1984, the craze had so affected the way Americans ate that Texas A&M professor Homero Recio obtained a fellowship to study the fajita. Recio found that the price of beef in 1976 was 49 cents per pound, compared to $2.79 in 1985, a figure he attributed to the massive consumption of fajita meat. Today fajitas can be found on almost every corner, in every shape and size, and filled with practically anything. Fajitas are one of the most popular dishes at Tex-Mex restaurants and are often viewed as a healthy alternative to the heavy "mixed plates" on the menu. Shrimp and chicken fajitas may be a far cry from the tough beef filled tortillas eaten by hungry West Texas ranch hands, but they would surely approve.

Tex-Mex Recipes

Texas Black-Eyed Pea Dip

Ingredients:
¼ cup bell pepper, chopped
7 jalapeño peppers, chopped
2 stalks celery, chopped
1 large onion, chopped
1 teaspoon black pepper
2 tablespoons Tabasco
½ cup ketchup
1 teaspoon salt
3 cubes chicken bouillon
¼ teaspoon nutmeg
¼ teaspoon cumin
2 cans black-eyed peas
1 can tomatoes
1 teaspoon garlic
½ cup bacon drippings
3 tablespoons flour

Combine peppers, celery, and onion. Place in a stockpot with the next seven ingredients and simmer. Add black-eyed peas, tomatoes, and garlic and cook another thirty minutes. In a separate bowl, blend together bacon drippings and flour. Slowly stir mixture into heated dip. Cook until thoroughly heated. Serve hot with corn chips.

Pico de Gallo

Ingredients:
2 garlic cloves, minced
½ teaspoon salt
1 teaspoon vinegar
1 teaspoon olive oil
6 roasted Anaheim chilies,
    chopped
6 ripe tomatoes, chopped
1 large onion, chopped
½ teaspoon salt
1 teaspoon course black pepper

Mix together the garlic, salt, vinegar, and oil.
Add the remaining ingredients, mix, and chill before serving.

Guacamole

Ingredients:
4 large avocados (pits removed), mashed
4 large tomatoes, diced
½ cup roasted Anaheim chilies, chopped
1½ teaspoon garlic salt
¼ cup chopped white onion

Combine ingredients in a large bowl, mixing well.
Cover, chill, and serve.

Hill Country Black Bean Salsa

Ingredients:
1 15-ounce can black beans,
   rinsed and drained
1 11-ounce can whole kernel
   corn, drained
4 large tomatoes, chopped
1 bell pepper, chopped
1 bunch green onions,
   chopped

2 garlic cloves, chopped
1 large jalapeño pepper,
   chopped
⅓ cup fresh cilantro,
   chopped
¼ cup lime juice
2 tablespoons olive oil
1 teaspoon salt
2 teaspoons ground cumin

Combine ingredients in a large bowl, mixing well.
Cover, chill, and serve.

Simple Salsa

Ingredients:
1 28-ounce can diced
   tomatoes with garlic
1 small red onion, chopped
1 large jalapeño pepper,
   chopped
1 cup fresh cilantro,
   chopped

2 tablespoons lemon juice
2 tablespoons lime juice
1 teaspoon ground cumin
1 teaspoon chili powder
¼ teaspoon salt
1 teaspoon sugar

Combine ingredients in a large bowl, mix, chill, and serve.

Sangria

Ingredients:

1 bottle burgundy wine
1 cup brandy
¾ cup orange juice

¾ cup grapefruit juice
¾ cup cranberry juice
Juice from 5 limes

Mix, chill, enjoy!

Classic Margarita

Ingredients:

2 ounces Cuervo 1800
½ ounce Cuervo White
1¼ ounce Rose's Lime Juice

½ ounce Bols Triple Sec
Fresh limes
Salt (optional)

Place ingredients and two fresh lime wedges in a shaker. Shake twice. Serve over ice in a salt-rimmed margarita glass. Garnish with a lime wedge.

A Texas Classic... Chicken Fried Steak

Many Texans agree that along with chili and barbecue, chicken fried steak stands at the top of the list of all-time popular foods in the Lone Star State. Recipes for this wonderful dish are legion, but here is a simple, yet slightly different, one that you might like to try.

1 egg, beaten

Milk

1 cup all-purpose flour

Salt and black pepper to taste

1 large round steak that has been "tenderized" by the butcher

Olive oil

Worcestershire sauce

Combine the egg with ¼ cup plus 2 tablespoons of milk. Combine the flour, salt, and black pepper. Cut the round steak into several pieces. Moisten the meat with the milk-egg mixture, then drag the pieces through the flour mixture, being sure that coverage is complete. Save the seasoned flour.

On medium-high heat, warm about ¼ inch of olive oil in a large, cast-iron skillet. When the oil is hot, reduce the heat and add the steak pieces. Cook for about five minutes, or until the meat is done. Drain the steak on paper towels.

Keep about three tablespoons of oil and the dregs of the cooked meat in the skillet. Return heat to medium. When oil is hot again, add four tablespoons of the seasoned flour and stir rapidly until the flour browns. Mix together ¾ cup of milk, ¾ cup of water, and two tablespoons of Worcestershire sauce. Add the combination to the skillet. Stir continuously until all lumps disappear. Lower the heat and simmer the gravy until desired thickness is reached.

Enjoy!

Whew, That's Hot!!!!!

There's nothing better than a hot pepper to wake you up or clear your head. For years, Texans have been using peppers in their cooking to heat things up. And let's face it—Tex-Mex wouldn't be Tex-Mex without the pepper.

The spiciness, or heat, from the pepper comes from a substance called capsaicin. In 1912, Wilbur Scoville decided to measure the amount of capsaicin in each pepper, giving us an idea of how hot different peppers actually were. The Scoville test measures the capsaicin in multiples of 100 units. The habañero pepper with 300,000 or more units is the hottest pepper of them all, while the sweet bell pepper has a rating of zero. At right is a list of some of the most popular peppers and their heat range in Scoville units.

Pepper	Heat Range
Sweet Bell	0
Pimento	0
Cherry	0–500
Pepperoncini	100-500
El-Paso	500-700
Santa Fe Grande	500-700
Coronado	700-1,000
Espanola	1,000-2,000
Poblano	1,000-2,000
Ancho	1,000-2,000
Anaheim	500-2,500
NuMex Big Jim	500-2,500
Jalapeño	2,500-8,000
Chipolte	5,000-8,000
Hot Wax	5,000-10,000
Hidalgo	6,000-17,000
Serrano	8,000-22,000
Tabasco	30,000-50,000
Cayenne	30,000-50,000
Thai	50,000-100,000
Bahamian	95,000-110,000
Carolina Cayenne	100,000-125,000
Jamaican Hot	100,000-200,000
Habañero	100,000-325,000
Scotch Bonnet	150,000-325,000
Red Savina Habañero	350,000-577,000
Pure Capsaicin	15 -16,000,000

Mine's Better. No, Mine's Better!

The Great Texas Chili Battle

Most culinary experts agree that Texas was the birthplace of chili. Even though hundreds of articles and stories were written by early visitors to Texas, no written record refers to chili before the publication in 1882 of *Gould's Guide to San Antonio,* so a pretty good case can be made for the "invention" of chili occurring around that time. Regardless of how long it has been around, chili, which native Texan Francis X. Tolbert once called "a haunting, mystic thing," has become one of America's most popular foods.

Originally, Texas chili consisted simply of beef, chile peppers, garlic, salt, oregano, and cumin, but over the years Texans have added such "foreign" ingredients as beans, tomatoes, beer, onions, broth, spaghetti, bell peppers, and even tequila. Today, the varieties of chili are as numerous as waves in the ocean, and residents of various sections of the nation staunchly defend their chili as being the absolute best. Probably the most noted difference among types of chili is whether or not the recipe calls for beans. Many chili gurus have defined a "bean line" running north and south across the nation that places most of Texas west of the imaginary boundary. People living west of the line, according to these authorities, prefer their chili without beans; those in the east like their chili with beans.

Here are several recipes for chili that clearly demonstrate the diversity of ingredients that can be used to make each bowl distinctive. In the final analysis, however, only one constant exists about chili…and that is the inconsistency of its contents. Indeed, as native Texan chili aficionado, writer, poet, and musician W. C. Jameson has declared, "The beauty of a recipe is that it is more of a guideline and less an absolute set of rules. Quantities can be altered as a result of preference. Substitutions can be, and often are, made."

★ All chili recipes in this article came from *The Ultimate Chili Cookbook,* by W. C. Jameson, published in 1999 by the Republic of Texas Press. Used with permission.

Blanco County Chili

2 tablespoons cooking oil	4 pounds beef, coarsely ground
1 large onion, chopped	2 garlic cloves, minced
6 to 8 tablespoons chili powder	1 teaspoon oregano
1 teaspoon cumin	1 16-ounce can tomatoes
2 cups water	Salt to taste

In a large cooking pot, heat oil and brown beef. Add onion and garlic and sauté. Add the rest of the ingredients, bring to a boil, cover, lower heat, and simmer for at least one hour, stirring and tasting occasionally.

Bunkhouse Chili

2 tablespoons bacon grease	1 teaspoon oregano
2 pounds coarsely ground chuck	1 teaspoon cayenne pepper
1 large onion, chopped	Salt and black pepper to taste
1 8-ounce can tomato sauce	1 teaspoon Tabasco sauce
2 teaspoons garlic powder	1 bottle dark Mexican beer
5 tablespoons chili powder	2 fresh jalapeño chili
1 tablespoon cumin	peppers, minced

In a cooking pot, heat bacon grease and brown the meat. Add onion and sauté. Add tomato sauce and garlic powder, bring to boil, reduce heat, and simmer for one-half hour. Add chili powder, cumin, oregano, cayenne pepper, salt, black pepper, Tabasco sauce, and beer. Stir and continue to simmer for another hour. Fifteen minutes before serving, stir in the minced jalapeño peppers. Serve with a side of pinto beans and fresh corn bread.

A perennial favorite among Texans.

Dallas County Jailhouse Chili

2 cups beef suet
2 pounds coarsely ground beef
3 garlic cloves, minced
1 tablespoon paprika
3 tablespoons chili powder
1 tablespoon cumin

1 tablespoon salt
1 teaspoon white pepper
1 sweet chili pod, chopped fine
3 cups water

Fry suet in cast-iron skillet. Add meat, garlic and remaining seasonings. Cover and simmer for four hours, stirring occasionally. Add water as needed and cook for another hour until slightly thickened.

A favorite of Southwest Texas outdoorsmen (and outdoorswomen).

TEXAS DEER CAMP CHILI

4 tablespoons olive oil
2 onions, chopped
5 garlic cloves, minced
3 ancho chile peppers, stemmed, seeded, and chopped
2 pounds venison, cubed
1 tablespoon coarse-ground red pepper

4 tomatoes, chopped
1 teaspoon cumin
2 cans beef or chicken broth
Salt and black pepper to taste

In a large cast-iron skillet, heat olive oil, add onions, garlic, and chile peppers, and sauté. Add venison and cook until meat has browned. Add red pepper, tomatoes, cumin, and broth. Stir and simmer for two hours. During the simmering time, stir the mix and adjust for taste. Serve with cheese and jalapeño quesadillas.

For those who like beans in their chili.

Black Bean Chili

2 tablespoons olive oil	2 to 3 cups chicken broth
1 large onion, chopped	Salt and black pepper to taste
2 garlic cloves, minced	1 tablespoon cumin
2 15-ounce cans black beans	Cooked rice
(frijoles negros)	Green onions, chopped

Heat oil in cooking pot, add onion and garlic, and sauté. Add beans, chicken broth, salt, and pepper; bring to boil, reduce heat, and let simmer for one-half hour. Add cumin, stir, and cook for additional ten minutes. Serve over rice and top with chopped green onions.

PEPPER FACT

Ever wonder why some people can eat the spiciest peppers without their eyes watering, their nose running, or wincing from pain? Capsaicin causes a long lasting selective desensitization to pain and discomfort brought on by consuming the substance. The more capsaicin you digest, the more tolerance you have, allowing those who choose to partake to go spicier and spicier. In fact, peppers can even be addictive. The spiciness of the peppers causes the nervous system to release endorphins, bringing about a natural high. For this reason eating peppers high in capsaicin often leaves lovers of peppers longing for more.

For years, there's been controversy over the correct spelling of the word, chili. Is it "chili" or "chile?" Actually, either spelling is legitimate, but not for the same item. "Chili" is correct when speaking of the dish; chile is proper when referring to any of a large variety of green or red peppers of the *Capsicum* genus.

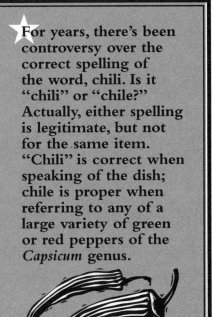

Tex-Mex Dictionary

Ancho Chili (AHN-choh) – Primarily used in making sauces, this slightly sweet, fruity chili pepper is the dried version of the popular poblano chili.

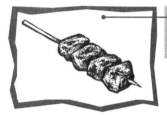

Anticuchos (an-tee-COOCH-os) – "Tex-Mex shish-ka-bob" made with sirloin chunks, marinated in a jalapeño and tomato mixture and grilled.

Arroz (AH-roz) – Rice.

Barbacoa (bar-ba-KO-uh) – Mexican pot roast usually served "taco style."

Bienvenidos (bee-in-vin-knee-THOSE) – Welcome, hello, howdy, and come on in…

Bolillo (bo-EE-yo) – Mexican rolls about 6 inches long.

Borracho (bo-ROTCH-o) – Usually refers to pinto beans simmered in beer for hours, similar to a soup.

Hon, did you know…?

The mesquite tree that dots South Texas actually provided a beverage for desperate early settlers. They reportedly dried and roasted the tree's beans to make a bitter sort of coffee.

Bunuelos (bun-WAY-los) – A fried, tortilla-like holiday desert, often sprinkled with cinnamon and sugar and sometimes served with ice cream.

Burrito (bur-EE-toe) – A flour tortilla filled with a combination of meat and beans. This Tex-Mex favorite is often topped with salsa, lettuce, cheese, or guacamole.

Carne (CAR-nay) – Beef.

Carne Guisada (CAR-nay GEE-sah-dah) – Meat stewed with onions and tomatoes, usually served over rice.

Chorizo (CHORE-ee-so) – Mexican sausage often made with pork and seasonings.

Chimichangas (chim-me-CHAN-gaz) – Deep fried burritos filled with a variety of ingredients.

Cilantro (SEE-lan-trow) – A slightly bitter seasoning used almost exclusively in Tex-Mex cooking.

Cocina (ko-SEE-na) – Kitchen.

Comino (KO-me-know) – Also known as cumin, a Tex-Mex seasoning.

Fajita (fah-HEE-ta) – Marinated and grilled flank steak or sometimes chicken breast, wrapped in a flour tortilla along with cheese, beans, guacamole, or pico de gallo.

Flan (flan) – A Mexican desert similar to custard.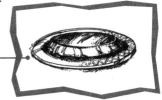

Flauta (FLOU-ta) – A corn tortilla stuffed with beef or chicken and then deep fried.

Frijoles (FREE-hole-ees) – Pinto beans, often refried.

Guacamole (GWOK-uh-mole-ee) – A dip made from avocados, lemon juice, diced onion, tomatoes, and cilantro.

Huevos (WAY-vose) – Eggs.

Jalapeño (hall-a-PEN-yo) – The most frequently used pepper in Tex-Mex cooking.

Margarita (mar-gur-EE-tuh) – A wonderful frozen concoction consisting of lemon or lime juice, tequila, and fruit liqueur.

Masa (MAH-sah) – Corn flour dough used to make tortillas.

Migas (me-GUZ) – Scrambled eggs mixed with chorizo or chicken, with corn tortillas.

Pan Dulce (pon-DUEL-say) – A dome-shaped Mexican sweet roll.

Pico De Gallo (PEEK-o DAY GUY-yo) – An uncooked salsa often used for dipping or as a topping.

Pollo (PO-yo) – Chicken.

Puerco (PWER-co) – Pork.

Queso (kay-SO) – Cheese, usually a variety of Cheddar, used in Tex-Mex cooking.

Ranchero (ran-CHAIR-o) – Describes a cooked salsa or something cooked with a combination of tomatoes, peppers, garlic, and onions.

Salsa (SAL-sa) – A broad term used to describe a variety of dips. If the salsa is uncooked it is pico de gallo. If it is processed into a purèe, it is chile, and if cooked and bottled, it is picantè.

Serrano Chile (sey-RRA-noh) – A small but fiery pepper which turns from red to yellow as it matures. It is usually used to make pico de gallo.

Taco (tah-KOH) – A soft or fried corn tortilla filled with a variety of ingredients, folded over and eaten sandwich style.

Tamale (tuh-MAL-ee) – Often eaten at Christmas and New Year, tamales consist of corn masa dough surrounding shredded pork. Tamales are wrapped in corn husks and steamed to cook. ————

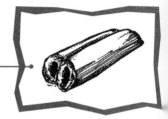

Tex-Mex – A wonderful blending of southern Texas and northern Mexico culture.

Tomatillo (TOM-a-tea-yo) – This small green Mexican fruit in the tomato family is generally used to make verde (green) sauces.

Torta (TORE-tah) – A Mexican sandwich made on a white or wheat roll.

Tortilla (tore-TEE-yu) – Thin bread made of corn or wheat flour and used to wrap, dip, or be layered.

Tostada (toast-AAH-tha) – Literally translated meaning "toasted chip," actually similar to nachos.

A Pepper A Day...

*T*hrough the years, pepper lovers have discounted the negative effects and touted the benefits of the pepper. Contrary to popular belief, research has shown that peppers do not cause ulcers. By studying cultures that use peppers extensively in cooking, such as in Brazil and Thailand and comparing them with those that don't, it has been shown that there is not an increased incidence of stomach ulcers. Better yet, the capsaicin in peppers has been found to work as an anticoagulant, thus possibly preventing heart attacks or strokes caused by blood clots. Peppers have also been found to be high in vitamin C, which is very effective in preventing cancer. Also, because capsaicin has been found to lower pain sensitivity, it is often applied as a counter-irritant in the treatment of arthritis.

Salsa Fights Salmonella!

CILANTRO
Coriandrum sativum

Salmonella, the ugly food-borne bacteria that causes sickness and sometimes even death, may have met its match in salsa. Scientists have discovered that dodecenal, a chemical found in fresh cilantro leaves, which are often used in making salsa, is effective in killing the bacterial cells in salmonella. Dodecenal has been shown to be twice as potent as the commonly used medicinal antibiotic at killing salmonella. This discovery could lead to dodecenal being used as a tasteless food additive to prevent food-borne illness or possibly as an agent in disinfectants. It also may help explain why the salmonella rate is low in countries such as Mexico that use salsa regularly. The lesson learned from this study is *to stay healthy, eat more salsa!*

Source: *Journal of Agriculture and Food Chemistry,* May 26, 2004

U.S. Measurement Equivalents

A few grains/pinch/ dash, etc. (dry)	= Less than ⅛ tsp.	⅛ cup	= 2 tablespoons
A dash (liquid)	= A few drops	¼ cup	= 4 tablespoons
3 teaspoons	= 1 tablespoon	¼ cup	= 2 fluid ounces
½ tablespoon	= 1½ teaspoons	⅓ cup	= 5 tablespoons
1 tablespoon	= 3 teaspoons	½ cup	= 8 tablespoons
2 tablespoons	= 1 fluid ounce	1 cup	= 16 tablespoons
4 tablespoons	= ¼ cup	1 cup	= 8 fluid ounces
5⅓ tablespoons	= ⅓ cup	1 cup	= ½ pint
8 tablespoons	= ½ cup	2 cups	= 1 pint
8 tablespoons	= 4 fluid ounces	2 pints	= 1 quart
10⅔ tablespoons	= ⅔ cup	8 quarts (dry)	= 1 peck
12 tablespoons	= ¾ cup	4 pecks (dry)	= 1 bushel
16 tablespoons	= 1 cup	1 kilogram	= approximately 2 pounds
16 tablespoons	= 8 fluid ounces	1 liter	= approximately 4 cups or 1 quart

LONE STAR
Tex-Mex Restaurants

Casa Rio – River House – San Antonio

The Casa Rio was the first business to open its doors on the historic and scenic Riverwalk in San Antonio. Serving the people of San Antonio for almost sixty years, Casa Rio provides guests with a wonderful dining experience along the beautiful and romantic Riverwalk. Casa Rio serves lunch and dinner daily and also offers cocktail boat service, a unique dining experience on board a Riverwalk river boat.

Casa Rio
430 E. Commerce Street
San Antonio, Texas 78205
210-225-6718
www.casa-rio.com

Caro's Restaurant – Rio Grande City/Fort Worth

www.caros.biz

*H*ome of the original puffy tostados, Caro's has been serving up their Tex-Mex specialties since 1937. Modesta Caro, the founding mother of Caro's, provided wonderful recipes including that of the puffy tostados. Her children carry on the tradition and legacy with the original restaurant in Rio Grande City and another in Fort Worth.

Caro's Restaurant
205 N. Garcia St.
Rio Grande City, Texas 78582
956-487-2255

Caro's Restaurant
3505 Blue Bonnet Circle
Fort Worth, Texas 76109
817-924-9977

Cisco's Restaurant Bakery and Bar – Austin

This laid-back local favorite has been serving a traditional Tex-Mex breakfast and lunch to politicians, college students, and movie stars for generations. Founder Rudy Cisneros, known to seat famous people, friends, and beautiful women in the front of the restaurant, often picked up the tab of close friends and important people. After Rudy's death in 1995, his son Clovis took over the business while his other son

Johnny runs the bakery. Still known as the best place for an Austin-style power breakfast, Cisco's is an Austin institution.

Cisco's Restaurant Bakery and Bar
1511 East 6th Street
Austin, Texas 78702-2420
512-478-2420

Dos Amigos Cantina – Odessa

*W*here else can you watch a bull ride while eating one of the best burritos in Odessa? Dos Amigos Cantina serves up a different kind of entertainment for those looking for a bit of everything. Combining a rodeo arena, a restaurant, and a bar can't be easy, but it is the standard at Dos Amigos. Depending on the day or night, you could be watching Willie Nelson or a bull-riding contest. Come here for great Tex-Mex food and a change of pace.

Dos Amigos Cantina
520 West 47th Street
Odessa, Texas 79764
432-368-7556
www.dosamigoscantina.com

El Azteca – Austin

*"S*erving Austin since 1963," El Azteca founders Jorge and Ninfa Guerra pride themselves with starting many Tex-Mex traditions. Noting that no one in Austin was serving Mexican beer, Jorge began

El Azteca
2600 East 7th Street
Austin, Texas 78702
512-477-4701
www.aztecarestaurant.com

driving to San Antonio twice a week to pick up cases of Corona, Dos Equis, and Tecate to sell in his restaurant. El Azteca was also one of the first restaurants to recognize the need for vegetarian entrees. In the early '70s, before vegetarian dishes were commonplace, Jorge and Ninfa were providing their non-carnivorous diners with interesting and tasty options. Jorge and Ninfa are now semi-retired and leave most of the business operations to their children and grandchildren, who carry on the same traditions and standards as their parents and grandparents.

El Fenix Mexican Restaurants – Dallas

*"A*n Idea so Innovative, and Food so Good, A City Grew Up Around It." Opened in 1916 by Miguel and Faustina Martinez, El Fenix Mexican Restaurant is one of Texas' oldest and most beloved Tex-Mex establishments. The El Fenix was so popular that it was originally open twenty-four hours a day, seven days a week. During World War II, the restaurant was required by law to be closed certain hours of each day. Never having been closed, new locks had to be installed because there was no key for the front door. With a reputation for wonderful food and excellent service, the El Fenix has provided generations of

Dallas - Fort Worth residents with authentic Tex-Mex recipes. The children, grandchildren, and great grandchildren of Miguel and Faustina Martinez carry on the traditions of their elders with a business that has grown to include fifteen restaurants and employs 800 people.

El Fenix Mexican Restaurant
1601 McKinney Avenue
Dallas, Texas 75202
214-747-1121
www.elfenix.com

Jacala Mexican Restaurant – San Antonio

*O*pening by offering their trademark puffy taco in 1949 and seating only sixteen, Jacala Mexican Restaurant is one of the oldest originally owned Mexican restaurants in San Antonio. Serving Tex-Mex at its best, you are always guaranteed to find at least one member of the family's four generations working at Jacala.

Jacala Mexican Restaurant
606 West Avenue
San Antonio, Texas 78201
210-732-5222
www.jacala.com

Joe T. Garcia's Mexican Restaurant – Fort Worth

*E*stablished on July 4, 1935, Joe T. Garcia's Mexican Restaurant is a Fort Worth tradition. The original restaurant, which was run by Joe, his wife, and five children, seated only sixteen people. The restaurant has gone through numerous renovations through the years to meet the needs of its customers, but the mouth-watering recipes Jessie (Mrs. Joe T.) used in 1935 are still followed to the letter. Joe T. Garcia's now has a seating capacity of over one thousand and continues to be run by the children and grandchildren of its founders.

Joe T. Garcia's Mexican Restaurant
2201 Commerce Street
Fort Worth, Texas 76106
817-626-4356
www.joets.com

Matt's El Rancho – Austin

*M*att Martinez came a long way from selling tamales for his father in 1923 from a wooden pushcart on Congress Avenue. Matt and his wife Janie opened Matt's El Rancho in 1952, working eighteen-hour days to make the restaurant the success it is today. Once a favorite of President Lyndon B. Johnson, Matt's El Rancho has a reputation for serving the best Tex-Mex in Austin. A combination of hard work, fresh ingredients, and wonderful recipes make this family restaurant an Austin tradition.

Matt's El Rancho
2613 S. Lamar
Austin, Texas 78704
512-462-9333
www.mattselrancho.com

Mi Tierra Café Y Panaderia – San Antonio

Mi Tierra Café Y Panaderia
218 Produce Row
San Antonio, Texas 78207-4554
210-225-1262
www.mitierracafe.com

*S*tarted in 1941 by Pete and Cruz Cortez as a three table café serving farmers and workers in El Mercado, Mi Tierra is today one of the oldest, biggest, and best Tex-Mex restaurants in San Antonio. Open twenty-four hours a day, this lively restaurant serves breakfast, lunch, and dinner, along with the "coldest beer in the Mercado." Year-round Christmas lights and strolling musicians provide a wonderful atmosphere to this San Antonio landmark.

Mexican Inn Café – Fort Worth

*I*n 1936, one of Fort Worth's most colorful residents and known gambler, Tiffin Hall, opened the first Mexican Inn Café in downtown Fort Worth. Hall, who had several gambling halls throughout the city, kept the Mexican Inn Café downstairs and a gambling establishment upstairs. Although he was known as "Fort Worth's Kingpin of Gambling," Hall knew how to run a restaurant and his business flourished. After Hall's death, the Mexican Inn Café was purchased and became part of the Spring Creek Restaurants. Touting their tortillas and chips as the best in Fort Worth, this wonderful Tex-Mex restaurant is a Fort Worth legend.

Mexican Inn Café (the original)
516 Commerce Street
Fort Worth, Texas 76102-5439
817-332-2772
www.mexicaninncafe.com

Molina's Mexican Restaurant – Houston

Molina's Mexico City Restaurant
7901 Westheimer
Houston, Texas 77063
713-782-0861
www.molinasrestaurant.com

*R*aul Molina, Sr.'s American dream began in 1941 with Molina's Mexico City Restaurant. Raul treated everyone who walked through the door like his next door neighbor, starting the "Good Neighbor" tradition. Currently run by the third generation of Molinas, the grandsons continue the traditions of their father and grandfather serving Houstonians the same recipes that have kept patrons coming back for over sixty years.

Spanish Village Restaurant – Houston

*B*oasting the best margaritas in Houston, this restaurant has been dishing up traditional Tex-Mex food for over fifty years. Year-round Christmas lights and a funky décor make this Houston tradition a popular haunt for locals and tourists alike. Known for their margaritas, which are quasi-frozen and served in a martini glass, the Spanish Village Restaurant is always a crowd pleaser.

Spanish Village Restaurant
4720 Almeda
Houston, Texas 77004
713-523-2861
www.spanishvillagerestaurant.com

TEXAS FOOD FACT

Tequila, the main ingredient in margaritas, is made from the agave plant. It takes between eight and ten years for an agave plant to mature. Once mature, one agave plant can produce up to five bottles of tequila.

The YANKEE and the

CHILI COOK-OFF

The following results from a recent
Chili Cook-Off in West Texas really shows
how far Yankees need to go to be true Texans!

Frank Walkenschmidt, the third judge, just happened to walk into the cook-off
when his Chrysler broke down along the interstate. Since one of the judges had called
in sick, Frank was asked to judge. From the notes that we have obtained from the
event, we probably do not have to worry about Frank buying any property in Texas.

Here are the scorecards from the event:

CHILI # 1 MIKE'S MANIAC MOBSTER MONSTER CHILI

JUDGE ONE: A little too heavy on tomato. Amusing kick.

JUDGE TWO: Nice, smooth tomato flavor. Very mild.

FRANK: Holy mother of pearl, what the hell is this stuff? You could remove
dried paint from your driveway. Took me two beers to put the flames out.
I hope that's the worst one. These Texans are crazy!

CHILI # 2 ARTHUR'S AFTERBURNER CHILI

JUDGE ONE: Smokey, with a hint of pork. Slight jalapeño tang.

JUDGE TWO: Exciting BBQ flavor, needs more peppers to be taken seriously.

FRANK: Keep this out of the reach of children. I'm not sure what I'm supposed to taste besides pain. I had to wave off two people who wanted to give me the Heimlich maneuver. They had to rush in more beer when they saw the look on my face.

CHILI # 3 FRED'S FAMOUS BURN-DOWN-THE-BARN CHILI

JUDGE ONE: Excellent firehouse chili! Great kick. Needs more beans.

JUDGE TWO: A bean-less chili, a bit salty, good use of peppers.

FRANK: Call the EPA, I've located a uranium spill. My nose feels like I've been snorting Drano. Everyone knows the routine by now… "Get me more beer before I ignite." Barmaid pounded me on the back; now my backbone is in the front part of my chest. I'm getting hammered from all the beer.

CHILI # 4 BUBBA'S BLACK MAGIC

JUDGE ONE: Black bean chili with almost no spice. Disappointing.

JUDGE TWO: Hint of lime in the black beans. Good side dish for fish or other mild foods, not much of a chili.

FRANK: I felt something scraping across my tongue, but was unable to taste it. Is it possible to burn out tastebuds?

CHILI # 5 LINDA'S LEGAL LIP REMOVER

JUDGE ONE: Meaty, strong chili. Cayenne peppers freshly ground, adding considerable kick. Very impressive!

JUDGE TWO: Chili using shredded beef, could use more tomato. Must admit the cayenne peppers make a strong statement.

FRANK: My ears are ringing, sweat is pouring off my forehead and I can no longer focus my eyes. I passed gas and four people behind me needed paramedics. The contestant seemed offended when I told her that her chili had given me brain damage. Sally saved my tongue from bleeding by pouring beer directly on it from a pitcher. I wonder if I'm burning my lips off? It really annoyed me that the other judges asked me to stop screaming.

CHILI # 6 VERA'S VERY VEGETARIAN VARIETY

JUDGE ONE: Thin yet bold vegetarian variety chili. Good balance of spice and peppers.

JUDGE TWO: The best yet. Aggressive use of peppers, onions, and garlic. Superb.

FRANK: My intestines are now a straight pipe filled with gaseous, sulfuric flames. No one seems inclined to stand behind me. Can't feel my lips anymore.

CHILI # 7 SUSAN'S SCREAMING SENSATION CHILI

JUDGE ONE: A mediocre chili with too much reliance on canned peppers.

JUDGE TWO: Ho hum, tastes as if the chef literally threw in a can of chili peppers at the last moment. I should take note that I am worried about Judge Number 3. He appears to be in a bit of distress as he is cussin' uncontrollably.

FRANK: You could put a grenade in my mouth, pull the pin, and I wouldn't feel a damn thing. I've lost sight in one eye, and the world sounds like it is made of rushing water. My shirt is covered with chili that slid unnoticed out of my mouth. My pants feel as if they are full of hot, bean-filled lava. At least during the autopsy they'll know what killed me. I've decided to stop breathing, it's too painful. I'm not getting any oxygen anyway. If I need air, I'll just suck it in through the 4-inch hole in my stomach.

CHILI # 8 BILLY BOB'S SMOKIN' CHILI

JUDGE ONE: A perfect ending, this is a nice blend chili, safe for all, not too bold but spicy enough to declare its existence.

JUDGE TWO: This final entry is a good, balanced chili. Neither mild nor hot. Sorry to see that most of it was lost when Judge Number 3 passed out, fell over, and pulled the chili pot down on top of himself. Not sure if he's going to make it. Poor Yank, wonder how he'd have reacted to a really hot chili?

FRANK: [Did not respond.]

TEN THINGS YOU WILL NEVER HEAR A REAL TEXAN SAY.......

1 Go Sooners!
2 I'll have a double decaf mocha latte.
3 I hate Bar-B-Q.
4 Nah, I've had enough beer tonight...
5 That's a real swell pair of loafers you have on there.

6 How do you spell Stabauch?
7 Turn off that Willie Nelson album!
8 I think I'll have a Guinness.
9 The hell with the Alamo!
10 I'm moving to Cleveland.

⋙ TEX-MEX ⋘

(tèks méks) adj.,designating the Texan variety of something Mexican;
also occas., of or pertaining to both Texas and Mexico

Today almost every home in America has a jar of salsa and a bag of chips thanks to the Tex-Mex craze that swept the country in the early '70s. Tex-Mex food first appeared on the American landscape in the border towns of south Texas in the early 1900s. A combination of flavors, cultures, and tastes came together with the influences of western and southern Texas and Mexico to create America's favorite regional cuisine. Immigrants to the United States at the turn of the century opened restaurants and began introducing hungry Texans to the flavors of their southern neighbor. After some experimentation, restaurant owners and cooks began to "Americanize" their dishes to better suit the tastes of the American palate. Texans flocked to Mexican restaurants to eat their favorite foods, lapping up tortilla chips, margaritas, and chili con carne.

Until the 1970s, Tex-Mex food remained primarily in Texas and was known only as Mexican food. It was not until 1972 when Diana Kennedy, an American writer living in Mexico City, published *The Cuisines of Mexico*, in which the term "Tex-Mex" was first used when referring to food. In her book, Kennedy spelled out the differences between authentic interior Mexican cooking and the "mixed plates" that were being passed as Mexican food at restaurants in Texas. Defiant restaurant owners decided to continue cooking what Texans craved, using the term to define the unique tastes of their cooking style.

The plan of the restaurateurs paid off. Due to the national attention gained by Kennedy's book, along with a campaign by Mexican restaurant owners, Tex-Mex cuisine was introduced into mainstream America and a food phenomenon was born. Not only did Mexican or Tex-Mex restaurants begin dotting the countryside, but a whole new fast food industry was born with companies such as Taco Bell, Taco John's, and Taco Tico's. In 1973 the term "Tex-Mex" as a food description was first entered into the *Oxford English Dictionary*. **¡Buen Provecho! Happy Eating!**

Source: *Oxford English Dictionary*. Second Edition, 1989

GREAT RECIPES

⊹≈ FROM ≈⊹
Great Writers

There's an old saying that some of the world's finest cooks are writers. The saying becomes reality when it comes to members of the **Western Writers of America**. WWA was founded more than fifty years ago by legends in the "pulp" era of writing when western novels and the movies made from them were at the peak of their popularity in the United States. Today, the organization numbers nearly 650 members, about twenty percent of whom reside in Texas.

Listed here is a tempting roundup of delicious recipes representing personal favorites of some of the WWA's most popular Texas members, past and present. We think you'll find these selections scrumptious and, best of all, easy to prepare. For more choices, take a look at *Buckskin, Bullets, and Beans: Good Eats and Good Reads from the Western Writers of America,* edited by Bob Wiseman, whence these hunger stoppers came. Used, of course, with permission

Old-Fashioned Peach Cobbler

½ cup butter, divided
1 cup self-rising flour
1 cup milk
¾ cup sugar
1 (16-ounce) can sliced
   peaches in heavy syrup
1 teaspoon ground cinnamon

Preheat oven to 350 degrees. Heat a Dutch oven or large skillet on top of the stove until a drop of water quickly sizzles away, then add half of the butter and swirl to coat. In a glass or ceramic bowl, mix flour, milk, and sugar and pour into the Dutch oven or skillet. Combine peaches and syrup with cinnamon and add to flour mixture. Dot with pats of remaining butter. Remove from stove and bake in the oven for 30 to 35 minutes or until crust rises and turns golden brown.

⊹≈⊷

The late **Fred Bean** from Austin was one of the state's most prolific novelists and wrote such Western classics as *Killing Season, Pecos River,* and *The Outlaw.* His recipe for **Old-Fashioned Peach Cobbler** is absolutely mouth watering and *soooo* simple.

TEXAS FOOD FACT

At *The Big Texan Steak Ranch Restaurant in Amarillo,* you can get a 4½ pound steak for free, if you can eat it in an hour!

Chicken Pot Pie Recipe

1 large roasting chicken
2 cups sliced carrots (4 to 5 medium-sized)
1 cup chopped onion
2 stalks celery with leaves, chopped
bouquet garni: (6 parsley sprigs and
   1 bay leaf, tied together)
¼ teaspoon thyme
1 cup quartered mushroom caps
salt and white pepper to taste
½ cup beer, at room temperature
2 tablespoons butter
½ cup heavy cream,
   whipped
2 tablespoons flour
12 ounces puff
   pastry (fresh or
   frozen)
1 egg yolk, beaten

When **Mike Blakely**, a former WWA president, novelist, songwriter, and musician isn't touring the West picking and singing, he's at home in Marble Falls writing such best-sellers as *Snowy Range Gang*, *Shortgrass Song*, and *Too Long at the Dance*. Mike's **Chicken Pot Pie** recipe will keep you going back to the table for more.

Pot Pie Instructions

Put chicken and enough hot water to cover it in a large, deep kettle or Dutch oven. Add carrots, onion, celery, and bouquet garni. Bring to a boil. Skim the residue from kettle. Reduce to a simmer, cover, and let cook for 15 to 20 minutes. Remove from heat and let cool for one hour, then pour into a large mixing bowl. Reserve broth in a bowl after removing carrots, onion, and celery; leave the bouquet garni in the broth.

Disjoint the chicken and remove meat from bones; discard bones and skin (or add back to broth and let simmer for a few hours until you have a nice, rich broth for other uses). Cut meat into large serving pieces.

Preheat oven to 400 degrees when you are ready to cook the pot pie.

To a deep pie or casserole dish, add chicken, carrots, onion, celery, thyme, mushrooms, salt and pepper, and beer. Cut butter into small pieces and dabble over chicken mix. Mix flour into whipped cream, making sure there are no lumps, then pour evenly over chicken.

Roll out puff pastry and place over the chicken mixture. Brush top with beaten egg yolk. Bake in preheated oven for 10 minutes, then reduce heat to 350 degrees and bake for 20 more minutes.

TEXAS FOOD FACT

*T*exans love their barbeque and can find it at 929 establishments statewide. Houston alone has 103 barbeque restaurants—more than any of the nation's top ten cities.

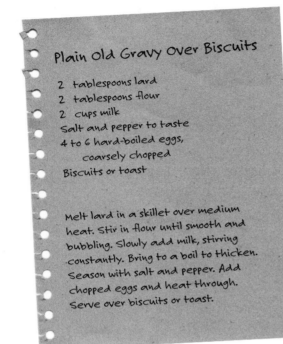

Plain Old Gravy Over Biscuits

2 tablespoons lard
2 tablespoons flour
2 cups milk
Salt and pepper to taste
4 to 6 hard-boiled eggs,
    coarsely chopped
Biscuits or toast

Melt lard in a skillet over medium heat. Stir in flour until smooth and bubbling. Slowly add milk, stirring constantly. Bring to a boil to thicken. Season with salt and pepper. Add chopped eggs and heat through. Serve over biscuits or toast.

Here's a simple, yet delicious recipe for those who enjoy just plain old **gravy over biscuits**. It's a favorite of author **Cindy Bonner**, whose books for juveniles have garnered two "Best Adult Books for Young Adults" awards from the American Library Association.

Preston Lewis has served as WWA's president and is an award-winning novelist with a number of works to his credit. The San Angelo writer shares with us here his grandmother's recipe for **pecan pie**. Deeeeelicious!

Great Texas Tastebud Teasers!

We're betting that you've got some great dishes tucked away in your family recipe book like the ones on this page. If you've got one or two that you're willing to share with Almanac readers in upcoming editions, we would love to hear from you. Just drop us a note for information about submitting your recipes. *Seconds, anyone?*

Pecan Pie

1   cup sugar
¾ cup light corn syrup
½ cup margarine
3   eggs, beaten
1¾ cups pecans
⅛ cup (or 2 tablespoons) salt
1   teaspoon vanilla
1   (9-inch) unbaked pie crust

Preheat oven to 375 degrees. In a saucepan, blend sugar, corn syrup, and margarine. Cook over medium heat, stirring constantly, until mixture comes to a boil. In a large glass or ceramic bowl, add the beaten eggs. Blend hot mixture slowly with beaten eggs. Stir in pecans, salt, and vanilla. Pour into the pie shell. Bake for 30 minutes.

How to Build a Cooking Fire

There's a lot to be said about sitting around a roaring fire and smelling the sweet scents of roasting meat or broiling fish. Although most American backyards now contain at least one grill—charcoal, gas, or electric—the lure of cooking over an open flame still attracts many self-proclaimed chefs.

Efficient fire-making dates back to the earliest days of mankind, shortly after some faceless individual discovered that the piece of animal flesh that was accidentally seared in a grass fire captured his senses of smell and taste like no mere vegetable or fruit offerings could. Indeed, fire was one of the primary items in early man's tool kit that separated him from the rest of the animal world. As Ellsworth Jaeger, a noted writer on woodcraft back in the mid-1900s, once declared, fire "enabled him [man] to rise from an animal existence to a plane where he could change night into day and winter into summer."

Fire-making for cooking— or just for the fun of it—can be rewarding and interesting, but it can also be dangerous. Therefore, one should always be keenly aware of the surroundings before selecting a spot upon which to build a blaze. Be sure all overhanging brush and tree branches have been cleared away so that escaping flames pose no hazard. If leaf mold, evergreen needles, or other flammable material is present, remove it—completely down to the bare earth—before laying the fire. Obviously, never build a fire against a tree or a log and, to be absolutely safe, even in a relatively open space, clear a spot measuring a few feet in diameter of all vegetable material.

1 Use small twigs, kindling, or other slivers of wood as the base for the fire and gradually surround this base with progressively larger pieces of split *dry* wood, shaping the entire pattern into a tipi.

2 When lighting the fire, put the flame at the bottom, among the pieces of tinder. Fan the flames slightly until the tinder and the smaller kindling are ablaze.

3 As the split wood catches fire, add additional, larger pieces to the flames as needed.

4 When putting the fire out, sprinkle the flames and burning embers again and again with water. Then dig up the coals with a shovel, being careful to combine them with the soil dug up from beneath the extinguished fire.

The Chuck Wagon

Texas Cattle Drive Necessity Gives Birth to Another Invention

That famous Panhandle cattleman, Charles Goodnight, is generally credited with being the "inventor" of the chuck wagon. In the early days, when cowboying was a local affair and herders were out for only a few days at a time, they generally carried their food with them. Sometimes, pack horses or mules might be utilized when additional supplies needed to be hauled. But, with the advent of the genuine cattle drive, when huge herds of longhorns were driven hundreds of miles from the home ranches in Texas northward to Kansas and, later, to the open ranges of Wyoming and Montana, a more complex and sophisticated method of feeding the men had to be developed.

The answer was the chuck wagon. Noted Texas ranch historian J. Evetts Haley has written that in 1866, Goodnight purchased "a government wagon, pulled it over to a wood-worker in Parker County, and had it entirely rebuilt with the toughest wood available, seasoned bois d'arc. Its axles were of iron instead of the usual wood, and in the place of a tar bucket he put in a can of tallow to use in greasing . . . . For the back end of the wagon he built the first chuck-box he had ever seen."

The lid on the chuck box was fitted with a swinging leg that allowed the lid to be used as a preparation table. The box was divided into conveniently sized compartments in which "Cookie," as the drive's chef was usually called, stored all sorts of rations and equipment, from salt and baking powder to beans and coffee to tin utensils and cooking ware.

The chuck wagon, driven by the cook, always went in advance of the cattle and the cowboys for two reasons: to avoid the

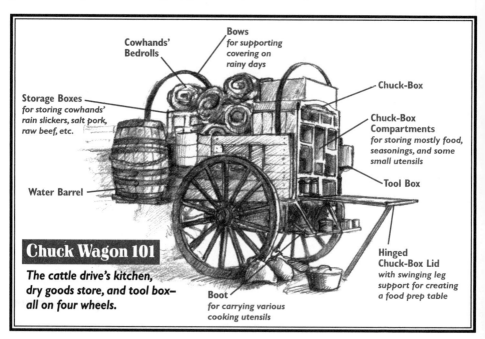

Cowhands' Bedrolls

Bows for supporting covering on rainy days

Chuck-Box

Storage Boxes for storing cowhands' rain slickers, salt pork, raw beef, etc.

Chuck-Box Compartments for storing mostly food, seasonings, and some small utensils

Water Barrel

Tool Box

Chuck Wagon 101

The cattle drive's kitchen, dry goods store, and tool box— all on four wheels.

Boot for carrying various cooking utensils

Hinged Chuck-Box Lid with swinging leg support for creating a food prep table

dust created by the thousands of hooves and in order to set up camp and get the evening meal underway by the time the tired cowboys arrived.

Skimpy as the food on a cattle drive might have been, eating was the highlight of each day for the weary cowboys after long hours in the saddle. Consequently, most cooks were hired for their ability to turn out a good meal on what little supplies they could carry in the chuck wagon. "There was no one particular type in wagon cooks, except that very few were young men," wrote Texas writer Ramon Adams. "One might be a Negro, a Mexican, or a white man from the dregs of the city, whose only knowledge of cow was that

it was 'dished up in a stew.' Many were broken-down punchers whose riding days were over, but who could not endure life away from cattle and horses, and thus took up cooking to follow the chuck wagon," he continued.

Like so many inventions, the chuck wagon was developed to solve a very real problem, in this case, the transporting of quantities of food and supplies across many miles and over a many-weeks period of time. Goodnight's redesign and perfection of a standard horse-drawn wagon into the utilitarian vehicle that it soon became contributed greatly to the success of the late 1800s cattle drive.

SWEET VICTORY!

The typical Texas cattle drive was for rugged men…even at meal time.

In the evening when the trail hands gathered aroung the chuck wagon, the coffee was hand ground. During the 1800s one popular supplier of coffee beans packed a stick of peppermint in each one-pound bag it shipped. This set the stage for the evening pre-meal entertainment. The cook would bellow out the question, *"Awright, who wants the candy tonight?"* This was the signal for some of the toughest Texans in the business to fight, bare-knuckled, for the privilege of grinding the coffee and getting the only sweets available on that long, dusty trail.

I Dare You To Eat That!

BEWARE!

What do you do when you unwisely bite off more than you can handle? Many people reach for a glass of water to extinguish the flames that rip through their mouths after accepting a dare to eat an extra hot habañero chile.

Those in the know, researchers as well as pepper aficionados, say that water is the worst thing for a burning hot mouth. Capsaicin, the substance in peppers that causes the heat, is not soluble in water and only washes through your mouth spreading the capsaicin. Because capsaicin is very soluble in fats and oils, experts say the best thing to cool your burning mouth is milk or ice cream. Eating rice or bread, which will absorb the capsaicin, is another option. An even more popular alternative to putting out the heat is a cold beer or frozen margarita. Alcohol is also known to help relieve the burn of capsaicin.

Waco is the "Home of Dr Pepper." In 1885, at Morrison's Old Corner Drug Store, pharmacist Charles Alderton concocted the formula for this unique and famous soft drink. The manufacturing plant that first produced Dr (no period) Pepper still stands in downtown Waco.

DID YOU KNOW?...

Best Biscuits I Ever Ate

Cow camps had an unwritten rule that it was all right not to like the food, but you had better not complain about it or else you would be assigned the job of cook. One cowboy broke a biscuit open and he exclaimed, "They are burnt on the bottom and top and raw in the middle and salty as hell, but shore fine, *just the way I like 'em.*"

TEXAS GARDENING

OUR DIVERSE STATE

Texas has four different hardiness zones, as shown on the United States Department of Agriculture (USDA) Cold Hardiness Zone map. The state reaches from Zone 6 in the Panhandle, where -10 degrees Fahrenheit is common, all the way down to Zone 9 in the Rio Grande Valley, where freezes are the exception. Few states in the country have this diversity.

The colder zones are in the northwest areas of Texas, including Wheeler, Randall, and Bailey counties in the Panhandle. The warmer zones are in the south and include Cameron, Hidalgo, and Starr counties of our Rio Grande Valley. Keep in mind that the USDA Cold Hardiness Zone map doesn't tell the whole story of temperatures in our state. Temperatures in urban areas may be 10 degrees warmer than those in rural areas due to asphalt, concrete, masonry, and a denser population—all of which create what are called microclimates.

Microclimates can also be created in our own home landscapes by fencing, shrubbery, and our homes and structures. You may discover that your yard has a location where particular plants will survive due to a microclimate that has been created, while your neighbor may not be able to grow the same plants.

Temperature range and rate of change greatly affect gardening in Texas. If, for example, one area were to drop to a sub-freezing temperature for a short period of time and climb right back up, plants in that area would most likely receive little harm. But if the temperature dropped suddenly and remained there for several days, great damage could occur. When an unusual freezing spell struck North Texas, some of its live oak trees, which would normally be considered quite hardy in that area, were severely damaged.

Facing the Wind

There is nothing like a Texas wind to affect your gardening activities. Make sure the plants that you select at your local garden center will be able to withstand the wind that is common in your area. Many Texans experience prevailing southwestern breezes, and in some locations they can be quite strong. I have seen large landscape plants growing at an almost 45-degree angle due to these prevailing breezes. Make sure that trees or other tall shrubs are staked properly until they are large enough to withstand the strong breezes and begin growing vertically. Trees that are properly selected and placed can serve beautifully as breaks to block out strong winds.

How to have a
GREAT TEXAS LAWN

Prepare the Planting Site

Before planting grass, eliminate all undesirable weeds or grasses either mechanically or chemically. Mechanical techniques for removing weeds include digging, hoeing, and smothering. Covering the soil with black plastic for three to five months prior to planting prevents sunlight from reaching the ground, smothering existing weeds and grasses, while generating ample heat to kill weed seed. Tilling to remove existing vegetation will not work with plants that form underground stems, such as bermudagrass. The rhizomes and stolons scatter, then later root and grow. Tilling also brings more weed seeds to the surface where they will germinate.

Chemical approaches that include very specific herbicides are often the most complete eradication methods. Use a non-selective herbicide like glyphosate (the active ingredient in herbicides such as Roundup®) or glufosinate-ammonium (the active ingredient in the herbicide Finale®) according to label directions to kill any existing vegetation. Non-selective

means the herbicide kills anything the spray reaches. But non-selective herbicides don't sterilize the soil, so you can replant once the existing vegetation is completely dead. Spraying herbicides should be done a few weeks, even months, before planting to allow the chemicals time to kill the entire plant, roots and all. Persistent weeds or grasses such as bermudagrass may require more than one spraying. Mixing an indicator dye (typically blue), available at turf or farm supply businesses, with the herbicide allows you to see where you have sprayed.

Remove large rocks, pebbles, or soil clods that may interfere with seed establishment. Large pieces of wood, tree branches, and bark should also be removed since they can contribute to a perplexing problem in lawns called "fairy ring." Once all vegetation is killed or removed, lightly work the top inch or so of soil just prior to planting by tilling very shallowly or raking by hand. Working the soil too deeply will stir up more weed seeds.

Take your soil seriously.

Poor, infertile soil means poor, non-productive plants, so a healthy lawn is a result of fertile, healthy soil. Since turfgrass receives its primary nutrition from the soil, having your soil tested is a must. Otherwise you are "growing by guessing," and that can be costly financially, nutritionally, and environmentally. A soil test will measure the fertility of your soil and tell you what needs to be added.

"When I was a kid, the dirt was so poor that we had to fertilize the house to raise the windows."

Former Houston Oilers Coach
"Bum" Phillips

When to Plant Your Lawn

Seed, sprig, sod, or plug at the appropriate times of year. For warm-season grasses, that means the soil temperatures need to be approaching 70° F. A good guide is to plant when other warm-season grasses start to green up and grow. There must also be at least two months allowed for warm-season grasses to become established before winter. April through July is the ideal planting time for warm-season grasses assuming you have adequate rainfall or supply supplemental irrigation. Dormant sodding of warm-season grasses is sometimes done, but the chances for winter-kill are much greater since the roots have not penetrated the soil, which provides extra protection.

DROUGHT TOLERANCE *of Texas Turfgrasses*

Bermudagrass	excellent
Carpetgrass	fair
Centipedegrass	fair
St. Augustinegrass	fair
Zoysiagrass	fair
Kentucky Bluegrass	fair
Tall Fescue	poor

MOW HIGH |||||||||||nnnnnn

One common mistaken belief is that the closer you cut the lawn, the slower it will grow, so you won't have to mow as often.

Almost 400 wildflowers bloom in Texas. With the help of Lady Bird Johnson, wild-flower enthusiasts founded the National Wildflower Research Center in Austin. Now, wildflowers are planted along public roads.

How Much Water?

Watering deeply for long periods of time and less frequently is best for your lawn. Light, frequent watering produces shallow, weak root systems. Apply enough water at one time to soak the soil to a depth of at least 6 to 8 inches, which is equivalent to 1 to 1½ inches of water per week. This may need to be increased at the peak of summer, depending on the soil type, sun, heat intensity, and slope of the yard. (Remember also to take into account water restrictions in your area.) For many sprinklers, this means letting them run for two or three hours.

★

When to Water

Without a doubt, the best time to water is before sunrise, between 2:00 and 8:00 in the morning. This is why an automatic timer comes in handy; otherwise you will need to be up before the crack of dawn.

Texas Turf Maintenance at a Glance

Warm-Season Grasses

	Jan	Feb	March	April
Establishment (planting, renovation, or reseeding)				
Mowing				
Low Maintenance Fertilization				
Watering				
Aeration			if needed for compac‣	
Soil Test				
Insect/Disease Management				
Pre-emergence Herbicide Warm Season Weeds			**if needed	
Post-emergent Herbicide Warm Season Weeds				
Pre-emergent Herbicide Cool Season Weeds				
Post-emergent Herbicide Cool Season Weeds		2nd application if needed		

*rate includes rainfall; higher amount in heat of summer

**earlier pre-emergent applications may be needed as much as 2 to 4 weeks in southernmost counties or with early warm sp‣

(Herbicides should be a last resort. Proper care is the best weed prevention. Make sure herbicide is labeled for your turfgrass

Cool-Season Grasses

	Jan	Feb	March	April
Establishment (planting, renovation, or reseeding)				
Mowing				
Low Maintenance Fertilization				
Watering				
Aeration				
Soil Test				
Insect/Disease Management				
Pre-emergence Herbicide Warm Season Weeds			**if needed	
Post-emergent Herbicide Warm Season Weeds				
Pre-emergent Herbicide Cool Season Weeds				
Post-emergent Herbicide Cool Season Weeds		2nd application if needed		

*rate includes rainfall; higher amount in heat of summer

**earlier pre-emergent applications may be needed as much as 2 to 4 weeks in southernmost counties or with early warm spe‣

(Herbicides should be a last resort. Proper care is the best weed prevention. Make sure herbicide is labeled for your turfgrass

May	June	July	August	Sept	Oct	Nov	Dec
raise height into late summer and fall							
	*1 inch per week depending on drought conditions						
	anytime - every couple of years						
	watch for subtle changes and investigate						
if needed							
				if needed			
					1st application, if needed		

and the weeds to be controlled. Follow all directions.)

May	June	July	August	Sept	Oct	Nov	Dec
						ideal	
higher in summer heat							
	*1 inch per week depending on drought conditions						
	anytime - every couple of years						
	watch for subtle changes and investigate						
if needed							
				if needed			
					1st application, if needed		

and the weeds to be controlled. Follow all directions.)

Preparing Your Lawn for Drought

The easiest way to deal with drought is to select a grass that is drought tolerant. Simple things like proper watering, raising the mowing height during drought and heat stress, mowing more frequently, and reducing or eliminating fertilizer and herbicides will also help.

The key to helping your grass survive or tolerate severe drought is to condition it so it doesn't need pampering. Remember that watering deeply and less often encourages deeper roots that are more drought tolerant. Gradually raising the mowing height 25 to 50 percent will also encourage deeper roots and help shade the soil. And by all means keep the lawn mower blades sharp; torn leaf blades cause even more moisture loss and stress to the plants.

Attempting to maintain your entire lawn during times of severe water shortage is not always practical. If water rationing should occur, determine the priority areas in your lawn. You may want to water the portion that receives the most traffic or is used for summer recreation. The lawn closest to the house may also be a priority to help filter dust or to serve as a fire retardant.

Of course, going dormant from drought is the natural way grass avoids stress. But during this dormancy your grass will not be green, sun-germinating weed seed can prevail, and with severe stress the plants can even die.

Ways to Save Water

- *Reduce Slopes or Berms in the Lawn*
- *Avoid Runoff Situations*
- *Test and Amend Soil*
- *Add Organic Material as Topdressing Whenever Possible*
- *Install a Water-Efficient Irrigation System*
- *Select Drought-Tolerant Grass*
- *Sod Rather Than Seed*
- *Water Early in the Morning*
- *Minimize Fertilizer*
- *Mow High*

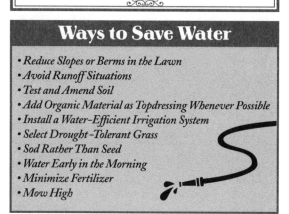

Reading a Fertilizer Bag

Fertilizers are sold based on the three main nutrients. The first number on the bag is the percentage of nitrogen (N), the second number is phosphorus (P), and the third is potassium (K). For example, a bag of 10-20-10 would have 10 percent of the total weight as nitrogen (NO_3 or NH_4), 20 percent phosphorus (P_2O_5), and 10 percent potassium (K_2O). The remaining weight to reach 100 percent could be secondary nutrients like iron, sulfur, and magnesium, and filler

materials to bind the nutrients into a form that is easy to apply. A fertilizer containing all three main nutrients is referred to as a "complete" fertilizer. Fertilizers with any nutrient missing, such as 45-0-0 or 13-0-44, are considered incomplete fertilizers. Fertilizer analyses are also referred to by the ratio of nutrients. For example, 10-20-10 would have a ratio of 1:2:1, 16-4-8 would be 4:1:2, and 17-17-17 would have a 1:1:1 ratio. If your soil test results suggest a fertilizer with a 3:1:2 ratio, you know you will need a fertilizer similar to 12-4-8.

Warm-Season Turfgrass Comparisons

Characteristics	Bermuda	Carpet	Centipede	St. Augustine	Zoysia
Growing Height	½-2 inches	1-2 inches	1-2 inches	2-3 inches	¾-1½ in.
Soil pH	5.5-6.9	4.5-5.9	5.0-6.5	5.5-7.0	5.5-6.9
Drought Tolerance	excellent	fair	fair	fair	fair
Salt Tolerance	good	poor	poor	good	fair
Partial Shade Tolerance	poor	fair	fair	good	fair
Heat Tolerance	excellent	excellent	excellent	excellent	excellent
Cold Tolerance	good	poor	good	fair	excellent
Cold Hardiness Zones	6a-9b	8b-9b	7a-9b	7b-9b	6a-9b
Wear Tolerance	excellent	fair	poor	fair	excellent
Spreading Rate	fast	slow	moderate	fast	slow
Color	dark	medium	light	dark	dark
Texture	fine	coarse	medium	coarse	fine

Cool-Season Turfgrass Comparisons

Characteristics	Kentucky Bluegrass	Tall Fescue
Growing Height	2-3 inches	2-3 inches
Soil pH	6.0-7.0	5.5-7.0
Drought Tolerance	fair	poor
Salt Tolerance	poor	fair
Partial Shade Tolerance	fair	good
Heat Tolerance	poor	fair
Cold Tolerance	excellent	excellent
Cold Hardiness Zones	6a-6b	6a-7b
Wear Tolerance	fair	fair
Spreading Rate	moderate	not applicable
Color	dark	dark
Texture	medium	coarse

High Traffic Sites

While it is true that bermudagrass and zoysiagrass can take more foot traffic than most varieties of lawn grass, it is only true within reason. It is not uncommon for paths to be worn, especially as a result of pets running back and forth frequently. Or you may be the culprit yourself, using the same route every day as a shortcut to the garden shed or the water faucet. Consider turning these high traffic areas into permanent hardscaped paths. Flagstone, brick, and concrete walkways are often expensive, but there are many other creative ways to turn worn grass paths into attractive, functional features.

Watering Your Lawn:

To cover 1,000 square feet with an inch of water takes 625 gallons

One gallon per minute (gpm) = 1,440 gallons per day

10.4 gallons per minute applies 1 inch of water over 1,000 square feet every hour

Gallons per minutes x 8.03 = cubic feet per hour

One gallon of water weighs 8.34 pounds

Botanists have identified over 5,000 species of flowers indigenous to Texas. In early spring, many cities sponsor flower "tours" that offer visitors a chance to enjoy the state's many varieties of blooming plants.

*L*earning about your soil is a matter of experience, talking to individuals who are knowledgeable about the soils in your area, and educating yourself. A great place to start is your local office of the Texas Agricultural Extension Service. Your County Agent will be able to familiarize you with the characteristics of the soil in your area. In addition, you can have your soil tested by the soil-testing laboratory in College Station for a modest fee. Kits to submit soil samples for analysis are available at your local Extension office. The soil laboratory at Stephen F. Austin University will also test your soil.

CALCULATING PLANT QUANTITIES

Determine planting bed area: (width x length = square feet)

Recommended Spacing (inches, from center to center)	Number of Plants (per square foot)
6	4.00
8	2.25
10	1.44
12	1.00
18	0.44
24	0.25

Example: 125 sq. ft. bed with 10 in. spacing = 180 plants needed (1.44 x 125 sq. ft. = 180)

Winter Protection

What Does "Winter Hardy" Really Mean ? ? ? ? ? ? ? ?

You'd think that worrying about cold protection would not be necessary during our relatively mild winters. And it wouldn't be if we used only hardy plants in our landscapes. But tender tropicals are, and probably always will be, part of most gardens; container plants in the landscape are often tender tropicals as well. The gardening term "hardy" refers to the ability of plants to withstand temperatures below freezing (32 degrees Fahrenheit) or colder with little or no damage. There are degrees of hardiness.

A plant that can tolerate 10 degrees is hardier than one that is hardy only to 20 degrees. In Zone 9 areas of the state, plants hardy to 15 degrees are considered winter hardy because the likelihood of lower temperatures is rare. In Zone 8, plants hardy to 10 degrees are considered winter hardy. In Zone 7, plants hardy to 0 degrees are considered hardy, and in Zone 6, plants hardy to minus 10 degrees are considered hardy. The term "tender" indicates plants that will be severely damaged or killed by temperatures below freezing. Factors such as how long the temperature remains below freezing, the moistness of the soil, how far below freezing it goes, and how protected is the plant's location in the landscape or microclimate will all affect the amount of damage that occurs. Cold protection is needed by tender tropicals whenever temperatures are predicted to go into the low 30s or upper 20s. Do not be concerned about wind-chill factors—look at the actual temperatures predicted.

Planning the Annual Flower Garden

Before you go to the nursery and buy annuals, **look carefully** at the growing conditions in the area to be planted. Most annuals do best with six to eight hours of sun a day (partial to full sun). Several will do well with two to four hours of direct sun (shade to partial shade). Make sure you select plants that will thrive in the light conditions they will receive. Annuals generally need good drainage, so plant in a raised bed if the area tends to stay damp. Measure the size of the bed and calculate how many plants you will need to create your desired effect. Although spacing varies with the plants' known average spread, about 8 inches can be used for estimating. It is also a good idea to **make some decisions on the color or colors** that will be used in the flower bed, as well as desirable heights (usually taller plants in the back of beds, shorter in front) and general layout to meet your desire. You can always make changes or adjustments if necessary, but it is a good idea to have developed your ideas as completely as possible before buying plants.

Planting Spring Bulbs

Most spring-flowering bulbs require excellent drainage, so avoid low, wet areas, or use raised beds as necessary. Prepare the area for planting:

- *Remove* any unwanted weeds.
- *Turn* the soil 8 to 10 inches deep.
- *Spread* 4 to 6 inches of organic matter (compost, rotted manure, ground bark, peat moss) over the area and blend thoroughly.
- *Rake* the area smooth, dig appropriate holes, apply slow-release fertilizer, and plant.

It is important to plant bulbs at the proper depth. Dig individual holes, or excavate the entire area to be planted to the recommended depth, and plant all the bulbs at once. Bulbs that are expected to rebloom reliably should be planted in areas that receive at least six hours of direct sunlight. This allows them to build up food reserves for next year's blooms. Bulbs that will be grown for just one season may be planted in shadier locations since they are discarded after blooming, although the same amount of direct sunlight is still preferred.

TIP

When cutting roses for indoor arrangements, avoid cutting long stems from roses just planted during the past spring. New roses need their foliage to get well established. Have a container of water in the garden with you when cutting roses, and place the stems in water immediately after cutting. For the longest-lasting cut flowers, harvest blossoms just as the buds begin to open.

Lawn Planning – Thatch Management

Lawns that feel too spongy when you walk on them may have developed a thick layer of thatch. Thatch is dead grass material that accumulates between the green leaf blades and the soil, and some is present and desirable in every lawn. But excess thatch reduces water penetration, creates shallow-rooted turf, encourages insect and disease infestations, and makes mowing difficult. Excessive fertilization, mowing infrequently, and mowing too high encourage this problem. Plan on dethatching with a vertical mower or core aerification during the summer if your lawn has this problem.

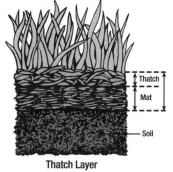

Thatch Layer

Steps for Repotting Houseplants

 **1 Choose** a new pot that is no more than twice as large as the original pot. Generally, 2 and no more than 4 inches larger in diameter is recommended.

 2 Add a layer of potting mix to the bottom of the new pot. It should be deep enough so that when the plant is placed into the new pot, the top of the rootball is about 1 inch below the pot rim.

3 Remove the plant from the old pot leaving root system intact. If roots are tightly packed, use your fingers to loosen them somewhat. Do not tear the root system apart.

4 Place the plant in its new container. If necessary, add more soil underneath the plant or remove some until the plant is positioned properly.

5 Add new potting soil in the space between the rootball and the pot. Use your fingers to firm the soil as you add it, but do not pack it tightly.

6 Fill to within 1 inch of the rim. Water the newly potted plant thoroughly to finish settling the soil.

DID YOU KNOW?

The only palm tree native to Texas is the Sabal palm. It can reach 20 to 48 feet in height and has a feathery crown and thick, bristly trunk. The Audubon Society grows it and other endangered species in a sanctuary in Brownsville.

PLANTING AND TRANSPLANTING SHRUBS

Proper planting will get your shrubs off to a good start. Here's how to plant in a well-prepared bed.

1 Place shrubs in their containers on top of the soil where they will be planted. Make sure the spacing and arrangement are correct before going on to the next step.

HEIGHT OF HOLE

2 Push down slightly on the pot to make a shallow depression, then set the shrub—in its container—aside.

3 Dig a hole into the depression as deep as, and a little wider than, the rootball. Do not dig any deeper than soilball depth.

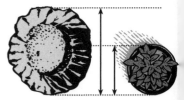

WIDTH OF HOLE

4 Remove the shrub from the container. If the roots are tightly packed in a solid mass, cut into the ball in several places or pull apart the root system somewhat. This will encourage the roots to grow into the surrounding soil.

5 Place the shrub's rootball into the hole. It is critical for the top of the rootball to be level with or slightly above the soil surface of the bed.

6 Use your hands to push and firm soil into the space between the rootball and the sides of the hole.

REMOVING CONTAINER

7 After planting all the shrubs in the bed, water them thoroughly by hand to finish settling the soil around their roots.

8 Apply root stimulators according to label directions.

9 Finally, mulch the bed 3 to 4 inches deep.

Follow the same procedure for balled-and-burlapped shrubs. Larger sizes are sometimes sold that way. After you set the rootball into the hole, remove any twine, nails, or wire securing the burlap. Remove the burlap (use a knife or scissors), being careful not to break the rootball.

DID YOU KNOW?

The Dallas Arboretum and Botanical Garden showcases thirty species of ferns and 66 acres of blooming plants at its location on Garland Road. On its grounds is a spectacularly ornate mansion built in 1940 by oilman Everett DeGolyer. The 21,000-square-foot house is definitely Texas-sized!

PERENNIALS

The first step in planting perennials is excellent bed preparation. It is important to do a good job at each of the following stages:

1 *Remove weeds and other unwanted plants from the bed.* Growing weeds may be eliminated with a non-selective weed-control aid that does not leave residue in the soil.

2 *Turn the soil* to a depth of at least 8 to 12 inches.

3 *Spread a 4-inch layer* of compost, rotted leaves, aged manure, finely ground pine bark, or sphagnum peat moss over the bed. If needed, add sand, lime, or sulfur at this stage. Have your soil tested through your county office of the Texas Cooperative Extension Service to learn more about what will improve your soil's fertility.

4 *Thoroughly blend* the amendments into the top 4 to 6 inches, rake smooth, and you're ready to plant.

Perennials are most often planted using purchased transplants or divisions. Transplants may be purchased in 4-inch to gallon-sized or larger pots. Generally, spring- and early summer-flowering perennials are planted in October through early December, and late summer- or fall-flowering perennials are planted from February through early April (they may also be planted in fall). Many gardeners plant perennials throughout the winter when weather is mild, especially in the south part of Texas.

Care for Your Shrubs

In an effort to make a landscaped area look full from the beginning, shrubs are often planted too close together. Even professionals do this. Eventually, the shrubs begin to crowd one another. Overcrowding can create stress through competition and increases insect and disease problems. In extreme cases, it might be necessary to remove some of the shrubs to make room for the rest. Sometimes regular pruning can keep things from getting out of hand. Avoid this problem by spacing shrubs properly at the beginning, even if the bed doesn't look full.

Pest Control

Holes in vegetable leaves may mean caterpillar or snail and slug activity. If you see small dark-green or black pellets on the foliage, the culprits are likely to be caterpillars. Silvery trails on the leaves indicate snails or slugs have been there. If in doubt, one discovery method is to put out a beer trap. Place a plastic bowl in the soil up to its rim near the plants and fill half full with beer. Snails and slugs will crawl into the beer and not be able to crawl out. They are not after the alcohol—it is the smell of the yeast that attracts them. If you catch a lot of snails and slugs in the trap, you have a problem with these pests—continue to put out traps, or apply bait to the area. If you don't catch any or catch just a few, your problem is probably caterpillars.

*T*here is nothing that speaks to a Texan's heart the way roses do. We Texans take great pride in our roses, and there are many selections from which to choose.

Many of our nation's rosebushes are produced in the area of northeast Texas around Tyler—often rightly considered the "Rose Capital of the World." Texas roses are available to us in a rainbow of colors, forms, types, and growth habits. They come packaged or container grown. The American Rose Society (ARS) lists over fifty categories of roses. This can be a bit confusing, even intimidating. While many rose aficionados are very serious about classification, growing roses should be much like other gardening activities—fun! With this in mind, this information will assist you when selecting roses to enjoy in your home landscape. Classification can be simplified into eight groups: climbers or runners (which includes ramblers), floribundas, grandifloras, hybrid teas, miniatures, heirlooms, polyanthas, and species.

TEXAS SHRUBS

Shrubs can be thought of as the furniture in our home landscapes. Ranging from a dwarf height of only 12 inches up to shrubs that grow to 20 feet or more, we can move them around, arrange them, and use them to dress up our foundations.

We strongly recommend that when you're in search of shrubs, you ask the following questions when visiting your local garden center or nursery.

- How tall and wide does this shrub grow in my area?
- What specific sun/shade conditions are best? (Morning sun/afternoon shade, daylong dappled sun/shade, etc?)
- Does it have blooms, and if so, what are the colors?
- When does it bloom, and for how long?
- Does it have any special soil requirements (Acid or alkaline soil, well-drained soil, deep soil, or moist soil?)
- Does it require special bed preparation? (Azaleas nearly always require special beds in Texas gardens.)
- If deciduous, ask these two additional questions:
    1) Does it have fall leaf color? If so, what are the colors?
    2) Are there any special conditions necessary to obtain these colors? (Special conditions might be a gradually cooling fall season, sun/shade, relatively mild or harsh summers, or overall care.)

Hibiscus

This information will help you decide whether or not to purchase a particular shrub and where to place it in your landscape. If you are seeking more maintenance-free specimens, be sure to select shrubs that will grow to a desired height and width without requiring pruning.

When laying out your foundation landscape beds at home, be sure to make them at least 5 feet wide or in many cases wider to accomodate mature shrub width. Improve the soil thoroughly before planting.

*I*f your cool-season annuals are way past their prime and you are not ready or able to replace them, pull them up anyway, improve the soil by adding organic matter to it, and heavily mulch the bed until you can plant. An empty, mulched bed looks much better than one full of dying cool-season annuals.

Care for Your Shrubs

In order to do well, shrubs must be planted in the growing conditions they prefer. The wrong location can mean constant problems:

• Too much shade produces leggy, low-vigor shrubs that bloom poorly or not at all and are more susceptible to disease problems.

• Too much sun can cause a shrub to appear stunted, with bleached-out, burned foliage.

• Poor drainage leads to root rot.

• Soil that stays too dry can cause excessive wilting, scorched leaves, and even death.

Observe your shrubs carefully throughout the year. Those that are not thriving may be in the wrong location.

OUTDOOR
Gardening Tip

Working outside in especially hot weather places extra stresses on the body. Gardeners working outside may lose up to two quarts of water each hour. To prevent dehydration, drink before, during, and after working outside. Drink before you're thirsty, and drink cold liquids because they are absorbed by the body faster. Drink water if you can; if you choose other liquids, make sure they contain only a small amount of sugar, as sugar slows down liquid absorption by the body. Avoid beverages containing alcohol and caffeine.

Work in your garden in the early morning or late afternoon when it is cooler, and stay in shady areas as much as possible. Follow the shade in your landscape as the sun moves across the sky; leave areas as they become sunny and move into areas as they become more shaded.

Wear a hat and loose, comfortable clothing, and use sun screen. Take frequent breaks and try not to stay outside in the heat for extended periods.

Tomato Cage Solution

*T*omatoes may also be grown in cages. The plants can grow quite large (5 to 6 feet is not unusual), and unfortunately the small commercially available tomato cages are usually inadequate. Here's a better solution:

- Purchase concrete reinforcing wire available at building supply stores—you'll need about 5 feet for each tomato plant.
- Cut into sections about 5 feet long, using heavy wire cutters.
- Form the pieces into cylinders and fasten their cut ends together.
- Place the cages over the tomato plants, pushing them into the ground.
- This activity results in cages that are 5 feet tall and approximately 18 inches across. They are ideal for growing tomatoes and the fruit is easier to harvest.

Planning the Herb Garden

Unlike vegetables, which require relatively large plantings in order to produce sufficient harvest, a single herb plant will often provide enough for a gardener's needs. Herbs may be grown in the vegetable garden, in their own area, or even among landscape plantings. Since few plants are needed, herbs are also excellent when grown in containers.

Most herbs require direct sun at least four to six hours a day (six to eight hours is best) and excellent drainage. Use raised beds or containers if drainage in your yard is questionable. Locate your herb-growing area as close to the kitchen as possible so the herbs are convenient to use while you are cooking. Those you choose to grow may initially be those you are familiar with and like to use in cooking.

Fall Colors
HELPFUL HINT

In mid- to late November, trees begin to show off their fall colors. Although not as spectacular as the fall color up North, there is still enough to appreciate. The following trees are some of the most reliable for fall color (those marked with a plus sign [+] will show good fall color even in the warmest parts of the state): **red oak, willow oak, Shumard oak+, flowering dogwood, Japanese persimmon, ginkgo+, sourwood, sassafras, flowering pear, Chinese pistachio+, tallow tree+,** and **sweetgum+.**

★

Onions are the Lone Star State's leading vegetable crop with sales reaching $100 million per year.

Harvesting Your Vegetables

Harvest bell peppers when they reach full size but are still green. You may leave them on the plant until they turn red, but this runs the risk of fruit rot. Harvest tomatoes anytime after they begin to turn pink to get them out of harm's way. Ripen at room temperature. They do not need light to ripen, so there is no need to put them in a window. Harvest snap beans when pods are the diameter of a pencil. Pick frequently. Squash and cucumber produce prolifically and need to be harvested almost daily. Their fruit is harvested immature, so don't let them get too big before you pick them. To see if sweet corn is ready to harvest, pull back the shuck partway. Puncture a kernel with your thumbnail. If the juice is clear, leave it for a few more days; if the juice is milky, it's time to harvest; and if there is no juice, it is too old. Dig up Irish potatoes in late May through June when the tops have turned mostly yellow. Save the smallest potatoes to use in planting a fall crop.

Live Oaks

HELPFUL HINT

Although considered evergreen, live oaks drop some, most, or all of their leaves in late February and early March. Almost immediately, new growth, often with a reddish tint, appears to replace the lost leaves. The amount of leaf drop can vary from year to year but is no cause for alarm. Rake up the leaves and use them as mulch, put them in your compost pile, or store them in plastic bags for later use.

Did You Know?

The Tigua tribe came to the El Paso area from New Mexico in the 1680s, and some of their fields have been in continuous cultivation since that time.

Excellent Heat-Tolerant Annuals and Tender Perennials

Under 2 feet:

Bachelor's Button	Ornamental Peppers
Blue Daze	Periwinkle
Celosia	Portulaca+
Coleus	Purslane
Dahlberg Daisy+	Salvia 'Lady in Red'
Dusty Miller	Scaevola
Dwarf Cosmos+	'VIP' Petunias
Gaillardia	Wax Begonia
Gomphrena	Zinnia
Lantana	
Marigold+	
Mexican Heather	

Over 2 feet:

Butterfly Weed
Canna
Cigar Flower
Cleome+
Cosmos+
Four o'Clock+
Hardy Hibiscus (Mallow)
Mexican Sunflower (Tithonia)+
Rudbeckia
Salvias such as 'Mealy Blue Sage'
Shrimp Plant
Sunflower+

+Seeds may be planted in flats or direct-seeded where the plants are to grow.

VEGETABLE PLANTING CHART

Vegetables	Seed or Plants per 100 feet (pl.=plants)	Depth of Seed Planting in Inches	Inches of Distance Between Rows	Plants	Average Height of Crop in Feet	Spring Planting in Regard to Average Frost-Free Date (FFD)
Asparagus	66 pl., 1 oz.	6–8, 1–1½	36–48	18	5	4 to 6 wks. before FFD
Beans, snap bush	½ lb.	1–1½	30–36	3–4	1½	on FFD to 4 wks. after
Beans, snap pole	½ lb.	1–1½	36–48	4–6	6	on FFD to 4 wks. after
Beans, Lima bush	½ lb.	1–1½	30–36	3–4	1½	on FFD to 4 wks. after
Beans, Lima pole	¼ lb.	1–1½	36–48	12–18	6	on FFD to 4 wks. after
Beets	1 oz.	1	14–24	2	1½	4 to 6 wks. before FFD
Broccoli	¼ oz.	½	24–36	14–24	3	4 to 6 wks. before FFD
Brussels sprouts	¼ oz.	½	24–36	14–24	2	4 to 6 wks. before FFD
Cabbage	¼ oz.	½	24–36	14–24	1½	4 to 6 wks. before FFD
Cabbage, Chinese	¼ oz.	½	18–30	8–12	1½	4 to 6 wks. before FFD
Carrot	½ oz.	½	14–24	2	1	4 to 6 wks. before FFD
Cauliflower	¼ oz.	½	24–36	14–24	3	not recommended
Chard, Swiss	2 oz.	1	18–30	6	1½	2 to 6 wks. before FFD
Collard (Kale)	¼ oz.	½	18–36	6–12	2	2 to 6 wks. before FFD
Corn, sweet	3–4 oz.	1–2	24–36	9–12	6	on FFD to 6 wks. after
Cucumber	½ oz.	½	48–72	8–12	1	on FFD to 6 wks. after
Eggplant	1/8 oz.	½	30–36	18–24	3	2 to 6 wks. after FFD
Garlic	1 lb.	1–2	14–24	2–4	1	not recommended
Kohlrabi	¼ oz.	½	14–24	4–6	1½	2 to 6 wks. before FFD
Lettuce	¼ oz.	½	18–24	2–3	1	6 wks. before FFD to 2 wks. after
Muskmelon (Cantaloupe)	½ oz.	1	60–96	24–36	1	on FFD to 6 wks. after
Mustard	¼ oz.	½	14–24	6–12	1½	on FFD to 6 wks. after
Okra	2 oz.	1	36–42	12–24	6	2 to 6 wks. after FFD
Onion (plants)	400–600 pl.	1–2	14–24	2–3	1½	4 to 10 wks. before FFD
Onion (seed)	1 oz.	½	14–24	2–3	1½	6 to 8 wks. before FFD
Parsley	¼ oz.	1/8	14–24	2–4	½	up to 6 wks. before FFD
Peas, English	1 lb.	2–3	18–36	1	2	2 to 8 wks. before FFD
Peas, Southern	½ lb.	2–3	24–36	4–6	2½	2 to 10 wks. after FFD
Pepper	1/8 oz.	½	30–36	18–24	3	1 to 8 wks. after FFD
Potato, Irish	6–10 lb.	4	30–36	10–15	2	4 to 6 wks. before FFD
Potato, sweet	75–100 pl.	3–5	36–48	12–16	1	2 to 8 wks. after FFD
Pumpkin	½ oz.	1–2	60–96	36–48	1	1 to 4 wks. after FFD
Radish	1 oz.	½	14–24	1	½	6 wks. before FFD to 4 wks. after
Spinach	1 oz.	½	14–24	3–4	1	1 to 8 wks. before FFD
Squash, summer	1 oz.	1–2	36–60	18–36	3	1 to 4 wks. after FFD
Squash, winter	½ oz.	1–2	60–96	24–48	1	1 to 4 wks. after FFD
Tomato	50 pl., 1/8 oz.	4–6½	36–48	36–48	3	up to 8 wks. after FFD
Turnip, greens	½ oz.	½	14–24	2–3	1½	2 to 6 wks. before FFD
Turnip, roots	½ oz.	½	14–24	2–3	1½	2 to 6 wks. before FFD
Watermelon	1 oz.	1–2	72–96	36–72	1	on FFD to 6 wks. after

Fall Planting in Regard to Average Autumn Freeze Date (AFD)	No. Days to Maturity	Average Length of Harvest Season (Days)	Average Crop Expected Per 100 Feet	Approx. Planting per Person (Storage)	
				Fresh (pl.=plants)	Canning or Freezing
not recommended	730	60	30 lb.	10–15 pl.	10–15 pl.
to 10 wks. before AFD	45–60	14	120 lb.	15–16 ft.	15–20 ft.
4 to 16 wks. before AFD	60–70	30	150 lb.	5–6 ft.	8–10 ft.
to 10 wks. before AFD	65–80	14	25 lb. shelled	10–15 ft.	15–20 ft.
4 to 16 wks. before AFD	75–85	40	50 lb. shelled	5–6 ft.	8–10 ft.
to 10 wks. before AFD	50–60	30	150 lb.	5–10 ft.	10–20 ft.
0 to 16 wks. before AFD	60–80	40	100 lb.	3–5 pl.	5–6 pl.
0 to 14 wks. before AFD	90–100	21	75 lb.	2–5 pl.	5–8 pl.
0 to 16 wks. before AFD	60–90	40	150 lb.	3–4 pl.	5–10 pl.
2 to 14 wks. before AFD	65–70	21	80 heads	3–10 ft.	—
2 to 14 wks. before AFD	70–80	21	100 lb.	5–10 ft.	10–15 ft.
0 to 16 wks. before AFD	70–90	14	100 lb.	3–5 pl.	8–12 pl.
2 to 16 wks. before AFD	45–55	40	75 lb.	3–5 pl.	8–12 pl.
to 12 wks. before AFD	50–80	60	100 lb.	5–10 ft.	5–10 ft.
2 to 14 wks. before AFD	70–90	10	10 doz.	10–15 ft.	30–50 ft.
0 to 12 wks. before AFD	50–70	30	120 lb.	1–2 hills	3–5 hills
2 to 16 wks. before AFD	80–90	90	100 lb.	2–3 pl.	2–3 pl.
4 to 6 wks. before AFD	140–150	—	40 lb.	—	1–5 ft.
2 to 16 wks. before AFD	55–75	14	75 lb.	3–5 ft.	5–10 ft.
0 to 14 wks. before AFD	40–80	21	50 lb.	5–15 ft.	—
14 to 16 wks. before AFD	85–100	30	100 fruits	3–5 hills	—
10 to 16 wks. before AFD	30–40	30	100 lb.	5–10 ft.	10–15 ft.
12 to 16 wks. before AFD	55–65	90	100 lb.	4–6 ft.	6–10 ft.
not recommended	80–120	40	100 lb.	3–5 ft.	30–50 ft.
8 to 10 wks. before AFD	90–120	40	100 lb.	3–5 ft.	30–50 ft.
6 to 16 wks. before AFD	70–90	90	30 lb.	1–3 ft.	1–3 ft.
2 to 12 wks. before AFD	55–90	7	20 lb.	15–20 ft.	40–60 ft.
10 to 12 wks. before AFD	60–70	30	40 lb.	10–15 ft.	20–50 ft.
12 to 16 wks. before AFD	60–90	90	60 lb.	3–5 pl.	3–5 pl.
14 to 16 wks. before AFD	75–100	—	100 lb.	50–100 ft.	—
not recommended	100–130	—	100 lb.	5–10 pl.	10–20 pl.
12 to 14 wks. before AFD	75–100	—	100 lb.	1–2 hills	1–2 hills
up to 8 wks. before AFD	25–40	7	100 bunches	3–5 ft.	—
2 to 16 wks. before AFD	40–60	40	3 bu.	5–10 ft.	10–15 ft.
12 to 15 wks. before AFD	50–60	40	150 lb.	2–3 hills	2–3 hills
12 to 14 wks. before AFD	85–100	—	100 lb.	1–3 hills	1–3 hills
12 to 14 wks. before AFD	70–90	40	100 lb.	3–5 pl.	5–10 pl.
2 to 12 wks. before AFD	30	40	50–100 lb.	5–10 ft.	—
2 to 12 wks. before AFD	30–60	30	50–100 lb.	5–10 ft.	5–10 ft.
14 to 16 wks. before AFD	80–100	30	40 fruits	2–4 hills	—

When to Water

When droughts occur in Texas they remind us just how important water is to us. There are many demands on our water supply and water is not available in unlimited quantities. Described as "the essence of life," water is as necessary to plants as to humans in order to survive.

Water your plants deeply and thoroughly. Lawns, for example, need to be watered to a soil depth of six inches, and they prefer to be watered to eight inches. Don't set any of your plants, including your lawn, on a watering schedule. We have all seen folks who want to turn on their lawn sprinklers, for example, every morning at 6:38 a.m. for ten minutes. That is not desirable for individual plants, grass, shrubbery, or any other plant.

After watering, don't re-water until your plants tell you they need it. Grass will tell you when it needs to be watered by changing from a nice pleasant green color to a kind of bluish gray. Or perhaps its sides will roll up, or it will lie flat when you walk across it, not springing back. When you see these signs, water the lawn thoroughly. You can tell when shrubs need to be watered by simply sticking your finger in the soil. If the soil is dry, then irrigate or apply water thoroughly…did I mention to water thoroughly? Be sure that you soak the entire root zone of your plants when watering. If you water your plants frequently and very lightly, they will develop undesirable shallow root systems. When watering containers, water until there are no more air bubbles coming out of them. You will then know that all the pores have been saturated with moisture. The excess water will drain out. Be sure that all your containers drain properly.

★

Questions to ask retailers before purchasing any type of plant:

- How tall and wide does this plant usually grow in my area?
- How much sun or shade is required?
- Does this plant have special soil requirements, and if so, what are they?
- Does this plant require well-drained soil, or will it grow in poorly drained or damp soil?
- Does it bloom? If so, when, for how long, and in what color(s)? In spring, summer, fall, or winter? For two weeks, six months, or longer?
- Does it have fall color? If so, what are the colors?
- Is it resistant to insect and disease pests that usually occur in my area?
- What are the watering/soil moisture requirements? Moist at all times? Tolerant of relatively dry soils?
- How often should it be fertilized, with what, and when?
- Are there any special pruning requirements? (Roses and certain other landscape plants usually require special pruning and/or training to realize maximum benefits.)
- Is it deer resistant (if that's important in your area)?

Remember that there are nurseries that specialize in native Texas plants. For more research on native Texas plants, contact the

Native Plant Society of Texas
P.O. Box 891
Georgetown, TX 78627
www.npsot.org
email: coordinator@npsot.org

The **NPSOT** is an excellent source for more recommendations. Find a chapter near you, and have fun with our native Texas plants!